The Washington Nationals
Flying Saucers over the Capital

By

Kevin D. Randle, Lt. Col. USAR (Ret)

Published by
FLYING DISK PRESS
4 St Michaels Avenue
Pontefract, West Yorkshire
England
WF8 4QX

Author's Note

This work is an update of the earlier *Invasion Washington*. New Information has been added, some conclusions have been changed and illustrations have been added. This provides the best information available in September 2022.

Table of Contents

Introduction

The radar and visual sightings of UFOs over the Washington, D.C. National Airport on two consecutive Saturday nights in July 1952, have taken on mythic proportions in the history of Ufology. These sightings, made on separate radar sets in separate locations, and verified visually by both military and civilian pilots, as well as military and civilian personnel on the ground, provide many clues about the nature of UFOs and the people who see and report them.

Washington National Airport circa 1944.

To understand the importance of these sightings, it is important to understand the context in which they were made. The Washington Nationals did not evolve in a vacuum, but into a situation in which UFOs were being reported frequently and in which a number of popular magazines had just published lengthy, and for the most part, very favorable stories about UFOs as they were being called at the time. Flying saucers were being talked about all during the summer of 1952, though other events including the nominating conventions of both political parties and the Olympic games, were also being widely reported which sometimes captured the front pages.

5

Flying saucers have been around publicly since the summer of 1947 when the first American reports were publicly acknowledged. Kenneth Arnold, a businessman from Boise, Idaho, saw nine strange crescent-shaped objects flying near Mt. Rainier in Washington on June 24, 1947, and for some reason,

The Kenneth Arnold flying saucer.

the national media was captivated. Arnold's report was carried in newspapers around the country. Soon, the flying saucers were a hot topic of discussion with newspapers filled with stories about them.

But the interest in the flying saucers faded after a few weeks during that summer of 1947, and it was only the occasional sighting and the occasional magazine article that kept the idea of flying saucers alive in the public arena. In September 1951, a series of sightings was made over Lubbock, Texas. The Lubbock Lights, as they became known, were national news, with the pictures of the V-shaped formations taken by Carl Hart, Jr. published in newspapers and magazines around the country. If it had been believed that UFOs were gone, that they were a summer fad several years earlier, it was now clear that they, whatever they were, had returned.

Then, in April 1952, *Life* magazine published a thoughtful examination of flying saucer mystery. While the *Life* editors didn't conclude that UFOs were from other planets, they did suggest that it was a real possibility. If nothing else, the sightings in Lubbock and the article in *Life* reintroduced the concept of the flying saucer into the public mainstream.

As noted, there were other important events happening that summer. Both the political parties were holding their nominating conventions to create their platforms and nominate their candidates for the presidency. The summer Olympic games were in full swing. The war in Korea was still being fought and would continue into 1953. In other words, there was a great deal of both important and frivolous information published that summer. There was something for everyone.

But there were also flying saucer reports. They appeared on the front pages of the newspapers around the country. At first these were small stories, in the right-hand columns of the newspaper. Then, after the second night of UFO sightings over Washington, the *Cedar Rapids Gazette*, in a banner headline that could have been lifted from a science fiction movie, reported "Saucers Swarm over Capital."

But UFOs weren't only being spotted by radar and intercepted by fighters over Washington, D.C. It was a scene that was being played out around the country. UFOs appeared in the skies, were being "painted" by radar, and chased by fighters everywhere. Hundreds of people were seeing UFOs and reporting them to the Air Force. For the first time, the topic was being treated with some semblance of respect by those in the government, the military and by the newspapers.

Although there had been photographs of UFOs taken in the past, it was during the summer of 1952 that some of the clearest were offered as evidence. These were also provided to the Air Force, and most were carefully investigated. Some of the pictures were later established to be hoaxes, but a few have withstood the test of time and show us what was being seen far better than a word picture painted by a reluctant witness.

Although there had been movie footage of UFOs taken in the past, one of the best films, in color, was taken in July 1952, by a Naval officer. The Air Force, the Navy, and those in the Department of Defense were impressed with this film. The military investigators and analysts worked long and hard to identify the bright objects maneuvering in the deep blue sky over the Utah desert.

They came up with up some suggestions, but nothing that was universally accepted by UFO researchers and military officers.

It was also during this time that some of the first reports of alien creatures were made to the Air Force. The Air Force did investigate the tale told in Flatwoods, West Virginia, but like so much of the UFO story, there was no physical evidence to corroborate the tale. There were just the stories told by a number of citizens who seemed to have no reason to invent such a tale, who seemed to lack the imagination to carry it off, and who seemed to wish that the reporters and investigators would go somewhere else to ask their questions. The importance of the Flatwoods case was not that it was just another UFO story but the fact that an extremely weird creature was reported. The Air Force seemed to take the story somewhat seriously originally. After 1952, the Air Force would find excuses not to investigate alien occupant sighting reports.

While it can be argued that the flying saucers of 1947 set the tone for the investigations and sightings to come, it can also be said that the Washington Nationals set the tone for all that would come after them. The Air Force investigation seemed to be quite serious in 1952. Project Blue Book, the official investigation, was headed by one officer and staffed by a number of other officers, as well as enlisted men, who supported the investigation. A small staff of consultants including scientists and civilian technicians was also available. Within a year that investigation would be reduced to a single, low-ranking enlisted man. Yes, within weeks of that low point, there would be another officer assigned, and in months it would again have a small staff, but after the most massive wave of UFO sightings known to that time, the only official, acknowledged, government investigation was allowed to deteriorate to the point where it could barely function at all.

Eventually, Project Blue Book would be staffed by two officers, a sergeant and a civilian secretary but they would not investigate UFO sightings with the same enthusiasm as had been done in 1952. The whole situation changed after the summer of 1952 and that is probably a result of the number of sightings, the increased interest by the public and the news media, and the failure by the Air Force to determine exactly what the flying saucers were, especially those over Washington, D.C. Yes, they would offer an explanation, but it wasn't a very good one.

This work was constructed in an attempt to understand just what had happened and how we arrived at the point where we now find ourselves. Although the main focus is the sightings from Washington National Airport, this is also a look at some of the activities during that summer. This is an attempt to put the UFO sightings into the context of the times

If we can understand some of what happened during the summer of 1952, then we might understand a little more about UFOs. This is the story of what happened that summer and how it affected all of UFO research.

Chapter One: Beginnings

Captain Edward J. Ruppelt, the chief of Project Blue Book in 1952, wrote in, *The Report on Unidentified Flying Objects*, that the year had begun slowly with only a few UFO sighting reports being made. In his attempt to revitalize the stagnant UFO investigation, and to ensure that the Air Force was receiving as many UFO sightings as possible, he had subscribed to a newspaper clipping service. That service would search the nation's newspapers and send to Ruppelt, and Project Blue Book, anything that related to his interest in flying saucers, alien craft, UFOs and other associated anomalies.

Captain Ed Ruppelt

According to Ruppelt, "In March [1952] the clipping service was sending the clippings to us in letter-sized envelopes. The envelopes were thin - maybe there would be a dozen or so clippings in each one. Then they began to get thicker and thicker, until the people who were doing the clipping switched to using manila envelopes. Then the manila envelopes began to get thicker and thicker. By May we were up to old shoe boxes."

In April 1952, *Life* magazine, one of the most respected of the national publications, reviewed the flying saucer situation in an article entitled, "Have We Visitors from Outer Space?" The article, according to press releases from the Air Force and the Pentagon, had used official sources including Project Blue Book and had been, more or less, approved by the Air Force. Key to this article, as opposed to others that had run in other magazine in the five years since the Kenneth Arnold sighting in Washington state had put flying saucers onto the front pages in June 1947, was the question that was being posed in the article's title, "Have we visitors from Outer Space?" *Life*'s answer seemed to be a qualified, "Maybe."

Ruppelt, as well as many others in the Air Force, thought that the treatment by *Life*, that is, suggesting that the government was taking the idea of flying saucers seriously, would lead to an increase in UFO reports. According to Ruppelt, the day after the article appeared, Project Blue Book received nine new reports. The next day, the numbers dropped back to what had been considered normal at the time.

The _Life_ magazine UFO article from 1952.

Ruppelt's theory, as well as the expectation of the Air Force, that more sightings would be reported after the _Life_ article, is fairly standard in the UFO field. Publicity, according to the theory, inspires many people to make UFO sighting reports. Whenever a big-name, respected magazine reports on the topic of UFOs with only what could be thought of as a serious attitude, people begin to feel more secure in their observations and make their reports to the authorities rather than keeping the information to themselves.

The theory, however, has been tested in the past and has failed to produce a new wave of sighting reports. _True_, a men's magazine of the 1950s that had a good reputation for expose, high quality articles and even some top fiction, had reported on flying saucers in articles by Major Donald E. Keyhoe. Those articles suggested that the Air Force had been less than candid with the public in their investigations and findings about UFOs. Keyhoe, in a theme that he would exploit for decades, suggested a cover-up, suggested secret studies and secret conclusions, and an attempt, by the government in general and the Air Force in particular, to mislead the public. Keyhoe's articles, appearing in the then reputable magazines, did not spark waves of sightings.

The Lubbock Lights

In late August and early September 1951, there was a series of interesting sightings over Lubbock, Texas that received widespread publicity, especially in the southwestern United States. Newspapers articles about the sightings begin when four college professors saw a group of glowing, dim lights one evening over Lubbock. After the group of objects had disappeared, the professors, W.I. Robinson, A.G. Oberg, and W.L. Ducker, discussed what they had seen, trying to figure out what the lights might have been. They also tried to determine what they should do if the lights returned. An hour or so later, the lights reappeared, and this time the professors were ready to make a few coordinated, scientific observations.

The lights, on this second pass, were softly glowing, bluish objects in another loose formation. It seemed to the college professors that the first group had been in a more rigid and structured formation than second, or the later groups they saw that night. That was, of course, their first scientific observation.

To the professors the next logical move was to learn if anyone else had seen the lights that night. Ducker called the local newspaper, the *Avalanche-Journal*, and spoke to the managing editor, Jay Harris, who expressed little interest in the sighting. Ducker, however, convinced Harris that a story should be printed which might draw out additional witnesses. Harris reluctantly agreed but only if Ducker allowed his name to be printed. Ducker refused.

But then, a few minutes later, Ducker called Harris again and agreed. In fact, Harris could print the names of all the professors, but only if Harris called the college public relations department and cleared it with them first. Harris had no trouble in getting permission to use the names of the professors, and the story was reported in the next issue.

The newspaper story was considered successful because it did result in additional reports. There were several others who called the editorial offices and claimed to have seen the lights on the same night. That seemed to be some corroboration of the lights seen by the professors. But, the important sighting, at least in the minds of the Air Force officers who later investigated, was made by Joe Bryant of Brownfield, Texas.

Bryant told Air Force officers that he was sitting in his backyard, watching the night sky, when a group of the dim lights flew overhead. He described them as having a "kind of a glow, a little bigger than a star." Not long after that, a

12

second small group appeared. Neither of the groups was in any sort of a regular formation, an important clue that the Air Force officers chose to ignore.

Bryant reported there was a third flight, but instead of flying over his house as before, they dropped down and circled the building. As he watched, one of them chirped quietly and he recognized them immediately. He identified the lights as plover, a bird common in west Texas. When he read the account of the professors' sightings in the newspaper the next day, he knew immediately what they had seen. If he hadn't been able to identify that last flight, if one of the birds hadn't chirped, he would have been fooled, too.

The professors, unaware of what Bryant had seen and believed, set out to obtain additional, scientific information. Joined by other professors and professionals including Grayson Meade, E.R. Heineman and J.P. Brand, they equipped teams with two-way radios, measured a baseline from the location of the original sightings, then staked out the Lubbock area. They hoped for additional sightings along the baseline. Knowing the length of that line, the time of the sighting, and the location and direction of flight, they would be able

Carl Hart, Jr.

to calculate a great deal of very important and useful information that might help them identify what they had been seeing.

The problem for the professors was that none of the teams ever made a sighting. On one or two occasions, the wives of the men, who had remained at one of the professor's house or another, had seen the lights but the men, at the bases, saw nothing. The flight paths of the objects seemed to be limited to the area near specific houses and over limited areas of Lubbock. The plan for calculating the data fell apart because none of the data were collected.

Then, on August 31, just days after the initial sightings, the case took an amazing turn. Carl Hart, Jr., a nineteen-year-old amateur photographer and resident of Lubbock, managed to take five pictures as the lights flew over his house in the middle of city. Lying in bed about ten o'clock, he saw the lights flash overhead. Knowing that they sometimes returned, as had been reported in the newspaper, he prepared for that. When the lights appeared a few minutes later, he was ready, snapping two pictures of them. Not long after that, a third group flew, and he managed three additional pictures.

Harris, the Lubbock newspaper editor, learned about the pictures when a photographer who worked for him periodically called to tell him that Hart had used his studio to develop the film. Harris, the ever-reluctant newsman, suggested that Hart should bring the pictures by the office so that Harris could get a look at them.

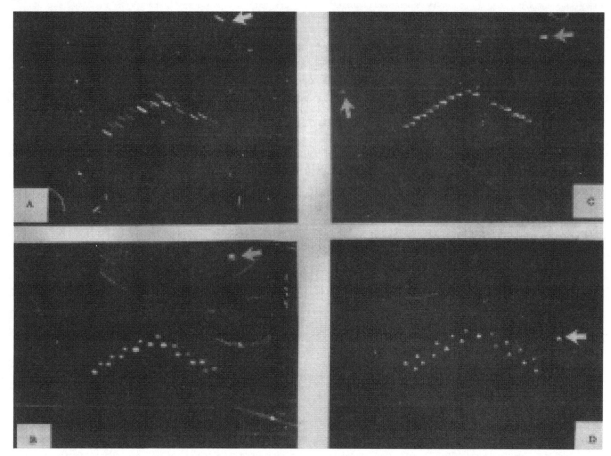

Four of the five photographs taken by Carl Hart, Jr.

Naturally, the newspaper feared a hoax of some kind. Harris, and the newspaper's lead photographer, William Hams, talked to Hart on a number of occasions over the next several hours. Harris bluntly asked if the pictures were faked. Hart denied it. More than forty years later, Hart told Mein 1995 that he still didn't know what he had photographed but that he had not faked anything that night.

Hams later decided to try to duplicate Hart's pictures. From the roof of the newspaper office, he attempted to photograph, at night, anything that flew overhead. He thought, that if he could duplicate the pictures, he would be able to figure out what they showed. He waited, but all he saw was a flight of birds that were barely visible in the glow of the sodium vapor lamps on the streets below him. The birds were dimly outlined against the deeper black of the night sky and flew in a ragged V-formation.

He took photographs of the birds, but when he developed the film, the image was so weak that he couldn't make prints. In fact, the images were so dim that he could barely see them. He repeated his experiment on another occasion but was no more successful. From his experience, he was convinced that what Hart photographed couldn't have been birds under any circumstances because they just didn't reflect enough light and just weren't bright enough.

Serious Air Force investigations were conducted throughout the fall of 1951. Investigators were dispatched from Reese Air Force Base on the west side of Lubbock. They spoke to Hart on a number of occasions. They forwarded copies of their reports to both Project Blue Book headquarters at Wright-Patterson Air Force Base and to Air Force Office of Special Investigation headquarters in Washington, D.C. Ed Ruppelt even made a trip to Lubbock to speak to the major witnesses including Carl Hart.

The Air Force investigators tried to pick apart Hart's story to prove that he had somehow faked the pictures. Between November 6 and 9, during still another investigation of the Lubbock Lights, Ruppelt and AFOSI Special Agent Howard N. Bossert interviewed Hart. In their report, they wrote, "Hart's story could not be 'picked apart' because it was entirely logical. He [Hart] was questioned on why he did certain things, and his answers were all logical, concise, and without hesitation."

What must be done here is to separate the Hart photographs from the rest of the Lubbock case because the photographs might not show what the professors had seen during their initial sightings. In fact, all the sightings must be individually examined, realizing that a solution to one is not necessarily the solution to another or to all the reports.

A Cascade of Solutions

First, are the sightings made by the professors. Clearly this was something that was unusual, at least to them. They were unable to identify the lights. Then, using their scientific training, they set about to find out what they had seen. Although their plan was good, the phenomenon did not cooperate with them. There were some facts obtained and these facts can lead us to some basic conclusions.

For example, the professors had originally estimated the objects as being very large and flying at a very high altitude. They based this assumption on the fact they had heard no noise associated with the lights and they assumed that any

15

sort of manufactured craft would make some noise which they would hear. If they couldn't hear it, then it meant, to them, that the objects were far away. If they were far away, they had to be fairly large to be seen. This line of thought establishes their conclusions about the altitude of over fifty thousand feet and a size of about one hundred feet in diameter.

Later, after they established their baselines, they never saw the objects again. The wives, however, reported the objects over the houses in the center of their observation zone. That would seem to indicate the lights were much smaller and much lower than originally believed. The door is now open for birds, though the problem, once again, is the lack of a bird species flying in a "V" shaped formation in the Lubbock area at that time of the year.

Or is it? Joe Bryant claimed that he saw the lights too, but that one of them, or several of them, swooped out of the sky to fly around his house. At that point he identified them as plover.

From Bryant's claim, the Air Force investigators extrapolated that all the Lubbock sightings could be explained by birds. In one of the reports filed with Project Blue Book, the investigators wrote, "It was concluded that birds, with streetlights reflecting from them, were the probable cause of these sightings... In all instances the witnesses were located in an area where their eyes were dark-adapted, thus making the objects appear brighter."

The problem is, and one with which the Air Force investigators never dealt, that similar sightings, that is, strings of lights in the night skies, were seen all over west Texas. From as far north as Amarillo to as far south as the Midland-Odessa area, reports of these sorts of sightings were made. Birds and the newly installed sodium-vapor lamps in specific areas of Lubbock, which the Air Force investigators believed contributed to the sightings, do not provide an adequate explanation because none of those other cities had the newly installed sodium vapor lamps.

That is relevant here, however, is that Air Force officers made a long, complex investigation of the sightings. Ruppelt flew down from Wright-Patterson Air Force Base and officers and investigators were dispatched repeatedly from nearby Reese AFB. The investigators actually spoke to the witnesses in person, searched for evidence, analyzed the photographs carefully using the latest equipment, and conducted many follow-up interviews. Ruppelt made it clear that he believed there to be a plausible, mundane explanation for the sightings, but never officially said what it was. Later, by searching his personal files including the rough drafts of his book *The Report on Unidentified Flying*

Objects, investigators learned that Ruppelt thought, personally, the Lubbock Lights were explained by fireflies.

Of course, that explanation, like the bird explanation, didn't explain the photographs. Ruppelt wrote that he never found an explanation for them. "The photos were never proven to be a hoax, but neither were they proven to be genuine." According to Ruppelt, "There is no definite answer."

Menzel Provides another Solution

That didn't stop Harvard astronomy professor, Dr. Donald Menzel, from offering an answer. In fact, he offered many answers, but was particularly annoyed by the photographs Hart had taken. Here was a form of physical evidence that something unusual was seen over Lubbock, and it was evidence that not all the sightings were of birds. Menzel finally decided that the photographs were a hoax. He had no other solution for them, and since he couldn't explain what the photographs showed, the only explanation left for him was a hoax.

But Menzel didn't offer his explanations for Lubbock in late 1951. In fact, most of the reporting done about the Lubbock Lights in 1951 was of a fairly objective nature in which the writers told what had been seen and engaged in very little speculation. The various newspaper accounts did not ridicule the witnesses, and there were no crank calls made to their homes. With the reporting being so even-handed, that would seem to inspire others to see UFOs, or lights in the sky, or flying saucers, but the numbers of reports being submitted to the Air Force didn't dramatically increase in the wake of the Lubbock sightings. People might have been interested in the Lubbock Lights, but apparently, they weren't interested enough to go outside to look for lights in their night skies.

Air Force records indicate that the number of UFO reports did increase slightly, however, in April 1952, after the *Life* article, which carried an objective analysis of the Lubbock sightings. At about the same time, Air Force policy changed with the issuance of Air Force Letter 200-5 and Project Blue Book again became a legitimate and important military activity. In fact, the letter allowed the officers of Project Blue Book to contact any Air Force base or unit without having to follow the chain of command. This one point gave Blue Book a great deal of prestige because such authority was rarely given.

With that letter, the number of UFO reports did increase, but the real cause seemed to be that more Air Force units were actively reporting the sightings. The *Life* article also alerted the general public to the existence of the UFO investigation, telling people where to send their UFO reports, if only indirectly.

Once people knew that an official agency was gathering the reports of UFOs, and they knew where to direct their letters, they began to write.

Ed Ruppelt reported that, in early May 1952, he was called by Thomas K. Finletter, in the Office of the Secretary of the Air Force, to brief him on the status of the UFOs. When the briefing ended, Finletter released a statement to the press. "No concrete evidence has yet reached us either to prove or disprove the existence of the so-called flying saucers. There remain, however, a number of sightings that the Air Force investigators have been unable to explain. As long as this is true, the Air Force will continue to study flying saucer reports."

Even such a statement, suggesting that UFOs were something to be seriously studied did not increase the sighting reports. Ruppelt noted that in May, after Finletter's statement, and several weeks after the *Life* article, the number of sightings reported was seventy-nine, down from the ninety-nine made during April 1952.

It seemed, based on the public reaction to the *Life* article, and the reports from Lubbock, and from the other forums in which UFOs were discussed, that flying saucers created little more than an amused detachment. If people thought about them at all, it was more in the category of "Whatever happened to..." They had heard that UFOs were hoaxes, misidentifications, or that they were only reported by those whose education or intelligence was suspect. People had many other, more important things to worry about.

The Air Force kept collecting the sighting reports, and some of them were interesting, but most of them did, in fact, fit into the categories that people thought they did. Balloons, aircraft, stars, meteors, unusual weather phenomena, and people who just wanted to see their names in the newspaper, were responsible for the majority of reports. There didn't seem to be anything solid to UFOs, and no one was talking about them. That is, until the middle of July 1952.

Chapter Two: Early July 1952

July 1952 would be the big month for the UFO sightings that year. It would be the month in which some of the most important cases would be reported and it would be the month that provided some of the best physical evidence that UFOs were not just illusions or delusions, but something solid enough to be filmed and photographed and even displayed on radar. Unfortunately, it would also be a month in which the hoaxes would continue with some spectacular results clouding the already misty picture.

Delbert Newhouse

The month began with one of the best of the movie footage cases ever made because the photographer was a Naval officer, his wife provided additional corroboration, as did his children, and he had nearly a minute of film showing bright, white objects maneuvering against a brilliant blue summer sky. On July 2, 1952, Navy Warrant Officer Delbert C. Newhouse, a trained Navy photographer, was heading toward a new duty station with his wife and two children. Just after eleven in the morning, as they were driving away from Tremonton, Utah, his wife noticed a group of bright objects that she couldn't easily identify. Newhouse, in a statement given to military intelligence officers, said:

> She asked me to stop the car and look. There was a group of about ten or twelve objects - that bore no relation to anything I had seen before - milling about in a rough formation and proceeding in a westerly direction I opened the luggage compartment of the car and got my camera out of a suitcase. Loading it hurriedly, I exposed about thirty feet of film.

According to Newhouse, by the time he got the camera out, the objects had moved away from the car. Newhouse said later:

> [T]here was no reference point in the sky and it was impossible for me to make any estimate of speed, size, altitude or distance. Toward the end one of the objects reversed course and proceeded away from the main group. I held the camera still and allowed this single one to cross the field of view, picking it up again and repeating for three or four such passes. By this time all the objects had disappeared.

The exact details of the story vary, depending on the source. Air Force files, based on the information supplied by others, do confirm that Newhouse and his wife saw the objects at close range. Later Ruppelt, after he had ended his association with Project Blue Book and was out of the Air Force, had an opportunity to speak with Newhouse, apparently for the first time. Ruppelt wrote that Newhouse had told him, "[T]hey [the UFOs] were close to the car, much closer than when he took the movie... he didn't just think the UFOs were disk-shaped; he knew they were; he had seen them plainly."

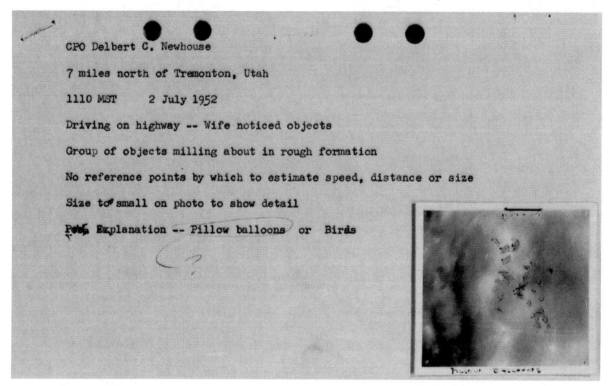

CPO Delbert C. Newhouse

7 miles north of Tremonton, Utah

1110 MST   2 July 1952

Driving on highway -- Wife noticed objects

Group of objects milling about in rough formation

No reference points by which to estimate speed, distance or size

Size too small on photo to show detail

Prob Explanation -- Pillow balloons or Birds

Page from the Project Blue Book file with information about the sighting.

In an interview I conducted in 1976, Newhouse confirmed for me that he had seen the objects at close range. He said they were large, disc-shaped, and brightly lighted. And Dewey Fournet, the Pentagon spokesman for UFOs in the early 1950s, and who was heavily involved in UFO investigations in 1952, told me that Newhouse had said much the same thing to him long ago. Fournet's interview was conducted in 1952, Ruppelt's sometime in the mid-1950s, and mine more than twenty years later. What is important here is that Newhouse's claim about the shape and size of the objects has remained consistent and provides a clue about the shape of the objects that is not available on the film. Newhouse's description of the UFOs would be ignored by some of the official investigators.

After filming the objects, Newhouse stored his camera, got back into the car and drove on to his new duty station in California. Once there, he had the film processed and sent a copy to the Air Force suggesting they might find it interesting. He had done that simply because he knew the Air Force was conducting an investigation into UFOs and he thought the film might be a valuable bit of evidence for them.

Fournet, at the Pentagon, arranged for a group of high-ranking military officers and civilian government officials to see the film. Once they finished with it, the film was returned to Wright-Patterson Air Force Base, home of Project Blue Book, for the proper photographic analysis. That analysis took several weeks, and although the Air Force analysts searched for a conclusive answer, interviewed fighter pilots about the maneuvering of aircraft in dogfights for comparison purposes, noticed the periodic fluctuations in the brightness of the objects, and considered several additional possibilities, they failed to identify the objects. According to Ruppelt, the Air Force photo labs had told him, "We don't know what they are, but they aren't airplanes or balloons, and we don't think they're birds."

Air Force and Navy Study the Film

Fournet then arranged for the Navy to examine the film at their Anacostia Naval Station just outside of Washington, D.C. The Navy made a frame-by-frame analysis that took more than a thousand-man hours and over two months. They studied the motion of the objects, their relation to one another in the formation, the lighting of the objects, and every other piece of data they could find on the film. In the end, like their Air Force counterparts, they were left with no explanations.

But, unlike their Air Force counterparts, the Navy experts were not restricted in their praise of the film. Their report said that the objects were internally lighted spheres that were not reflecting the sunlight. They also estimated the speed at 3,780 miles an hour if the spheres were five miles away. At twice the distance, they would have been moving twice as fast. At half the distance, half the speed. If the objects were just under a mile distant, they were still traveling at 472 miles an hour. The Navy also noted that if the objects were less than a mile away, they would have been identifiable as birds and, according to their analysis, birds simply did not fly at 472 miles an hour.

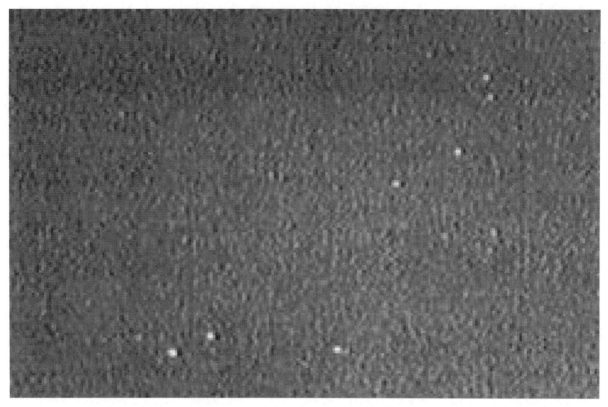

One frame from the Tremonton film showing the objects seen by the Newhouse family.

That is not how the situation would remain, however. In January 1953, in the aftermath of the 1952 wave of flying saucer sightings, the CIA sponsored a scientific inquiry into the UFO question. The panel of five scientists was chaired by Dr. H. P. Robertson. They spent a week looking at some of the best of the UFO information and evidence, including the Tremonton movie taken by Newhouse. As the "Robertson Panel" reviewed the film, Dr. Luis Alverez, one of the scientists, said that he thought the objects might be birds. Fournet told me, in an interview conducted in the mid-1990s, "Dr. Alverez suggested that [birds] as a possible solution to that Tremonton [Utah] movie..."

The next morning, according to Dr. Michael Swords who has studied the Robertson Panel and its historical implications for a number of years, after the scientists on the panel had seen the Tremonton film, "the Air Force, the CIA, has mysteriously produced this film of sea gulls to show them [the panel members] and you just wonder [how they found it so quickly]." He asked, "Wasn't that convenient? They just happened to have that sea gull film handy in the stacks somewhere."

In the years that followed, the Tremonton movie's suggested "possible" explanation of sea gulls became the final solution. Donald H. Menzel and L.G.

22

Boyd, in their book, *The World of Flying Saucers,* wrote of the Tremonton film, "The pictures are of such poor quality and show so little that even the most enthusiastic home-movie fan today would hesitate to show them to his friends. Only a stimulated imagination could suggest that the moving objects are anything but very badly photographed birds."

The University of Colorado's Air Force sponsored UFO investigation known as the Condon Committee had their investigator on the Tremonton film, William K. Hartmann, re-examine the case years after the Robertson panel had made its pronouncement and Menzel believed that he had found the solution. After reviewing the evidence, Hartmann concluded, "These observations give *strong evidence that the Tremonton films do show birds* (emphasis in original), as hypothesized above, and I now regard the objects as so indentified (sic)."

So, a possible answer, first suggested by the Robertson Panel became the final explanation for the film as the years passed. However, in the analyses that have appeared in the years after the Robertson Panel decided on birds, one important fact has always been left out. Newhouse, his wife and children saw the objects at very close range. Fournet told me that he did remember that fact and said, "...when you look at what Newhouse said when he was interviewed after that [by Ruppelt, by Fournet, and later by me] ... When you put all that together, the seagull hypothesis becomes flimsier and flimsier."

Ruppelt, in fact, mentioned that fact in his book. According to him, no one at Project Blue Book had asked Newhouse what the objects looked like because there were pictures of them available. It was only later, after Ruppelt had gotten out of the Air Force, that he talked to Newhouse about what he had seen. Remember Ruppelt wrote, "He didn't *think* the UFO's (sic) were disk-shaped; he *knew* that they were." If that is true, then the bird's explanation is eliminated, though the evidence for that elimination does not appear on the film. For many, it means that the Tremonton film is unidentified. That certainly does not mean that it shows physical spacecraft, but it does suggest that the bird explanation fails badly.

The Newhouse film was only the beginning of the reports made in July 1952. During the next two weeks several dozen additional, solid UFO reports were made to Blue Book headquarters. Pilots, both civilian and military, as well as other military officers, were sighting the UFOs and they were reporting those sightings to their bosses at the airlines or their commanders at their bases. As mentioned, the regulations had been changed and that meant that the military personnel knew what was required of them.

Nash/Fortenberry Sighting

One of the more interesting, and one of the most widely reported of those airliner sightings was that made by two Pan American Airways pilots on July 14, 1952. At the time of the sighting, Captain William B. Nash was in the left seat and next to him was William Fortenberry. It was just after 8:00 p.m., and they were near Norfolk, Virginia, heading toward Miami, Florida, when they spotted the UFOs.

The official Air Force report, as it appears in the Project Blue Book files, states:

Nash on left and Fortenberry on right. A DC-4 type a/c [aircraft], nr. 88901 [meaning the tail number of the airplane] piloted by 2 airline pilots, was approaching Norfolk, Virginia, about 20-25 miles out on the NE leg of the range, at 8,000' when 6 unidentified objects were first sighted approaching a/c on a heading of about 60 deg [northeast] approximately 2,000'. When the objects reached a point under & slightly to the right of the a/c, one of the observers saw them roll up on edge and instantly shoot off on heading 270 deg [due west]. After change of direction, two more objects appeared from behind and joined the formation. Speed of the discs was estimated at well over 1,000 mph. When first seen, they were glowing on top side, with intense amber-red light. Diameter was approximately 100' (estimated) and they were perfectly circular. They approached DC-4 in narrow echelon and appeared to decelerate before changing direction. With deceleration, dimming of glow was noted; immediately after changing direction and flattening out, glow disappeared entirely. They reappeared once, glowing brightly again, this time in sequence rather than simultaneously, and they were lost from view. Sighting occurred at 2012 EST [8:12 p.m.] on 14 July 1952. Total duration of sighting was 15 seconds.

The Air Force officer who wrote the report made a few additional notes under a section titled, "Air Force Comments: Five jet a/c were in vicinity of Langley AFB at the time of the observation. After various checks with surrounding AF agencies, it was concluded that the objects were not the 5-jet a/c. Other checks for known airborne objects were made with negative results. Air Force Conclusion: Unidentified."

In later interviews, Nash added some details. He described the objects' maneuvering, saying, "They flipped on edge, the sides to the left of us going up and the glowing surfaces facing right. Though the bottom surfaces did not become clearly visible, we had the impression they were unlighted. The exposed edges, also unlighted, appeared to be about fifteen feet thick, and the top surface, at least seemed flat. In shape and proportion, they were much like coins."

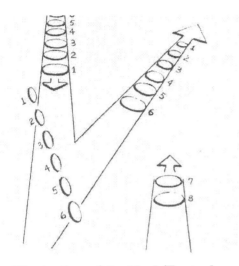

Illustration of the Nash/Fortenberry sighting.

Nash said that the original six disks had dimmed just before the turn, and then brightened again. The two disks that joined the formation later were the brightest of them all. Once the objects disappeared, Fortenberry and Nash made a radio report of the sighting to be sent on to the Air Force.

Nash told researchers, "At seven a.m. the morning after the sighting, we were telephoned by the Air Force... to come in for questioning. There were five men, one in uniform; the others showed us ID cards and badges of Special Investigators, USAF. In separate rooms, we were questioned for one hour and forty-five minutes - then about half an hour together... They had a complete weather report... [and] our flight plan. The investigators also advised us that they already had seven other reports. One was from a Lieutenant Commander..." That would mean he was a Naval officer and not a member of the Air Force.

Donald Menzel was not as enthusiastic in his praise of the case. He carried on a long dialog with Nash that resulted in several letters that ran to pages and pages. Menzel tried to be complimentary about Nash's qualifications as a pilot and an observer, but Nash seemed convinced that Menzel was only interested in "debunking" his report. Nash concluded one of his long letters to Menzel saying, "It would be a pleasure to have you aboard my aircraft. I think, however, that when I invited you to the cockpit, it would behoove us to avoid this subject [the UFO sighting] until on the ground where we'd have hollering room."

Menzel, in *The World of Flying Saucers,* offered what he believed to be the solution to the case. He noted, early on, "As a pilot spending much of his life in the air, Captain Nash had long been interested in the question of UFOs, and during the long night hours of over-water flights he had often cut down the cockpit lights to search the sky. In five years of watching, he had observed hundreds of meteors, various types of auroral display, the lights of other aircraft, and the multicolored images of stars and planets distorted by [atmospheric] refraction, but he had never seen any unidentifiable aerial phenomenon that appeared to be under intelligent control - until this particular night, when he was not watching for UFOs."

Menzel recounts the sighting in some detail in his book, adding a few colorful adjectives and produces a very readable history of the case. He notes that although Nash had said that Air Force investigators told him of seven witnesses on the ground, none are mentioned in the Blue Book files, which is true. Menzel also said that Nash had told him that the visibility was "unlimited," but the weather records, available in the Blue Book files show the visibility at eight miles with a slight indication of haze. These sorts of facts are always of interest to Menzel.

Menzel then explains that when a sighting can't be explained, and "when puzzling observations in a laboratory seem to point to a conclusion that contradicts the main body of scientific knowledge, the researcher first tries to repeat the experiment and duplicate the observations. If this is impossible, as with the Chesapeake Bay phenomena [the Nash/Fortenberry case], he next re-examines the assumptions on which the conclusion is based." Menzel then proceeds to do exactly that.

Having looked at the observations by the pilots, Menzel assumed that they are simply wrong. He is not suggesting that either man had attempted a hoax, only that they had been inaccurate in some of their basic observations, especially those that would have required some instrumentation to be accurate. Menzel then attacks the sighting from another angle, finally offering his solution for it.

Menzel wrote, "A thorough study of the situation showed that inversions of both temperature and humidity must have been present." I will note here, only because it seems to be in direct opposition to what Menzel had written about re-examining assumptions, that he has made an assumption. He wrote that the inversion layers "must" have been present, not that they were present. No meteorological evidence existed for these inversions. Menzel worked around that, suggesting, "Small in extent, existing only briefly in one place, constantly changing location, such inversions may not be detected by radiosonde [that is, balloon-borne meteorological observations made by the weather service] observations. During July and August [1952], temperature inversions occurred almost every night in the coastal regions and accounted for the radar angels [blips] so frequently observed in the Washington [D.C.] area during those weeks.

Even with the explanation, as provided by Menzel, in the Project Blue Book files, the case was still labeled as "unidentified," in the final index of UFO reports made by Air Force officers. This means, quite simply, that the Air Force officers charged with explaining the UFO sightings, had not found Menzel's explanation to be persuasive. And, in July 1952, they didn't have time to concentrate on a single case. There were always others being reported.

More Unidentified Sightings

Just two nights later, on July 16, more UFOs were seen in the Washington, D.C. area, this time by two men on the ground. According to the "Air Intelligence Information Report" prepared by Paul Hill and 2Lt Alfonse R. Russo:

> Two amber lights, further apart than they would be on a plane, were flying northwards. Size Unknown. No noise, no sound. The two amber lights made 180 degree turn towards the West. The apparent altitude varied from about 10 degrees when first sighted to about 20 degrees altitude at the middle of their turn. When these two lights made the turn, they jockeyed for position in a jagged movement. About this time a third light came up and joined them, placing itself right beneath the other two. They were a strong amber or straw color. There was no variation of intensity or change in the appearance of the lights when they turned. There was an airplane coming from the Southeast, the direction of Norfolk Airport, toward the Northwest and, as it came across Hampton Roads, it seemed to cut right between the lights. The noise of the airplane was heard, and its green and white lights seen. This placed the fact that the yellow lights were apparently well in the background of the airplane. Other than this no estimate of their distance or size was possible. As they went South, they held constant altitude for a while and then seemed to be climbing until they were possibly twice as high as when they first were seen. After traveling South about a minute, three other lights appeared to join them as they went away, seeming to form more or less of a circle and faded out in the distance.

The sighting lasted for about three minutes and both of the observers, neither of whom was identified in the Blue Book file, were technically trained people. Ruppelt noted that one of the men was "a high-ranking civilian scientist from the National Advisory Committee for Aeronautics Laboratory at Langley AFB."

In attempting to identify these lights, the Air Force tried all their normal explanations and rejected them one by one. Ruppelt eventually wrote, "We investigated and found that there were several B-26's from Langley AFB in the area at the time of the sighting, but none of the B-26 pilots remembered being over Hampton Roads [Virginia]. In fact, all of them had generally stayed well south of Norfolk until about 10:30 p.m. because of thunderstorm activity northwest of Langley."

The Blue Book file contains the weather records for that day and that location, and they don't mention thunderstorms. There is a mention of cloud-to-cloud lightning in the area. The Air Force suggestion is that the lightning "might have affected these sightings."

Ruppelt continued his report, writing, "There were other factors... airplanes carry just one or two amber lights, and the distance between the two lights was such that had they been on an airplane the airplane would have been huge or very close to the observers. And last, but not least, the man from the National Advisory Committee for Aeronautics was a very famous aerodynamicist and of such professional stature that if he said the lights weren't airplanes they weren't."

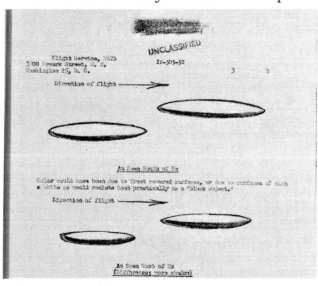

Illustration from the Project Blue Book files.

Ruppelt's opinion about the man's stature notwithstanding, the official explanation, as listed in the Blue Book files is, "Aircraft."

Out west, in Las Vegas, Nevada, another formation of UFOs was sighted on July 15. According to the statement in the Project Blue Book files, a man (his name redacted by Air Force officers in 1976) reported:

> About 8:45 a.m., I was sitting at our breakfast table talking with my wife. Also present in the kitchen adjoining, were my

28

daughter..., age 11, two employees..., adult and..., age 16 [all names removed by Air Force censors]. My wife was seated facing the window, South. Suddenly she cried out, "Flying saucers!"

I made a remark, jokingly, in disbelief, and then seeing her intent gaze and apparent sincerity, I jumped up, and with my wife, daughter and followed by ... dashed into the yard at the South side of the house. At this time, I first sighted two flying objects. Bearing S. W., azimuth 25 degrees about the horizon. This by subsequent estimation against large trees, looking from the point of observation. Course of the objects apparently Westerly, slight down glide, very smooth and apparently very rapid. I realize that speed could not be judged without knowing distance of object, which could not be estimated....

"My description of the objects would be two discrete lens shaped objects, the leading one above the following one, color identical to that of small dense clouds. Under shadow same as under a cloud. Top, silvery, white same as cloud. No fringe, tails, lights, sound or other manifestations. I will state that at the time I considered first that I might be looking at a gunnery target towed by an aluminum-colored jet plane. But this concept was discarded while the objects were still under observation, due one, to the short length and two, to the large angle off the line of flight which a tow rope would have had to make. I have seen gliders pulled off and do not believe even a glider could have made the relative position to its towing plane that was made by these two objects.

Air Force investigators also took a statement from the wife. Her story, of course, matched that told by her husband, though she did add some interesting detail. She wrote, "I saw two very small objects glide into view from 'behind' the next house chimney. At first, they looked like gulls gliding but I realized they were no such things here.... A re-enactment of our motions and words from the time I first spotted them until we saw them disappear was 30 seconds."

The male witness had a long background at weather stations in the southwest. His vision was better than average and there is no reason to suspect that he misidentified the objects, especially with the corroboration of his wife and the others. However, the Air Force investigators noted that "Nellis AFB, [Las Vegas, Nevada] reported jet a/c in the area at time." The official explanation was marked as "probably aircraft."

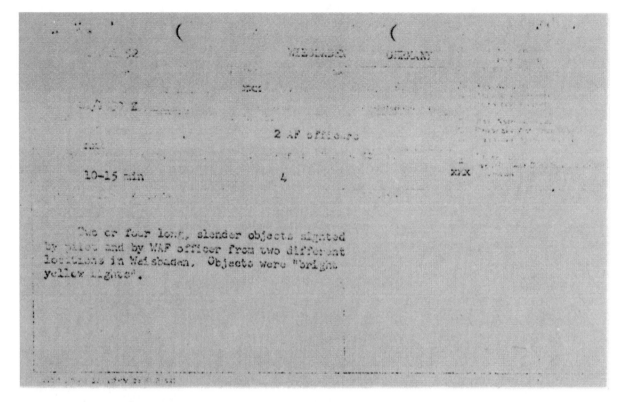

The badly faded Project Record Card but the important information is visible.

On July 21, 1952, two officers, Captain Edward E. Dougher and Lieutenant Josephine J. Strong, who were both considered "absolutely reliable. Inasmuch as their observations were very similar and were made from two completely different locations in Wiesbaden, [Germany] at the same time and in the same area, it can be safely assumed that they both observed the same demonstration."

According to the once classified Air Intelligence Information Report found in the Blue Book files, the observation by Captain Dougher was described this way:

> No object as such was sighted. "Object" was a bright yellowish-white light of indefinite size. Four (4) were seen in the NNW direction from Wiesbaden, and they appeared to be travelling from NNW to SSE and climbing. Suddenly they burst apart, two (2) climbing until they went behind the branches of some trees under which Captain Dougher was standing, and the other two (2) leveling off and going in two opposite directions, generally East to West. The one going East went behind a small hill in about one (1) minute, whereas the other remained in sight for about fifteen (15) minutes, or enough time for Captain Dougher to drive home (about

30

2 miles), park his car, go into the apartment, and out on his porch where he and his wife watched the light, now getting very dim, disappear behind some small hills to the East. Captain Dougher believes that the light was several miles away. No sound was heard and there were no other unusual features. Flight appeared to be straight and level after the initial "burst" of four (4) lights.

It was noted in the official report that the time of the sighting was about 7:26 to 7:40 p.m. and that Dougher made the observations from the ground. It was also noted that Dougher was a pilot who was not on flying status at the time of the sighting. There was a C-47 flying in the area at the time, but Dougher was certain that what he saw was not an aircraft.

Lieutenant Strong also made a statement that was reported on the same document as that of Dougher. It said:

Lt Strong also reported that she saw no object as such, but that she saw to "reddish" colored lights going in opposite directions, approximately East and West. When first sighted they were close together, but in about two (2) minutes the one going East disappeared behind a building. The light going West, however, continued in the same general direction for about ten (10) minutes, finally nose-diving over and disappearing into the clouds. Lt Strong would not give an estimate of the speed because she had no idea of the distance to the light. She did say that from her observation point the light travelled about 45 [degrees] in five (5) minutes. Nothing unusual was noted concerning the flight characteristics, and no noise was heard. Lt Strong did say that shortly after observing this light she observed a C-47 in the same general direction. Comparing relative sizes, she said the light appeared to her to be about four (4) times the length of the fuselage of the C-47.

There were, of course, a few additional facts. She reported the times of the sighting as 7:25 to 7:35 p.m. She was in downtown Wiesbaden and that the lights were first in the NNW. The altitude and distance are unknown but Strong did say the objects to be about 30 degrees to the horizontal.

Captain Gerald M. Jones was the preparing officer and he added one additional comment. "Lt Strong was about one (1) mile closer to the initial "burst" of lights than was Captain Dougher. Lt Strong's position was almost exactly between Captain Dougher's original position and the direction in which the burst was observed."

31

Analysis

There are a number of things that all these cases, as well as many of the others that were reported, have in common. They are multiple witness, though all the witnesses in each were together when the sightings were made. The sightings were all of multiple craft, sometimes flying in a formation and sometimes merely "milling about." All were made by people with some technical expertise, so that it can't be said that the sightings were made by the unschooled or by those who were easily fooled.

What is most important here is that the sightings were made from around the country. It wasn't a localized phenomenon, but something that could appear just about anywhere at any time. The sightings provided an interesting perspective for the major cases that would follow in a few days.

Donald Menzel, in his analysis of the situation, that is, what was happening in July 1952, suggested that the two major magazine articles, first in *Life* and then in *Look* suggested UFOs to the people. When confronted with something strange in the sky, their first reaction, because of those national publications, was to assume that what they were seeing were flying saucers. Other evidence, including the timing of the events, as examined earlier, suggests otherwise. The articles had been published months earlier, and if there was a causal relation, it would have been generated earlier.

It should also be noted here that these were not the only sightings to have been made. As mentioned earlier, the total number of sightings reported to the Air Force had not significantly changed after publication of the articles. The totals for April, as reported by Ruppelt were up, but then the totals for May were down. Fewer than a hundred sightings had been reported in either April or May.

That, however, changed in June. The numbers jumped significantly. In June there were 129 sightings reported to Project Blue Book. In July the numbers jumped again. In the past, a month's reports might be found on a single page in the index. June was broken down into three pages. July covered sixteen pages with the sightings for July 27, 28, and 29 each listed on a single page. On July 28 alone there were 31 sightings reported. By the end of the month, more than 400 sightings had been logged into Project Blue Book. Of course, the staff had not increased so that the investigations were directed toward the best of the crop. Sometimes, according to the Blue Book files, little was done, once the report had been made. There were simply too many sightings and too few investigators.

The types or sightings being reported, of multiple craft in some kind of formation foreshadowed the events that would take place over Washington, D.C. Late on the evening of July 19, the first of the sightings that would become known as the Washington Nationals began. These were the events that would demand the lion's share of the investigative resources because before the sightings ended, President Truman had asked for some answers.

Chapter Three: July 19/20, 1952

The stage was now set for the most spectacular of the UFO sightings during the summer of 1952. In fact, Ed Ruppelt, in his book, *The Report on Unidentified Flying Objects*, said that the sightings, which would later become known as the Washington Nationals, had been predicted by a scientist who told him, Ruppelt, "Within the next few days, they're [the flying saucers] going to blow up and you're going to have the granddaddy of all UFO sightings. The sighting will occur in Washington or New York, probably Washington."

Just a few days later, the Washington Nationals, so named because the radar facilities in which the majority of the sightings were made were located at Washington National Airport, later was renamed as Ronald Reagan Washington National Airport, began there. According to the CAA's (forerunner of the Federal Aeronautics Administration) logbook, two radars at the Air Routing and Traffic Control Center (ARTC) picked up eight unidentified targets near Andrews Air Force Base at 11:40 P.M. on the evening of July 19. Air Traffic Controller Edward Nugent spotted seven blips clustered together in the corner of his radar scope. Nugent believed that they were in an area about fifteen miles south-southwest of Washington, D.C. These were not airplanes because, at one point, they accelerated far faster than conventional aircraft could fly. First, they moved along at only a hundred miles an hour, then suddenly would seem to accelerate to fantastic speeds. One of the objects was tracked, according to the calculations made at the Center, at 7,000 miles an hour. In 1952 there was nothing that could fly at that speed that would be in the skies above Washington, D.C.

Nugent then called the senior air traffic controller on duty, Harry C. Barnes. Barnes later wrote, "We knew immediately that a very strange situation existed.... They [the unidentified blips on the radar] followed no set course [and] were not in any formation, and we only seemed to be able to track them for about three miles at a time. The individual pip would seem to disappear from the scope at intervals. Later I realized that if these objects had made any sudden burst of extremely high speed, that would account for them disappearing from the scope..." And that would put them in the range of the 7,000 mile an hour bursts noticed by Nugent.

The first thing for the controllers to do was check the radar equipment to make sure that it was functioning properly. Two other controllers, both trained in basic maintenance found nothing wrong with the gear. Barnes then called his counterpart at the airport at Tower Central. The facility was located about a quarter mile away, on the same airfield, and if the radars at the ARTC were malfunctioning, those at Central should not be affected. Howard Cocklin told Barnes that they had spotted, and were tracking, the same objects that he was. Cocklin also said that he had looked out the windows of the control tower and saw one of the objects high overhead. He described the object later as a bright orange light, but he could see no shape behind the light and could offer no other details about it.

The Washington National Air Traffic Controllers.

Barnes next called Andrews Air Force Base, now known as Joint Base Andrews, which is nearby and asked if they had anything on their radars but was told that the only thing they were tracking was a C-47 that was about an

35

hour away from Washington and scheduled to land at Andrews. The radar operators weren't seeing anything out of the ordinary on their screens. Moments later, Barnes made another call to Andrews and suggested that they look outside because there was something strange in the sky near the Air Force base. Airman William Brady looked out, to the south, and saw, what he later described as "an object which appeared to be like an orange ball of fire, trailing a tail. It appeared to be about two miles south and one-half miles from the Andrews range. It was very bright and definite and unlike anything I had ever seen..."

Other Facilities Involved

He tried to get the others in the Andrews facility with him to look to verify the sighting, but even as he shouted at them, the brightly glowing object stopped moving and then just seemed to vanish. According to Brady, it "took off at an unbelievable speed," as it disappeared in a split second.

Moments later, according to Brady "I saw another one, same description. As the one before, it made an arc-like pattern and then disappeared. I only saw each object for about a second." Again, he was the only one to see either of these objects.

No one else in the tower saw any of those lights even with Brady's help. Later, there would be other sightings in the tower, but for the moment, Brady was alone in his observations. That might have been a result of the events happening so quickly, or it might have been that what Brady thought unusual was nothing more mundane than stars seen through a thin layer of haze that would periodically obscure them. That suggestion would later be offered by Air Force investigators as an explanation for his sightings.

Joseph DeBoves, who was also on the scene as a civilian control tower operator at Andrews, said that Brady became excited during one of his telephone conversations, yelling, "There one goes." DeBoves believed that Brady was watching nothing more interesting than a meteor.

On the other hand, there is a memo in the Project Blue Book files that notes a sighting from the ATRC, that is Washington National Airport, at about 12:30 a.m. of "an orange disk about 3,000 feet... at 360 degrees [due north]." That could be independent confirmation of Brady's sightings made at Andrews and evidence of something more real than illusion.

Just after midnight, Airman Second Class (A/2c) Bill Goodman, called the Andrews control tower to tell them he was watching a bright orange light about the size of a softball that was gaining and losing altitude as it zipped through the night sky. This seemed to be further confirmation that something unusual was in the sky over the Washington, D.C. area and it seemed to corroborate the visual sightings made by Brady.

About two in the morning on July 20, the Radar Officer, Captain Harold C. Way, at Andrews Approach Control learned that the ARTC had a target east of Andrews. He went outside and saw a strange light which he didn't believe to be a star. He said that he thought it was changing colors, from "red to orange to green to red again." He said that it seemed to rapidly lose altitude, and then climb again. Later, however, he went back out, and this time, according to what he told Air Force investigators later, decided that he was, in fact, looking at a star.

Bolling Air Force Base, another Air Force installation in the Washington, D.C. area, became involved briefly about the time Way went outside. The tower operator there said that he saw a "roundish" object drifting low in the sky to the southeast of Bolling. There were no radar confirmations of the sighting. It did, however, now involve a third government facility in the sightings that were being made that evening.

The ATRC radar operators at National Airport began to detect targets near Bolling and informed the tower operators, including SSGT Richard Lacava, the operations dispatcher, at Bolling. In the mobile control tower, that is a truck mounted control tower that can be repositioned around the airfield, SSGT Don Wilson spotted a round, white-amber-colored light that he believed was about seven miles to the southeast of the airfield. He said that it was about the intensity of a star. It drifted slowly and though visible for a few minutes, Wilson could see nothing other than the bright light.

In still another sighting from that area, a guard going off-duty saw, in the southwest, an object that he said, "Looked to be the size of a golf ball... bright orange in color. The object moved from the west to the northeast in a half circle pattern and was traveling at such speed that I knew that it could not be a jet aircraft.... It would be hard to judge the altitude the object was flying because it seemed to lose and gain altitude. The object moved in this pattern several times and then disappeared into the west. From the time I saw the object and then lost it, I would say it was about 15 to 20 minutes." This meant that the guard had gotten a very good look at the object. This was no fleeting light seen for only a few seconds.

Back at Andrews, Staff Sgt. Charles Davenport spotted an orange-red light to the south of the base. According to his statement, "It would appear to stand still, then make an abrupt change of direction and altitude." Davenport called the tower and the men there also saw the object before it vanished in a burst of speed.

The ARTC again told the controllers at Andrews that they still had the targets on their scopes. There is conflicting data in the files, and in other source documents, because some of the reports suggest that the Andrews radar showed nothing, while other reports claim they did. Now DeBoves, and two others in the tower, Monte Banning and John P. Izzo, Jr., swept the sky with binoculars but could see no lights other than the stars.

There were some multiple radar facility sightings. At one point during the night, the radars in the ARTC, the National Airport Tower, and at Andrews all were fixed on an object hovering over the Riverdale Radio beacon. For thirty seconds it remained there, giving the radar operators in all three locations the chance to check their readings and their equipment against one another. The target vanished from the three radar screens at the same time. This suggested to the men that they were looking at something real and not some sort of a weather-related phenomenon.

Interceptors Brought In

The sightings lasted through the night, and during that time, the crews of several airliners saw the lights right where the radars showed them to be. Tower operators also saw them, and jet fighters were brought in for attempted intercepts to identify the objects. Associated Press stories written hours after the sightings claimed that no intercepts had been attempted that night, but those stories were inaccurate. Documents in the Project Blue Book files, as well as eyewitnesses, confirm the attempted intercepts. Barnes, in fact, believed that the UFOs were monitoring the radio traffic because, about 3:00 a.m. all the mysterious targets suddenly disappeared. Moments later, two F-94 jet interceptors, scrambled from New Castle Air Force Base, appeared. Although the interceptor pilots searched for the UFOs, they found, and saw, nothing. Low fuel finally forced them to return to their base. As the jets disappeared, the UFOs reappeared.

F-94 Fighter like this was used in the intercepts.

At about 3:30 a.m., SSGT C. T. Davenport, an aircraft mechanic, saw an object at treetop level. This one was bluish-white in color and moved erratically. He said, "Three times I saw a red object leave the silver object at a high rate of speed and move east, out of sight."

It wasn't just the men on the ground, in the towers at Andrews and Washington National, or at the radar screens who were seeing the UFOs. Airline pilots were also spotting the lights. Typical of the sightings were those made by Captain Casey Pierman on Capital Airlines flight 807. He was on a flight between Washington and Martinsburg, West Virginia, at 1:15 A.M. on July 20, when he, and the rest of the crew saw seven objects flash across the sky in front of them. Pierman said, "They were like falling stars without trails."

Capital Airline officials said that National Airport radar picked up the objects and asked Pierman to keep an eye on them. Shortly after takeoff, Pierman radioed that he had the objects in sight. He was flying at 180 to 200 mph, and reported the objects were traveling at tremendous speed. Official Air Force records confirm this, which means that Pierman did make the report to military officers.

Another Capital Airlines pilot, Captain Howard Dermott, on Capital Flight 610, reported a single light followed him from Herndon, Virginia, to within four miles of National Airport. Both the ARTC and the National Tower confirmed that an unidentified target followed the aircraft to within four miles of landing. At about the same time, an Air Force radar at Andrews AFB was tracking eight additional unknown objects as they flew over the Washington area.

Repeatedly, throughout the night, Barnes attempted to alert various military authorities about the series of UFO sightings. He wanted the closest Air Force intelligence officer alerted so that a military record of the sightings, at the civilian facilities, could be created. He spoke to the duty officers who would only tell him that the information was being forwarded up the chain of command and that they had no authority to do anything else. It is clear, however, that military officials were responding to the sightings, otherwise, there would have been no attempted intercepts.

Later, Barnes would tell investigators, both for the military and for the University of Colorado's Condon Committee, that the experience of finding unidentified radar and visual targets, where there was supposed to be nothing in the air, frightening. Barnes also mentioned that the UFOs had flown in the vicinity of the White House, which would later become a point of interest to many.

Barnes also said that, at the time, no one in the facility with him believed they were watching Russian aircraft, military experiences, or visitors from another world. Instead, all the men were puzzled by the events. And, though Barnes seemed to have ruled out manufactured craft, he said that everyone believed that the objects were under intelligence control.

The radar returns, and UFO sightings, continued almost to dawn. At about 5:30 a.m., seven or eight of the UFOs were seen on the scopes at the ARTC. They faded from sight quickly. At about this same time, E.W. Chambers, a radio engineer, saw five huge disks circling in a loose formation over the Washington, D.C. area. He clearly saw shapes of the objects, rather than just lights in the distance. The disks tilted upwards and disappeared climbing steeply.

Just before daylight, about four in the morning, after repeated requests from the ARTC, another F-94 interceptor arrived on the scene, but it was too little too late. All the targets were gone. Although the flight crew made a short search of the local area, they found nothing unusual or exciting and returned to their base quickly.

During that night, apparently the three radar facilities only once reported a target that was seen by all three radars at the same time. There were, however, a number of times when the ARTC radar and the Washington National tower radars had simultaneous contacts. It also seems that the radars were displaying the same targets that were seen by the crews of the Capital Airlines flights. What it boils down to is that multiple radars and multiple eyewitnesses were showing and seeing objects in the sky over Washington where each other suggested they were.

Barnes would later write, "[The UFOs] became most active around the planes we saw on the scope... [T]hey acted like a bunch of small kids out playing... directed by some innate curiosity. At times they moved as a group or cluster, at other times as individuals over widely scattered areas... There is no other conclusion that I can reach but that for six hours there were at least 10 unidentified flying objects moving above Washington. They were not ordinary aircraft. I could tell that by their movement on the scope. I can safely deduce that they performed gyrations which no known aircraft could perform. By this I mean that our scopes showed that they could make right angle turns and complete reversals of flight. Nor in my opinion could any natural phenomena such as shooting stars, electrical disturbances or clouds account for these spots on our radar."

Barnes would confirm that opinion later, as he talked with the investigators for the Condon Committee. It was nearly fifteen years after the events, and Barnes told the investigators that, "A number of objects, some seven or eight, would be in a place as a group, then seem to go over to an aircraft to take a look. If the aircraft attempted evasive action by turning, the objects would turn too. They seemed, furthermore, to have monitored messages between the aircraft and the tower. When a particular pilot was told to look for an object the pilot would see it but would report that it was zooming off at just about the time at just about the time at which the target also disappeared from the radar set. Many of the objects were extremely maneuverable."

Barnes told the Condon investigator that he didn't believe that the objects they had detected were "ghost" or weather-related phenomena. Barnes ruled out a malfunction as well, telling the investigators that Washington National, Andrews, and Andrews Approach Control had all independently sighted the objects in the same place about the same time. Barnes said that all the radars were operating normally and that men at all three facilities were in contact with one another and confirming the other sightings.

The only downside was that none of the radars used that night had height finding capability. They could record the direction to the object, and by knowing the sweep time of the scope's antenna, they could determine the speed. They just didn't know how high the objects were. That made the attempted intercepts a little more difficult to manage.

Importantly, the Condon Committee investigator learned that during one of the attempted intercepts, the radar onboard the jet fighter obtained a lock on one of the objects. That increased the number of radars involved in the night's activities. The pilot, however, did not have a visual sighting at that time.

The first night of the Washington Nationals had ended with the controllers frustrated by the lack of response by the military. Both visual and radar sightings were made, often with an object seen in the sky where the radar suggested that it should be. Radars at three different locations picked up the returns, but only once, as mentioned, did all three radars display the same objects. And, only once, as mentioned, did an aircraft's onboard radar acquire an object.

Importantly, there were attempted intercepts made, but the fighters were required to scramble from Air Force bases outside the Washington, D.C. area because the runways at Andrews were closed for repairs. That certainly slowed the response time, and required that requests for the intercepts travel, somewhat slowly, through the military chain of command, first up toward the Pentagon, and then down to the local base. However, the fighters did reach the area, but, unfortunately, those pilots, on those intercepts didn't see anything unusual.

The night had ended and the sightings on the radars at the various facilities had ended. But that was only for a short period of time. And, although, many would report on the second night of sightings at Washington National, and, although, military representatives would be at the airport to watch the activity, there were other sightings in the area between those two nights. Some very interesting sightings came out of the interim.

Chapter Four: The Air Force Investigation, Part I

After the first night of the Washington Nationals, Air Force intelligence, including ATIC and the officers assigned to the UFO project, that is Project Blue Book, had no idea that these sightings had taken place. They learned of the Saturday night - Sunday morning UFO show when the information was published in several newspapers on Monday, July 21. Ruppelt, on business in Washington, D.C. with Colonel Donald Bower and unaware of the sightings, reported, "I got off an airliner from Dayton and I bought a newspaper in the lobby of Washington National Airport Terminal Building. I called the Pentagon from the airport and talked to Major Dewey Fournet, but all he knew was what he read in the papers. He told me he had called the intelligence officer at Bolling AFB and that he was making an investigation. We would get a preliminary official report by noon."

So, the official Air Force investigation was not off to a running start. The chief of that investigation, Ruppelt, hadn't even been alerted during the sightings, nor had he been informed the following day. He had to learn about the string of sightings from the newspaper.

Harry Barnes had tried to find an intelligence officer during the first night of sightings but was unable to alert anyone. It would have been better for the investigation had an Air Force officer been either at the ARTC or in the tower that night to make personal observations. That officer would have been able to observe things firsthand rather than have to rely on the testimony of those who had been there, some of whom were lower ranking enlisted personnel. The perspective, from a trained intelligence officer, might have been a little crisper.

It was about one in the afternoon on that Monday when Fournet called Ruppelt and told him that the intelligence officer from Bolling was now available for a briefing. Ruppelt found Bower, and together they went to Fournet's office. They  received the preliminaries, including a brief rundown on where each of the facilities was in relation to the other. Washington National was, and is, about three miles south of the heart of Washington, D.C., Bolling AFB is on the other side of the Potomac River, and farther along, about ten miles away, on a line with Bolling and Washington National, was Andrews AFB. All three had radars, though the capabilities of those radars varied from location to location and depended on the mission of the facility. All the airfields were linked by an intercom system so that they could coordinate the air traffic in and around Washington, D.C., and in and around each of their airfields.

Dewey Fournet

Ruppelt, after sitting in on the briefing, knew exactly what had to be done, knew what questions should be asked, and where to go to get the statements and evidence he needed for a complete investigation of the UFO sighting that were fast becoming front page news in various parts of the country. Bureaucracy, however, was no more interested in flying saucers than the Pentagon seemed to be at the moment. There were regulations to be followed, regardless of the consequences, there were orders to be issued, and when every other roadblock had been hurtled, there was the standard bureaucratic inertia that slowed everything to a near standstill and stopped all creative and independent thought.

Ruppelt reported that "Feeling like a national martyr because I planned to work all night, if necessary, I laid the course of my investigation."

Unfortunately, his orders had called for him to return to Wright-Patterson after his regularly scheduled meetings at the Pentagon. That would be a hurtle to leap later in the day. He wanted to begin his investigation.

He tried to arrange a staff car, but in brass heavy Washington, only very senior colonels and generals could get staff cars on short notice. Ruppelt was neither a senior colonel nor a general and he was assigned to Wright-Patterson, so no one wanted much to do with him. Ruppelt called the colonels and generals he knew at the Pentagon hoping that they would understand the necessity for him to have a car, but none of them were available, and none answered his telephone calls, so no staff car could be had.

He was told, by the bureaucrats who cared nothing for flying saucers, or even national security if it wasn't written down somewhere so they could cite the appropriate authority, he could rent a car but not charge it as a travel expense because city busses were available. He could take cabs, but that wasn't a legitimate expense because city busses were available. Riding a bus was not the best way to conduct an important intelligence investigation, especially when the locations he had to visit were in widely separated parts of the city and he didn't know the city all that well. He would waste hours riding around Washington, trying to get from one end of the city to the other.

To make matters worse, Ruppelt was then told that his orders didn't cover an overnight stay in Washington. If he didn't get his orders amended, or return to Dayton that day, he wouldn't collect his expense money (per diem) and would be, technically, at least, absent without leave. And he couldn't talk to the finance officer because he was already gone for the day even though it was before four-thirty in the afternoon. In other words, there was no real way to get his orders amended so that he could stay in Washington to begin his investigation.

Ruppelt then called Colonel Bower, told him of the experience, and said that he would have to return to Dayton. Bower agreed that there was no other solution available to them. Bureaucracy had won out over investigation.

In a Memorandum for the Record, dated 23 July 1952 with a subject of "ATIC Participation in the Investigation of the Washington Incident of 20 July 1952," a slightly different version of these same events appears. According to the document, "3. Before the afternoon was over it appeared that this was going to be a 'hot' incident. Capt. Ruppelt called Col. Bower in Lt. Col. Teaburg's office and offered to stay over in Washington to get the investigation started but was advised that this should not be done."

Ruppelt was not without support in official Washington, however. Ruppelt had been told that the President, Harry Truman, was interested in the sightings and wished that a full investigation be made. Ruppelt, of course, wanted to comply, but there just wasn't time late on Monday afternoon for him to make the arrangements to stay, let alone begin his investigation, without getting into trouble with the Air Force.

Ruppelt then returned to Wright-Patterson where the number of UFO reports had risen to about forty a day. He was still concentrating on the Washington National sightings and asked the resident radar expert at Wright-Patterson, Captain Roy James, what he thought about the sightings. James, who Ruppelt described as having little interest in UFOs, suggested that the returns sounded as if they were weather related but since he hadn't studied the case, and he didn't have the finer details, he couldn't be sure. The weather theory was, at best, a guess based primarily on the theory that UFOs can't be real, solid objects, so there must be another explanation for the sightings. It was James' personal opinion without the benefit of investigation.

An "Official" Air Force Investigation

Although Ruppelt couldn't stay in Washington to investigate the case, the intelligence officer at Bolling did provide a complete account of his investigation which was forwarded, according to regulations, to ATIC and eventually to Ruppelt. Those reports, gathered within days, and in some cases, within hours of the sightings, are important documents. They have not been colored, for the most part, by the newspaper coverage of the sightings, by the repeated questions asked by various official and unofficial investigators, or the simple passage of time. They provide a glimpse into what was happening on those nights in July 1952.

Included in the statements submitted was one by Air Force Captain Harold C. Way. He told the investigating officer:

> At about 0200 EST Washington Center advised that their radar had a target five miles east of Andrews Field. Andrews tower reported seeing a light, which changed color, and said it was moving towards Andrews. I went outside as no target appeared on Andrews radar and saw a light as reported by the tower. It was between 10 degrees and 15 degrees above the horizon and seemed to change color, from red to orange to green and red again. It seemed to float, but at times to dip suddenly and appear to lose altitude. It did not have the appearance of any star I have ever observed before. At the time of the observation there was a star due east of my position. Its brilliance was approximately the same as the object and it appeared at about the same angle, 10 degrees to 15 degrees about the horizon. The star did not change color or have any apparent movement. I estimated the object to be between three and four miles east of Andrews Field at approximately 2,000 ft. During the next hour very few reports were received from

Washington Center. [According to Washington Center's account, however, the 0200 EST object was seen on radar to pass over Andrews and fade out to the southwest of Andrews - G.D.T. (parenthetical statement in original)] At approximately 0300 EST I again went outside to look at the object. At this time both the star and the object had increased elevation had increased elevation by about 10 degrees. [The azimuth would have also increased about 10 degrees, so that the observed change was apparently equal to the sidereal rate, 15 degrees of right ascension per hour - G.D.T. (parenthetical statement in original)] The object had ceased to have any apparent movement, but still appeared to be changing color. On the basis of the second observation, I believe the unidentified object was a star.

Way wasn't alone in his evaluation of the visual sightings. Other documents included in the Blue Book files suggest a similar explanation. An unidentified control tower operator (his name was redacted, but who was apparently Joseph DeBoves) at Andrews reported to investigators:

I reported for duty in the tower at 2300 EST on 19 July 1952 for my eight-hour tour of duty. About 1230 [0030 using military time] A/1C [Airman First Class] Brady, [an unidentified civilian] and myself started talking about flying saucers. [Two unidentified men] were inclined to believe there were such objects. I was and still am skeptical. The tower maintenance man T/SGT Izzo was listening to the conversation over the intercom on the 6th floor as he worked there and commented jokingly now and then.

These preliminary statements by the tower operator, DeBoves, are important because they set a tone. According to the man, they were talking about flying saucers before they had received any communications from National Airport and before anyone saw anything that suggested a flying saucer to them.

Again, according to the statement provided to the official investigation by DeBoves:

At approximately 0100 hrs [named removed] answered the ringing telephone and spoke to someone unknown to me who was apparently watching the sky from the hardstand [meaning the ramp areas adjacent to the airfield] ... Brady became excited during the conversation and suddenly yelled there goes one. I saw a falling star go from overhead a short distance south and burn out. About two minutes later [name removed] said there's another one 'Did

47

you see the orange glow to the south'. I said I thought I saw it, but he pointed south, and I was looking southwest. I went up on the roof after that and watched the sky in all directions. In the meantime, Wash Center [ARTC at National Airport] was reporting targets on their radar screen over the Andrews range. Andrews Approach Control observed nothing.

DeBoves, according to his official statement, obviously believed that there was nothing going on of interest. He had seen, what to him had been a meteorite but that some of the others had thought strange. They didn't believe it was a meteorite. DeBoves was handing out the Air Force party line, as it would develop over the next several days.

DeBoves continued, "[Name redacted] was in the tower talking on the phone and interphone. He was watching a star and telling various people that it was moving up and descending rapidly and going from left to right and Banning [one of the others in the tower] and I listening to him from the roof believe we saw it move too. Such is the power of suggestion."

Actually, such is the power of autokinesis, which is the apparent motion of an object such as point of light or star due to the small, involuntary movements of the eye. The object appears to be in motion when it is not.

> This star was to the east slightly to the left of and above the rotating beacon. Brady reported the star as two miles east of Andrews and at an altitude of two thousand feet.
>
> A short time later approx 0200 hrs I saw a falling star go from overhead to the north. A few minutes later another went in the same direction. They faded and went out within two seconds. The sky was full of stars, the milky way was bright, and I was surprised that we did not see more falling stars.
>
> At about 0230 hrs I descended to the tower and observed from there the rest of the night but saw nothing more. All night Wash Center was reporting objects near Andrews or over the Andrews range, but Andrews Approach Control could see nothing, however they could see the various aircraft reported so their screen was apparently in good operation.
>
> About 0400 hrs a jet (GAS BAG) [the call sign of the interceptor] called Wash Center on 121.5MC's and said he had been assigned to contact Wash CAA to investigate the unknown objects reported

in the sky, but he was almost out of fuel and was returning to his home base.

At 0500 hrs Wash Center called me and reported an unknown object five miles southeast of Andrews Field. I looked and saw nothing. That was the last report I heard.

The intelligence officer also interviewed T/SGT John P. Izzo, who, according to DeBoves, was on another floor in the same building, listening to the same conversations. According to Izzo's statement:

At about 0015 [12:15 a.m.] I called the tower on our intercom as I overheard them talking about flying saucers. Curiously, I went up to the tower and I heard Wash Center call us on the intercom advising that they had five unidentified targets over the Andrews range. Mr. [named removed, but probably Banning] and Mr. [name removed but probably DeBoves] went to the tower roof while I stayed inside the tower. I, myself, couldn't see any targets at that time over the Andrews range. I went to the tower roof about ten minutes later. Mr. [name removed but probably DeBoves] and myself saw what appeared to be two falling stars directly overhead falling in a south to northerly direction. They did not occur at the time, about ten minutes apart. The first one was quite bright and orange in color. In my estimation, all those were, were just falling stars. At about the same time, A/1C Brady said he spotted a strange light near our beacon which is atop our water tower east of our control tower. I spotted the same from the tower roof but to me it appeared to be just a distant star and it changed position due to the rotation of the Earth on its axis. To me it didn't appear to be moving around. At 0230 Wash Center called and said that a Capital Airlines spotted three objects near Hendron, Va and he stated they were like nothing he had ever seen. At about 0400 a jet with the call sign (gas bag) called Wash Center on 121.5MC (A). Mr. [name removed] asked me if I could monitor it and I said I would it up on our spare... received down on the sixth floor. I heard the jet (gas bag) advise Wash Center he was at 21,000 ft and was running low on fuel. We advised he was going back to base. That was all that I heard from the jet. From... to 0500 I stayed down on the sixth floor (radio room) and I then back to my shop... at 0600. I went off duty at 0700.

William Brady, the airman to whom the others referred, provided a brief description of what he had seen without the speculations that others had made. Brady merely described the event without suggesting stars, meteors, Air Force pressure, or the power of suggestion. He told the investigators:

> Airman Goodman called the tower and reported he had seen some objects in the air around Andrews, while we were discussing them, he advised me to look to the south immediately, when I looked there was an object which appeared to be like an orange ball of fire, trailing a tail. It appeared to be about two miles south and one half mile east of the Andrews range. It was very bright and definite, and unlike anything I had ever seen before. The position of something like is hard to determine accurately. It made kind of a circular movement and then took of (sic) at an unbelievable speed. It disappeared in a split second. This took place about 0005. Seconds later I saw another one same description as the one before it made an arc like pattern then disappeared. I only saw each object for about a second. The second one was over Andrews range, the direction appeared to be southerly.

Other reports from the other observers at Andrews said much the same thing. They described lights in the distance, almost always moving in an erratic manner that seems move reminiscent of autokinesis rather than intelligent control. They all suggested that the objects were in sight for short periods, often only seconds, before they disappeared. They provided little in the way of description of the objects.

The exception here seems to be the report made by A/2C (Airman Second Class) William Goodman. He told the investigators that:

At this time, I noticed an object to the Southwest of Andrews, it looked to be about the size of the softball, and it was bright orange in color. The object moved from the west to the Northwest in a half circular pattern and was traveling (sic) at such a speed that I knew that it could not be a jet aircraft, my estimation of the speed is from 1000 miles an hour to 2000 miles an hour. It would be hard to judge at what altitude the object was flying because it seemed to lose and gain altitude. The object moved in this pattern several times and then disappeared into the west. From the time I saw the object and then lost it I would say it was about 15 or 20 minutes. But as far as saying that this was a flying saucer I would not because it looked to me to be more round in shape than flat.

There is one other important point that has to be made about the Air Force investigation of the Air Force personnel, both military and civilian, who

Ed Ruppelt in civvies.

reported UFOs that night. Ruppelt, who should have known what was happening inside the Air Force investigation, even if he was not physically present during all aspects of it, and who had access to all the relevant documents about the sightings, reported, "I heard from a good source that the tower men had been 'persuaded' a bit."

Reading carefully, and between the lines, it does seem that the higher ranking of the observers that first night said exactly what the Air Force would like them to say. In other words, those who could be considered career men in the Air Force were quick to pick up what their superiors had wanted them to say. The fiery orange objects were really just stars seen through a light haze and nothing unusual. It was the talk of flying saucers, especially after the calls from the radar men from National Airport, that suggested flying saucers that had turned the normal stars into something more exciting.

Harry Barnes Continues to Find Answers

While the Air Force investigators did interview the military personnel involved, it seems that they didn't talk to the civilian controllers at National Airport. An undated letter in the Blue Book files states, "Attached is a copy of the report written by the Senior Controller, [name removed, but apparently Harry C. Barnes] on duty from approximately 2330E [11:30 EST] July 19, to 0800 July 20, 1952."

The letter, obviously written by a civilian (because the name was removed) noted, "Parts of this report have been given to Major Williams of Air Force Intelligence, Lt. Col. Searless, Office of Public Information, Department of Defense and to Mr.... [whose name has been redacted]."

Barnes' letter confirms the reports that had been made by others that night. It confirmed that the radar operators had spotted several targets and "...although an occasional strong return was noted, most of the targets would be classified as fair to weak." When the controller attempted to alert military authorities, the buck was passed from one location to another. The report noted, "There was some confusion for awhile as to whether Andrews or Bolling was going to make the report, but it was finally determined that [Andrews] would handle."

There was discussion about the possibility of an intercept attempt. The author wrote, "The targets were noticed east and south of [Andrews] so we asked the [Andrews] tower to look and see if they saw anything, also asked [Andrews] approach control to check scopes. [Andrews] had a lad on the roof with glasses who spotted an object that looked to be orange in color and appeared to be just hovering in the vicinity of [Andrews]. They saw others as time went on with varying descriptions. Most of this information was given... with the expectation that they would run an intercept."

According to Barnes' letter, the men at Washington National, as well as other locations, discussed the possibility of an intercept, but always someone wanted more information. Barnes wrote, "As time wore on, pilot reports were received - P807 [a commercial flight] saw 7 of the objects between Washington and Martinsburg variously described as lights that moved very rapidly, up and down and horizontally as well as hovering in one position and SP610 [Capital Airlines flight 610] saw one come in with him from Herndon and follow him to within 4 miles of touch-down. This was substantiated by Tower and Center radar."

Barnes had contacted various military agencies about 3:00 a.m. According to his letter:

> They were doing nothing about it, so I asked if it was possible for something like this to happen, even though we gave them all this information, without anything being done about it. The man who was supposed to be in charge and to whom I was talking, said he guessed so. Then another voice came on who identified himself as the Combat Officer and said that all the information was being forwarded to higher authority and would not discuss if further...

then [he] said that they were not really concerned about it anyway, that somebody else was supposed to handle it.

Another letter in the Blue Book files was a "Spot Intelligence Report" about the UFOs seen at Andrews on July 20. This, according to the heading, was a "Special Inquiry" that was forwarded to the Inspector General's office of the 4th District Office of Special Investigations, at Bolling Air Force Base. The letter was sent on to the Director of Special Investigations. This was a letter created at the highest levels of the Air Force and concerned the UFOs over Washington, D.C., on the first night. It included a copy of the tower log for that night.

According to the letter, "The following is a copy of the AACS [Andrews Approach Control] Control Tower Log… dated 20 July 1952:

> 0005 Phone call advsg that there was an object south of ADW [Andrews]. A/1C [named deleted] looked south and saw a (sic) orange object that appeared for just a moment then disappeared. The party on the phone saw the same thing. Wash Center also calling to advise they have five targets unidentified in the vicinity of the ADW range. TWR [tower] personnel used to observe from the roof of the TWR.
>
> 0120 While watching from the TWR roof Mr. [name deleted, but probably DeBoves], T/SGT IZZO and myself. Capt. H.W. REDDING observed what appeared to be two falling stars, but they had an orange hue and a tail and were traveling at a fast pace.
>
> 0125 T/SGT and Mr. [name deleted] also saw a third object that appeared like the first two objects (appeared like a falling star).
>
> 0235 ADW A/O making a full report including the report by the party on the phone. Wash Center received a call from Capital Airlines plane that he saw three objects near [name deleted] and reported that they were like nothing he had ever seen. He also reported three more between HRN and [Hendron] and Martinsburg. Wash Center first saw these targets around 2340 and then about ten minutes later they moved toward ADW.
>
> 0330 Wash Center advised the targets seemed to move more frequently when there were aircraft moving. As daylight was approaching, they seemed to move less frequently.
>
> 0530 Wash Center advised target north of ADW. Tower could not see it.

TWX [teletype message] sent to Director of Intelligence, Hq USAF, Washington, 25, D.C.

Air Technical Intell Center, Wright-Patterson AFB, Ohio

ATTN: ATIAA-26

Commanding General, Ent AFB, Colorado Springs, Colo.

Commanding General, Headquarters Command, USAF, Bolling AFB."

Under the section labeled action taken, it was reported, "No investigation of this matter was conducted by this office inasmuch as no request for investigation was received." Of course, Barnes was burning up the telephone lines trying to find someone somewhere who would respond to the situation.

That seemed to summarize the attitude of the Air Force after the first night of watching UFOs over Washington, D.C. Various officers couldn't be bothered with forwarding the reports, no one requested any sort of intercept be attempted until the night was nearly over, and then, alerted that something had happened, no one cared to investigate because no request had been received. That, of course, explains how Ruppelt could leave ATIC at Wright-Patterson a day after the sightings and not know a thing about them until he arrived at Washington National Airport and read about them in the newspaper.

Had that been all of it, then the situation might never have come to the attention of the President. Had the UFOs not returned later and had there not been so many other sightings around the country, that might have been the end of it. However, the UFOs had just begun to gain attention. Soon everyone would know about their overflights of Washington.

Chapter Five: Interim

At the close of the first round of Washington National sightings, it might have seemed as if the wave had peaked. How could any sightings improve on the radar, airborne and ground-based observations of the UFOs that came from Washington National? Sightings from other parts of the country just couldn't live up to this standard of multiple witnesses including military and civilian pilots, as well as multiple radar facilities. In the interim, before the saucers returned to the radars of Washington National Airport, there were other UFO sightings. Some of them involved radar, some involved airborne observations, and in a few cases, there were attempted intercepts that were no more successful than those tried over Washington, D.C.

On July 21, over Alhambra, California, a private pilot and two of his relatives saw a round, silver-colored object. The pilot thought the UFO was at about 40,000 feet and was heading north but was changing direction in an irregular fashion so that it seemed, at times, to be heading east-northeast. The object was in sight for about four minutes. The Air Force originally marked the case as a possible balloon but later, after a policy change, they dropped the possible and wrote it off as a balloon.

Also on July 21, at Robbins Air Force Base in Georgia, an unidentified "blip" made several passes on a wind-finding target being tracked by radar. The Air Force didn't do much in the way of an investigation, but given the timing, and that there were no corresponding visual sightings, that isn't surprising. There wasn't much they could learn with an investigation, and they left the case marked as "insufficient data."

It was also on July 21, 1952, that there was another report from a military flight crew that involved radar. According to a brief statement included in the Project Blue Book files, Captain Henry S. Anthony, Jr., and First Lieutenant John T. Larkins, were airborne in the Beluga Lake area when the first contact was made at 18,000 yards. "Lock-on was accomplished at 12,000 yards and an intercept started. Target was level with the aircraft's speed greater than 100 knots to 6,000 yards. At this point the target disappeared and could not be re-established. Pilot did not make visual sighting."

A little less than an hour later, they made another attempt to contact the target. They had remained in the area searching for the UFO.

While at 16,000 feet, contact was made at 12,000 yards. Lock-on was accomplished and target overtaken at 50 - 60 knots. At 1500 yards, set action resembled normal break-lock and target was lost due to an abrupt upward motion as seen in pilot's scope. Contact was re-established at 6,000 yards and followed to 700 yards where target and aircraft speed appeared the same - 300 knots. Intercept was continued to 400 yards at which time the target moved out rapidly to 3200 yards where speeds again synchronized with the target moving down. Pilot nosed the aircraft down and as speed increased to approximately 400 knots, the target was overtaken to 1500 yards. At this time the radar broke lock due to a rapid downward movement of the target. Again, no visual sighting was accomplished.... During this incident, the weather was exceptionally clear with practically a cloudless sky.

The Air Force found no explanation for this sighting. Again, the information was sketchy, at best. The pilots made no visual sighting but were chasing an object seen only by their radar operators. There wasn't much that an investigation could accomplish, unless it could be proven that the radar had malfunctioned.

The following day, on the morning of July 22, a series of sightings began in the Boston area. According to a report written by Lieutenant Colonel Robert S. Jones, "[R]eports of sightings of unidentified phenomena... were received from five (5) separate sources. No activity or condition developed that accounts for sightings."

According to Jones, he had received a telephone call telling him of a sighting by "Lt. Commander W. J. ADAMS... to the effect that he and several others had observed unidentified phenomena during the night of 22 July 1942... GUY W. BAILEY, weather observer... advised that he observed strange lights between 2315 and 2326 [11:15 p.m. and 11:26 p.m.] ... Additional calls reporting similar phenomena were received..."

In the first Boston (seen here) area sighting, there were two round, bluish-green lights, one following the other. Adams could see no features on either of them and described them as brighter than a first magnitude star. They moved without sound or exhaust. The lights moved through about 90 degrees of sky, then reversed themselves and back before reversing themselves a third time. It should be noted here that the long flights by the objects tended to rule out bright stars or planets. The reversal of the course would rule out artificial satellites, but then, none had been launched in 1952. That explanation wouldn't be possible until after October 1957.

Adams said that the lights didn't seem to dim with the distance, and they eventually just disappeared, as if a light had been switched off. The lead object disappeared first, and when the second reached that point in the sky, it too, vanished.

In the second sighting, there were four small, red and green lights. At times a single light would come on, washing out the smaller, colored lights, suggesting to the observer, that he was seeing a single object with various lights on it being illuminated and extinguished in some ill-defined sequence. Again, it was just lights in the night sky and not a sighting of a physical object.

The observer, who looked at the lights through a small telescope, could see nothing to suggest an object behind the light. He believed that if the lights were on an aircraft, he would have been able to see it clearly and would certainly have been able to hear it.

Project Blue Book records list both sightings in a single file and both as "insufficient data for a scientific evaluation." Given that there were but single observers in both cases, and no obvious explanations appeared, the Air Force conclusion is not without merit.

In Uvalde, Texas, on July 22, there was a sighting that was labeled as unidentified. According to a document in the Blue Book files:

> This is an interesting case, with two witnesses. Chief witness [Don Epperly] was the weather observer for Trans-Texas Airlines, who was thoroughly familiar with planes, weather balloons, etc. Object covered an arc of approximately 100 degrees in 45 seconds, had no visible aerodynamic features, had a bright afterglow and gyrating movement. No sound. Object seemed to climb higher every second and move from in front of a cumulus cloud to in back of it, thus giving some estimate of distance. Object observed in broad daylight. It is too bad that this one was not much more thoroughly investigated since there were two adult witnesses and on 14-year-old witness. It much be carried as unknown.

There was also an Air Intelligence Information Report form in the file that provided some additional details. According to that:

> The observer described the object as being large and round, of silver color. The object was estimated to be approximately 30 feet

in diameter and at an altitude of 20,000 feet. The object had a very bright after-glow. No aerodynamic features were visible. The object had tremendous speed, estimated at well over 1,000 miles per hour; propulsion system was not visible, and no sound was heard by the observer. The movement of the object was described as "gyrating". The object was traveling from East, about 40 degrees from the horizon to Southwest. The object seemed to climb higher every second and was observed for approximately 45 seconds before it disappeared behind a large cumulus cloud.

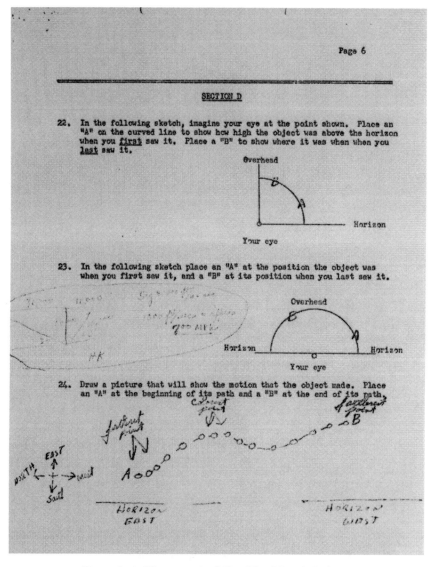

Page detailing part of the Uvalde sighting.

On July 23, an object was sighted over Misawa Air Force Base in Japan. Captain Norman C. Lamb, in an Air Intelligence Information Report, wrote:

> I was scrambled... at approximately 2015 [8:15 p.m.] hours.... [W]hile flying at 18,000 feet on a heading of 015 degrees [or almost due north], I witnessed a strange phenomena. Approximately five minutes (5) later... I saw a greenish blue light approaching my aircraft from my 5 o'clock position [the right rear], 15 degrees high. My first thought was that it was the navigation light from another aircraft. As it leveled off in formation with me just back of my right tip tank [an external fuel tank] I realized that I should be seeing a red navigation light if it was another aircraft. As I started a turn into the light it stopped its forward motion and made an erratic maneuver downward out of sight.

> This light had no strange glow nor tail behind it. It closed on me rapidly, and I was indicating about 285 knots. It appeared to be a navigation light on another aircraft flying 500 feet from my aircraft. No other aircraft were reported in my immediate vicinity. Visual contact was not made after its erratic maneuver. I am sure it was not a reflection from/or in my aircraft.... The entire incident lasted not more than 15 seconds.

Brigadier General Charles Y. Banfill, the deputy for intelligence for the United States Air Force in Japan, appended a personal statement to the report. He wrote, "The 'strange phenomena' referred to in the statement by Captain Lamb was a very bright light which appeared to be located along the coast of Hokkaido... This light appeared much brighter than the normal dull yellow lights displayed on the fishing boats in the area and was seen by both the pilot and the radar operator."

In what might be considered the more important part of the statement, Banfill wrote, "The radar operator was directing his attention to the scope at the time of the encounter. The object dove out of sight just as he looked out. The pilot rolled hard toward the object and tried to follow it down but reported that it disappeared very rapidly. A search of the area showed nothing unusual after the brief observation."

It was also on July 23 that F-94s from Dover Air Force Base in Delaware made fourteen different visual observations over a two-hour period from early in the morning to about 10:45 a.m. Only one of the sightings was corroborated by radar. The objects were at a very high altitude. The colors were described in one sighting as bluish-white, in another as orange, and in a third as just "very high, bright lights." According to some of the reports, the objects emitted a whistling noise. It should also be noted that flight crews from the same base were involved, and later would again be involved, in the sightings around Washington, D.C. UFOs were not unknown to them.

That same day, the radar at Jamestown, Rhode Island, detected one unidentified object about 25 miles south of the station and moving north at high speed and high altitude. Another radar made contact and vectored an airborne F-94 toward it, but the intercept attempt failed. Two additional jet aircraft, these from Westover Air Force Base, Massachusetts, were scrambled but did not intercept.

Interestingly, in the Project Blue Book index, these sightings are mentioned, but there is no conclusion listed for them. The project card is listed as missing from the files and that might explain why there is no final conclusion assigned to the reports. At any rate, there is not much information available for any of these cases.

All this suggests that there were many UFO sightings, many involving aircraft and radar in other areas of the world. Some of them were strange, but basically, lights in the sky are lights in the sky. To add radar to the mix certainly eliminates a wide range of nature phenomena, but that doesn't lead to a specific conclusion and certainly doesn't suggest that the UFOs are anything extraterrestrial.

There were, however, many sightings in, and around, the Washington, D.C. area at the same time. Again, given the nature and perceived importance of the sightings made at Washington National Airport, as well as the attention given to them, many of these other sightings have been overlooked. They didn't have the same number of observers, or the heavy involvement of radar facilities at so many other locations.

Typical of these sightings is one made on July 21 from Baltimore, Maryland, just after 1:00 p.m. Jacques Ayd and John Neuman saw what they described as a large cone-shaped object with a brilliant orange glow which was so bright it hurt their eyes to look at it. To them, it appeared to be about the size of a four-engine aircraft.

They thought the object might have been at about twenty thousand feet altitude when they first saw it. It dove suddenly, moving so fast they had a hard time following the motion. They had it in sight for about a minute, which provided them with enough time to get a very good look at it and rule out a number of mundane possibilities.

In the Wilmington, Delaware area, on July 24, three UFOs flying in a formation described as "1 directly above the other," were seen. The description of the objects was that the:

> Top object was circular or cylindrical in shape with the two objects below being reported by the four observers as cylindrical, rectangular, very flat, rectangular and very flat and long. All three objects appeared approximately the same size, with a rough estimate being 80 feet in diameter. [The] objects were shiny and reflected light. They appeared to remain in the same area and there was no indication of contrails, exhaust, propulsion methods, sound, maneuvers with the exception of 1 observer reported that the middle object appeared to move out and slightly away from the other two, remaining there for approximately 45 seconds and then returning to the original position.

What is interesting about the case is that the observers, whose names were so carefully avoided by the officer writing his report, were Air Force pilots, flying in two F-94B jet aircraft that were based at New Castle AFB. This is the same location from which aircraft had been scrambled during the Washington National sightings just a few days earlier. The UFOs, according to the file, were as much as 30,000 feet above the jets, and neither of the pilots could get the nose elevated high enough to expose any gun camera film, which would have provided additional evidence.

According to the Air Force file, there were other aircraft in the area, but none of those pilots saw anything. The weather, again according to the Air Force, was clear with the exception of a squall line, that is a line of thunderstorms, in the distance, which, according to the pilots, had no effect on their observations.

The Blue Book files have several special folders holding the reports that can be grouped together. One of those lists dozens of reports in the Washington, D.C. area. Many of them have no conclusions attached, meaning there is a blank space for that conclusion in the index. Many of the other cases are labeled as insufficient data for scientific analysis. Few are identified and many of those identifications are weak, suggesting a possible balloon, or a possible aircraft. That sort of answer comes out of the witness statements, meaning that someone had described the UFO as resembling an aircraft or that the witness had suggested a shiny spherical object that looked like a balloon. It also meant that the Air Force could find no record of an aircraft or balloon in the right place at the right time to account for the sighting.

As the interim week came to a close, UFOs were still much on the minds of the people and the military. Ruppelt wrote that on the same night as the second round of the Washington Nationals began, Blue Book received a "really good report from California. An ADC [Air Defense Command] radar had picked up an unidentified target and an F-94C had been scrambled. The radar vectored the jet interceptor into the target, the radar operator in the '94 locked on to it, and as the airplane closed in the pilot and RO [radar operator] saw that they were headed directly toward a large, yellowish-orange light. For several minutes they played tag with the UFO. Both the radar on the ground and the radar in the F-94 showed that as soon as the airplane would get almost within gunnery range of the UFO it would suddenly pull away at a terrific speed. Then in a minute or two it would slow down enough to let the F-94 catch it again."

Ruppelt did interview the pilot himself over the telephone. The pilot told Ruppelt that he, the pilot, felt as if they were involved in a big aerial game of cat and mouse with the strange object. The pilot said that he hadn't liked it and was afraid that at any moment, the cat would turn and pounce, possibly destroying his aircraft in the process. It was not a good position for the pilot and the radar operator.

Ruppelt noted in his book, "Needless to say, this was an unknown."

As the California fighter pilot was chasing his single UFO, the formations of strange lights had returned to Washington National. Focus changed as Air Force personnel, including a Naval radar expert assigned to assist them, watched the UFOs dance through the skies over the nation's capital from inside the radar room at Washington National. Before long, everyone, including President Truman, was demanding answers.

Chapter Six: July 26/27, 1952

The first round of the second wave of sightings over Washington, D.C., didn't begin at night, nor were they first seen by the radar operators at Washington National Airport. At about 2:30 p.m. two radar operators at Langley AFB, not all that far from Washington, D.C., watched an object on their radar scope for about two minutes. They estimated that it approached Langley from the south at a speed of 2,600 miles an hour at an altitude just under five thousand feet. It disappeared from the radar scopes when it was only eight miles away.

Twenty minutes later, at about ten minutes of three, those same radar operators watched another target for about four minutes as it headed toward the east. It suddenly stopped, hovered for two minutes, and then continued to the east, finally disappearing from the scope about fifteen miles away. The operators believed that the object had simply dropped below five thousand feet which was the lower limit of the radar.

They had also tried to spot the object using binoculars but had been unable to find it. They noted that the return on the radarscope was larger than that of an aircraft and that it had a fuzzy appearance, suggesting to some that the blip was the result of the weather rather than a solid object flying over the area.

At about 8:15 p.m., a pilot and stewardess on a National Airlines flight saw several glowing objects through the cockpit windows. They described them like the "glow of a cigarette." Both said the objects were high above them and were moving about a hundred miles an hour.

About 10:30 p.m. (though some sources suggest it was early as 8:00 p.m.) the same radar operators who had been on duty at Washington National the week before again spotted several slow-moving targets on their radarscopes. The objects were spread out over Washington in a large arc around the city. This time the controllers carefully marked each of the unidentifieds. When they were all marked, they called the Tower and learned the unidentified targets were on those scopes too. As had happened the week before, a call to Andrews confirmed that they, too, were watching the unknowns.

During this time, the ARTC requested that a B-25 in the area check on several radar targets. The crew saw nothing even after repeated attempts, and precise directions from the radar center. In what might be an important clue, one of the pilots said that "each time the tower man advised us we were passing the

63

UFO, we noticed that we were over one certain section of the Potomac River, just east of Alexandria. Finally, we were asked to visually check the terrain below for anything which might cause such an illusion. We looked and the only object we could see where the radar had a target turned out to be the Wilson Lines steamboat trip to Mount Vernon." The pilot was convinced that the radar was "sure as hell picking up the steamboat." It was a slow-moving object that could account for the sighting.

At some point, the senior controller, Harry Barnes, alerted the military that the unidentified targets were back. Given the circumstances the Saturday before and given the number of sightings reported in the area during the last week, a number of military people were on alert. The first to respond was Al Chop, the civilian Pentagon spokesman about UFOs. Later in the evening, Major Dewey Fournet, and a Naval officer, Lt. John Holcomb, made their way to National Airport. Holcomb was an electronics specialist temporarily assigned to the Air Force Directorate of Intelligence

Al Chop

An hour later, with targets being tracked continually, the controllers called for jet interceptors. Al Chop told me that he was in communication with the main basement command post at the Pentagon at that time. He requested that interceptors be sent. As a civilian, he could only make the request and then wait for the flag officer (general or admiral) in command at the Pentagon to make the official decision. Chop, however, did have a connection to the Pentagon so that those in the command post listened to what he had to say. The situation, at that point, was only mildly better than it had been a week earlier.

As happened the week before, there was a delay, but by midnight, two F-94s were on station over Washington. At that point, the reporters who had assembled to observe the situation were asked, by Chop, to leave the radar room at National Airport because classified radio and intercept procedures would be in operation. Chop felt that the reporters could do their jobs without being privy to the classified operational procedures that would be used that night.

Although that fact that the reporters had been chased from the radar room was well reported, Ed Ruppelt later wrote in his classic book about UFOs, "I knew this was absurd because any radio ham worth his salt could build equipment and listen in on any intercept. The real reason for the press dismissal, I learned, was that not a few people in the radar room were positive that this night would be the big night in UFO history - the night when a pilot would close in on and get a good look at a UFO - and they didn't want the press to be in on it."

Chop, however, suggested to me that "because an intercept is run under classified [regulations], it was not privy to the reporters, so I made them leave... We would allow them to come in there and look at the radar scopes until we ran into an intercept. At that time, they had to leave the room."

The situation then, wasn't quite as simple as Ruppelt made it out to be. Chop wasn't worried about the reporters overhearing the supposedly classified intercept conversations but watching the intercepts as they played out on the radar scopes. Whatever the reason, whether good or not, the reporters were not there to watch the intercepts.

Chop described the first of these intercepts. The fighters, according to what he told me, came from New Castle, Delaware:

> The first two that came in, when they came in, we had about, I'd say, fourteen or fifteen UFOs, targets that we could not identify on the radar scopes. We had them marked. Well, we didn't mark the unknowns. They marked the known flights. Everything else on the scope was a UFO, of course.... Now [Andrews] were tracking the objects or what appeared to be the same objects. We couldn't conclusively say they were exactly the same but the conversations between the flight controllers at Washington National and at [Andrews], they would say, "Do you have these four up at the southeast section of your scopes," and [Andrews] would say, "We have those."

> We had one pilot going north and one going south. And the pilot in the northern sector... he could see nothing although we did have UFOs, blips, there. The one in the south... the flight controllers kind of directed him to them, we had a little cluster of them, five or six of them and he suddenly reports that he sees some lights... He said they are very brilliant blue-white lights. And he was going to close on them to get a better look at them, which he did.

Eventually all the Pentagon representatives were assembled at National Airport. Holcomb was considered the resident expert on radar operations and was familiar with the equipment, as well as the types of returns that could be expect under the weather conditions that were being experienced in the Washington, D.C. area. His opinion about the quality of the targets and the possibility of some sort of weather-related phenomenon would be the important one.

In fact, Holcomb was getting the current meteorological data from the Washington National Weather Station as the UFOs were dancing across the scopes. The weather station personnel indicated that there was a slight temperature inversion over Washington, but Holcomb didn't believe it was strong enough to cause the problems, and the targets, that they were experiencing. Holcomb later said it did not explain all the good solid returns. As the expert on the scene, his opinion was an important one.

Holcomb, or Fournet, telephoned the analysis to New Castle AFB in Delaware, where the fighters were based. Again, the F-94s were scrambled, and on

New Castle Air Force Base circa 1954.

arrival, were vectored toward the various targets, which were now weaker. The pilots didn't see anything except for an object identified as an aircraft and a hovering white light that disappeared when approached.

With those men watching, as well as the controllers at various facilities using various radars, the F-94s arrived. And the UFOs vanished from the scopes immediately. The jets were vectored to the last known position of the UFOs, but even though visibility was unrestricted in the area, the pilots could see nothing. The fighters made a systematic search of the area, but since they could find nothing out of the ordinary, and because the targets on the radars had all disappeared, and with fuel running out, the fighters returned to their base. Their time over the target, giving the fact they had to travel from Dover, Delaware, and return to that base, was limited.

Chop, describing the situation years later, told me, "The minute the first two interceptors appeared on our scope all our unknowns disappeared.

It was like they just wiped them all off. All our other flights, all the known flights were still on the scope... We watched these two planes leave. When they were out of our range, immediately we got our UFOs back."

Later, Air Force officers would learn that as the fighters appeared over Washington, people in the area of Langley Air Force Base, Virginia spotted weird lights in the sky. Ruppelt, in his book, reported, "...people in the area around Langley AFB... began to call Langley Tower to report that they were looking at weird lights that were 'rotating and giving off alternating colors.' A few minutes after the calls began to come in, the tower operators themselves saw the same or a similar light and they called for an interceptor."

An F-94, in the area on a routine mission was diverted to search for the light. The pilot saw it and turned toward it, but it disappeared "like somebody turning off a light bulb." The pilot continued the intercept and did get a radar lock on the now unlighted and visually invisible target. The radar lock was broken by the object as it sped away. The fighter continued the pursuit, obtaining two more radar locks on the object, but each time the locks were broken.

In the Newport News, Virginia area, not that far from Langley AFB, people were also seeing lights in the sky. William W. Parkinson, Jr. was standing on the roof of the *Daily Press* building when he saw a bright, rotating object that

Langley Air Force Base

flashed silver, red and green lights. It hovered, according to Parkinson, over the James River Bridge for nearly thirty minutes and then drifted over a ballpark to the east. Gradually it rose to about five thousand feet and was in sight for two hours and fifteen minutes. Almost two dozen people called the newspaper to report seeing the UFO.

At 1:45 a.m., the Langley Tower operators sighted a bluish object that they said resembled a lighted cotton ball. They thought it was about ten miles from the tower and to the west. It climbed straight up, to about five thousand feet and disappeared. They only saw it for five or six seconds.

The scene then shifted back to Washington National. Again, the Air Defense Command was alerted and again jet fighters were scrambled. This time the pilots were able to see the objects, vectored toward them by the air traffic controllers. But the fighters couldn't close on the lights. The pilots saw no external details behind the glow, and saw nothing strange, other than lights where the radar suggested that something should have been seen.

After several minutes of failure to close on a target, one of them was spotted lopping along alone. A fighter piloted by Lieutenant William Patterson turned, kicked in the afterburner and tried to catch the object. It disappeared before Patterson could see much of anything.

Interviewed the next day, Patterson said, "I tried to make contact with the bogies below one thousand feet, but they [the controllers] vectored us around. I saw several bright lights. I was at my maximum speed, but even then, I had no closing speed. I ceased chasing them because I saw no chance of overtaking them. I was vectored into new objects. Later I chased a single bright light which I estimated about ten miles away. I lost visual contact with it..."

Chop said that he, along with the others in the radar room, watched the intercept on the radar scope. What the pilot was telling them about the ongoing intercept, they all could see on the radar.

Patterson finally had to break off the intercept, though there were still lights in the sky and objects on the scope. According to Chop, the pilot radioed that he was running low on fuel. He turned so that he could head back to his base to refuel.

Chop said that the last of the objects disappeared from the scope about the time the sun came up. He said, "They stayed [under] observation on our radar scope until dawn, about five or six o'clock [that morning]. When it got light, they just gradually disappeared."

Ruppelt later quizzed Fournet about the activities that night. According to Ruppelt, Fournet and Holcomb, the radar expert, were convinced the targets were solid, metallic objects. Fournet told Ruppelt that there were weather-related targets on the scopes, but all the controllers were ignoring them. Those watching the scopes, as well as Holcomb, could tell the difference between the weather-related targets caused by the inversion layers and those they believed to be solid. Everyone was convinced that the targets being chased were solid objects.

The situation was a repeat of the week before. Headlines around the world on Tuesday, July 29, told the whole story. In a banner headline that could have come from a science fiction movie, *The Cedar Rapids Gazette* reported, "Saucers Swarm over Capital."

The problem, however, is that no one was sure what had happened during the night. Both Fournet and Chop, interviewed years later, said that the returns were solid, not weather related, and that the objects seemed to react to the appearance of the jet interceptors. Like the radar operators, and the Navy expert, Holcomb, both thought they were looking at real objects and not echoes or refracted returns.

When the night ended, that chapter also ended. UFOs were still reported from all over the United States. More photographs were taken, but the arguments about what had happened in Washington were just beginning.

Chapter Seven: The Air Force Press Conference

After the second round of Saturday night radar and visual sightings, and after a number of failed intercept attempts, the Air Force found it necessary to call a press conference to explain the situation. Ed Ruppelt called the conference the largest and longest that had been held by the Air Force since the conclusion of the Second World War. Ruppelt also suggested that the cards had been stacked again Major General John A. Samford, the Director of Intelligence, who was the senior officer at the conference. Because Samford had to "hedge" on many of the answers to questions because the investigations had not been concluded, it seemed, to many of the assembled reporters, that the Air Force was attempting to hide the truth.

The press conference was held at the Pentagon, in room 3E-869, to be precise. Also attending for the Air Force was Major General Roger M. Ramey, then the Director of Operations for the Air Force and the same Roger Ramey who had been at 8th Air Force commander in Fort Worth during the Roswell UFO crash briefings in July 1947. Others there for the Air Force included Colonel Donald L. Bower, of ATIC, Captain Roy L. James, an expert in radar operations and also from ATIC, Ed Ruppelt, the chief of Project Blue Book, and Mr. Buroyne L. Griffing, from ATIC.

Conspicuous by their absence were Major Dewey Fournet, the military liaison officer between the Pentagon and Project Blue Book, Al Chop, the official Pentagon spokesman on UFOs, and Lt. John Holcomb, the Naval officer who was an expert on radar and electronics. Since all three had been at Washington National during the second set of sightings, their inclusion would seem to be a natural event. Apparently, the Air Force had other ideas because none were there to answer questions.

The press conference began with an introduction by a civilian Pentagon press relations official who said:

> Ladies and gentlemen, let me remind the military that, while they are welcome here, this is a press conference and let's be sure that the press is all seated before the conference begins.

> This refers to the fact that many military officers who had no role in the press conference were in the room to listen to it. They were being told to sit down and shut up.

From left to right, Colonel Bower, Captain Ed Ruppelt, Roy James and

B. L. Griffing. Seated are Major Generals Roger Ramey and John Samford.

Let me introduce General Samford, Air Force Director of Intelligence, and General Ramey, Director of Operations. General Samford.

Major General Samford: I think the plan is to have very brief opening remarks and then ask for such questions as you may want to put to us for discussion and answer. In so far as opening remarks is [sic] concerned, I just want to state our reason for concern about this.

The Air Force feels a very definite obligation to identify and analyze things that happen in the air that may have in them menace to the United States and, because of that feeling of obligation and our pursuit of that interest, since 1947, we have an activity that was known one time as Project Saucer and now, as part of another more stable and integrated organization, have undertaken to analyze between a thousand and two thousand reports dealing with this area. And out of that mass of reports that we've received we've been able to take things which were originally unidentified

71

and dispose of them to our satisfaction in terms of bulk where we came to the conclusion that these things were either friendly aircraft erroneously recognized or reported, hoaxes, quite a few of those, electronic and meteorological phenomena of one sort of another, light aberrations, and many other things.

It is important to note that there never was a Project Saucer in a real sense. When the Air Force created its first UFO investigation, code named Sign, it publicly called the project by the name of Saucer. Later, after the code name, Sign was compromised, the Air Force announced that it had ended its investigation but continued it as Project Grudge.

> Samford: However, there have remained a percentage of this total [of sighting reports], in the order of twenty per cent [sic] of the reports, that have come from credible observers of relatively incredible things. And because of these things not being possible for us to move along and associate with the kind of things that we've found can be associated with the bulk of these reports, we keep on being concerned about them.

> However, I'd like to say that the difficulty with disposing of these reports is largely based upon the lack of any standard measurement or any ability to measure these things which have been reported briefly by some, more elaborately by others, but with no measuring devices that can convert the manageable material for any kind of analysis that we know. We take some of these things and we try to bring to the good honest workmen of science a piece of material that has no utility because it doesn't have the kind of measurements on it that he can use. And, as a consequence, he has to reject these things and say, "Until you can bring me something more substantial than that, I can't make any progress."

> So, our need, really is to get the measurement value on these and, in the interim, lacking sufficient measure of these things to make them amenable to real analysis, we have to say that our real interest in this project is not one of intellectual curiosity but is in trying to establish and appraise the possibility of menace to the United States. And we can say, as of now, that there has been no pattern that reveals anything remotely like purpose or remotely like consistency that we can in any way associate with any menace to the United States.

To this point, Samford has said little of real value. He has admitted there is a problem and that they have studied it, but they found nothing for science to investigate. An examination of UFOs prior to this point reveals that such is not the case. There had been a number of photographic cases, including movie footage, which can be measured. There have been a number of radar cases, including the Washington Nationals which spawned the press conference, in which measurements could be made and examined by science. Samford was being less than candid, assuming that he knew what was in the Project Blue Book files, and as the Director of Intelligence, he should have known.

This statement also provides a clue as to the nature of the official investigation in the summer of 1952. The Air Force had attempted to learn if and had convinced itself that flying saucers posed no threat to the security of the United States. Satisfied that invasion fleets were not about to land; the Air Force attitude was that flying saucers did not warrant any sort of investigation by them. Air Force officers had fulfilled their mission when they determined there was no threat to national security. Besides, there was nothing they could about them anyway.

Investigative Emphasis Changes

> Samford: Now, we do want to continue in the interests of intellectual curiosity or the contributions to be made to scientific measurements, but our main interest is going to have to continue in the problem of seeing whether the things have [the] possibility of harm to the United States, and our present dilemma of lack of measurement that can be turned to analysis and a complete lack of pattern in any of these things which gives us any clue to possible purpose or possible use, leaves us in some dilemma as to what we can do about this remaining twenty per cent of unidentified phenomena.

> The volume of reporting is related to many things. We know that reports of this kind go back to Biblical times. There have been flurries of them in various centuries. 1846 seems to have had a time when there was quite a flurry of reporting of this kind. Our current series of reports goes back, generally, to 1946 in which things of this kind were reported in Sweden.

> There are many reasons why this volume goes up and down, but we can't help but believe that, currently, one of the reasons for volume is that man is doing a great deal more. There's more man-made activity in the air now than there was, certainly, in Biblical

times or in 1946. In addition to that, our opportunities to observe have been enhanced greatly.

The difficult part of it, as far as advancing the program is concerned, is that our ability to measure doesn't seem to have advanced in any way as well as our opportunity to observe and greater recurrence of more disturbing things of this sort that are actually in existence from man-made air participation that we know about.

So, our present course of action is to continue on this problem with the best of our ability, giving to it the attention that we feel it very definitely warrants in terms of identifying adequately the growing or possible or disappearing, if it turns out to be that menace to the United States to give it adequate attention.

While General Samford is giving lip service to the idea that Air Force officers treat the subject of UFOs seriously, the truth is that they didn't. In less than a year, the staff of Blue Book, as it had existed in July, had been reduced to the point where it could affectively do nothing. At its lowest, it was "commanded" by an airman first class, one of the lowest ranking of the enlisted grades. No officer was assigned.

Ruppelt himself wrote that in December 1952 he asked for a transfer for a new and better assignment. He agreed to stay with Blue Book until February 1953 so that a replacement could be assigned and trained but no replacement arrived. Ruppelt left Blue Book in the hands of a single officer and one enlisted man. By July 1953, the enlisted man was the sole soldier manning the office. When Ruppelt returned to Wright-Patterson Air Force Base he learned that the investigation had collapsed.

General Samford: Now, I think with those opening remarks I could invite questions. Questions, yes, sir?

Reporter: Have there been more than one radar sighting simultaneously -- that is, blips from several stations all concentrating on the same area?

Samford: You mean in the past?

Reporter: Yes, sir.

Samford: Yes. That is not an unusual thing to happen to this sequence at all. Phenomenon have passed from one radar to another and with a fair degree of certainty that it was the same phenomenon. To say that there have been simultaneous sightings, the same thing by different radar, I think that we could be quite sure that that has occurred simultaneously. Now, when we talk about down to the split second, I don't know, but simultaneously in time sufficient for us to argue that they've been two mechanical observations of the same thing.

Reporter: Enough to give you a fix so that you can be sure that it is right in a certain place?

Samford: That is most rare.

Reporter: Has there been any?

Samford: Most rare. I don't recall that we have had one that gives us that kind of an effect.

Reporter: Could that be due to ionized clouds?

Samford: There are thoughts that ionized clouds do have some influence on this. We do know that the thunderstorm activity is quite nicely identifiable by radar because we use the radar for the purposes of avoiding thunderstorms and we do have some that show the storm area that's coming in towards principal stations where protection is necessary in terms of high winds and thunderstorms.

Samford is avoiding the question here. The Washington Nationals were just the sort of sightings that the reporter had been trying to identify. The sightings involved multiple targets on multiple sets in which, those who attempted visual confirmation, found unexplained lights where the radars showed them to be. This question was the whole point of the press conference, but Samford just didn't answer it and the reporters, who should have known better simply did not follow up on it.

Reporter: How much money would you say the Air Force spends a year tracking down these flying saucer reports?

29 JULY 1952 SIGHTINGS

DATE	LOCATION	OBSERVER	EVALUATION
731 29	Osceola, Wisonsin	Multiple (PHOTO)	UNIDENTIFIED
732 29	Langley AFB, Virginia		UNINDENTIFIED
733 29	Otis AFB, Massachusetts		BALLOON
734 29	Chico, California		INSUFFICIENT DATA
	(CARD MISSING)		
1735 29	Atlanta, Georgia		BALLOON
	(CARD MISSING)		
1736 29	Red Bluff, California		INSUFFICIENT DATA
	(CARD MISSING)		
1737 29	Albuquerque, New Mexico		INSUFFICIENT DATA
1738 29	Merced, California		UNIDENTIFIED
	(CARD MISSING)		
1739 29	Wichita, Kansas		UNIDENTIFIED
	(CARD MISSING)		
1740 29	Miami, Florida		AIRCRAFT
	(CARD MISSING)		
29	Miami, Florida		
	(CARD MISSING)		
741 29	Dallas, Texas		
	(CARD MISSING)		
742 29	Detroit, Michigan		AIRCRAFT
	(CARD MISSING)		
743 29	United States		AIRCRAFT
	(CARD MISSING)		
744 29	Negro Mountain, Grantsville, Maryland		AIRCRAFT
745 29	Mapo, California		AIRCRAFT
	(CARD MISSING)		
746 29	Hickam AFB, Hawaii		BALLOON
	(CARD MISSING)		
747 29	Ennis, Montana		UNINDENTIFIED
748 29	Otis AFB, Massachusetts		BALLOON
	(CARD MISSING) CASE MISSING		
749 29	Los Alamos, New Mexico	Multiple	Other (PAPER IN WIND)
750 29	Montague, California		
	(CARD MISSING)		
1751 29	Palm Beach, Florida		Astro (METEOR)
	(CARD MISSING)		
1752 29	New Mexico (Walker AFB)	Military	
	(CARD MISSING)		
1753 29	Ashiya AB, Japan		Other (SEARCHLIGHTS)
29	Port Huron, Michigan	Military	Aircraft
	(CARD MISSING)		

ADDITIONAL SIGHTINGS REPORTED (NOT CASES)

	LOCATION	OBSERVER	EVALUATION
	Englewood, New Jersey		(PHOTO)

A single page from the Project Blue Book files devoted to the sightings for July 29, 1952, showing the number of missing cards. It is difficult to accept the conclusions without the other data available for review.

Given the circumstances of the press conference, and what had just been reported in the newspapers, the question is somewhat irrelevant. If the phenomenon is real, then regulations required investigation. If it posed a threat to national security, again, regulations required it. The investigation was something that was required to learn the truth, so the amount of money spent meant virtually nothing.

> Samford: Well, the energy that's going into it at the present time is outside of anything except the normal reporting procedures. Most of our reports come from individuals or, we might say, I think, on the order of sixty-odd per cent comes from the civilian population straight out. I think there might be something like eight per cent come from civil airlines pilots. You might find that another percentage, in the order of twenty-five, might come from military pilots. And the effort to further analyze them and profit in going after that in a big way is going to have in some way to be related to a standard measurement that makes this material for workman to work on.

I suppose that it not necessary to point out that Samford did not answer the question. Instead. he suggested the percentages of those who report flying saucer sightings to the Air Force. He offered no evidence that his statistics were accurate, and in reality, it makes no difference.

> Reporter: General, have you talked to your Air Force Intelligence Officer who is over at the National Airport when they were sighting all these bandits on the CAA screen?

> Samford: Yes, sir; I have.

> Reporter: And have you talked to the Andrews Field people who apparently saw the same thing?

> Samford: I haven't talked to them myself, but others have.

> Reporter: Well, could you give us an account of what they did see and what explanations you might attach to it?

> Samford: Well, I could discuss possibilities. The radar screen has been picking up things for many years that, well, birds, a flock of ducks. I know there's been one instance in which a flock of ducks was picked up and was intercepted and flown through as being an unidentified phenomenon.

> Reporter: Where was that General?

Samford: I don't recall where it was. I think it might have been in Japan, but I don't recall the location of that. That's just a recollection of what that sort of thing could happen, and I do know that at Wright Field there was one of these things on radar -- that was in 1950, I think -- maybe Captain James would reinforce that. Was that in 1950?

Captain James: That's correct.

Samford: -- in which the local radar produced the effect of the encircling phenomenon that caused quite a lot of concern and it was gone out and intercepted and found to be a certain kind of ice formation that was in the air in various parts of the atmosphere around Wright Field on that day.

Samford is on fairly safe ground here. There are any number of reports in which the capabilities of the radars were not fully understood at that time. During the Second World War, radars in Great Britain produced a strange phenomenon every morning as a blip came off the ground and then seemed to expand and fading until it disappeared. They found that birds, taking off in the morning were the cause.

Samford: Again, there are theories like the men whose theory of light refraction which says that temperature inversion in the atmosphere can cause an image from somewhere else to be reflected in positions where it is not. If that is a correct theory, related to it is another oddity with respect to the ground effect that you get in radar.

We have one instance in which a night fighter with radar is reported to have locked on, as they say, to an object in flight, which, after he'd followed it beyond this curve, found that he was locked on to the ground and he had only a very few minutes to recover because the ground target had gone up and then misplaced this phenomena (sic), and he locked on to it in a position where he wasn't, but, following it, he eventually found himself directed toward the ground.

Now, the conditions that seem to produce these temperature inversions and possibly the same kind of thing for ground targets being misplaced in altitude -- I don't know that it is worded that they're misplaced in azimuth -- is somewhat typical of the kind of hot humid weather that we've been having here in the last three or four weeks. There's no reason to relate those phenomena to those atmospheric conditions positively, but it is a possibility.

Please note here something that the reporters failed to understand. Samford suggested a possible explanation but also said that there was no reason to believe that the sightings were related to the weather conditions over Washington at the time. The reporters apparently didn't hear this part of Samford's statement.

Samford: Yes, sir?

Reporter: Did interceptors go up on any of the three occasions?

Samford: Here.

Radar Experts and Weather Scientists Challenge Air Force Saucer Theories

WASHINGTON (INS)—Radar experts and weather scientists Wednesday challenged the air force theory that flying saucers are ground objects reflected in the sky under freak atmospheric conditions.

Radar crews at Washington National airport, where mysterious "blips" have been tracked three times in the last two weeks, maintained they have recorded "unknown objects" twisting in a weird pattern, and not light reflections, as the air force suggested.

The U. S. weather bureau, while conceding that a "temperature inversion" has existed during the current hot spell, took issue with the theory expounded by Maj. Gen. John A. Samford, air intelligence chief.

A "temperature inversion" is a layer of warm air above cold air, and Samford suggested that under such conditions an auto headlight or airport beam could be reflected in the sky as a flying saucer.

A weather bureau official said, however, that reflections due to such an inversion ordinarily would appear on a radar screen as a steady line, rather than as single objects such as were sighted on the airport radarscope.

Other saucer developments included:

1. The air force, seeking an unshakable explanation of the mystery disks, rushed preparations to scan the skies with 200 astronomer-type cameras and powerful telescopes.

2. The Rev. Francis Hayden, director of the Georgetown university observatory, predicted that the saucer season will reach a climax Aug. 12, probable time of the annual Perseid shower of thousands of shooting stars.

3. The coast guard said it will allow the air force to inspect the negative of a photograph purportedly showing five "egg-shaped objects" flying in formation over Salem, Mass. The picture was taken at 9:35 a.m. (EDT) July 16.

4. Two Philadelphia scientists Drs. I. M. Levitt and T. K. Marshall, agreed with the air force explanation of the mystery visitors and blamed weird reflections resulting from the hot weather.

5. Jet fighter-interceptor pilots at bases throughout the country remained on a 24-hour alert.

6. The navy confirmed that on May 11, 1943, mysterious object sighted by radar were erroneously identified as enemy ships touching off a salvo of scores of rounds of ammunition fired at non-existent enemy off Alaska The navy said the error resulted from atmospheric reflection like that which sometimes make freak television reception possible.

A demonstration of the dichotomy between what the Air Force said and the weather experts. The argument about the cause of the sightings changed as the Air Force pushed the weather answer and the press agreed with that assessment.

Reporter: Yes.

Samford: Yes, sir.

Reporter: What did they see on their radar scopes?

Samford: I don't recall that they saw anything. Do you remember, Roger, whether anything was sighted on their radar scopes?

Air Force Calls Scientists To Solve 'Saucers' Mystery

July 29, 1952

WASHINGTON — (UP) — Mysterious objects swooped over the nation's capital again early today and the Air Force called in top scientists to find out what "flying saucers" are.

The Civil Aeronautics Administration traffic control center reported that its radar picked up the objects for about six straight hours early this morning.

The objects, a CAA official said were traveling about 100 to 120 miles an hour in a 10-mile arc around the capital, between Herndon, Va., and Andrews Air Force Base in nearby Maryland.

It was in this same area that radar screens recorded the strange "targets" the past two Saturday nights, setting off a new rash of "flying saucer" rumors in the capital.

Attitude Reversed

Top Air Force brass has decided to get to the bottom of the mystery. Forsaking an earlier attitude that "there ain't no such animal," they are enlisting top scientists in a major new saucer study, it was learned today.

A CAA official said the control center radar first started picking up the strange "blips" about 1:30 a. m. and that they continued showing up on the radarscope until 6 a.m. this morning. At some times, he said, there were as many as eight to 12 of the objects on the scope at the same time.

A pilot aboard an Eastern Air Lines Constellation was directed to check on the objects about 3 a. m., but he reported he saw no lights despite a 15-mile visibility. The CAA official said the objects disappeared from the radar screen when the plane was in the area where they had been tracked and "then came back in behind him."

Force officials said they considered it the service's "obligation" to continue to investigate saucer reports.

Favorite Theory Emerges

General Samford insisted, in the ace of recent reports here from

Three times in the last ten days it was disclosed, Air Force interceptor planes have been dispatched to the Capital area to hunt for reported flying objects, some of which were reported to be stationary, others moving at various speeds. General Samford's staff attempted to explain the supposedly moving objects as sightings of separate phenomena some distance away from each other.

Radar operators for the Civil Aeronautics Administration at the Washington National Airport had reported that the "blips" of light on their radar screens had appeared and disappeared.

One Pilot Chased Too Far

As an example of how ground objects or lights can be reflected into the clouds and mistakenly identified, one Air Force expert told of a pilot who nearly crashed his plane into the ground while chasing an "object" that had appeared in his airplane's radar screen. Of this General Samford said: "Ground targets [objects] can be misplaced in altitude" for a pilot during hot, moist weather.

The Air Force experts said that although they had run down more than 1,000 supposed sightings of "saucers" or other objects in recent years, only 20 per cent of the reports from creditable sources remained unexplained.

Recalling that signs in the sky of one sort or another dated at least to Biblical times, General Samford said that one reason for the "saucer" flurries was undoubtedly the great increase in manmade activity in the air. He also cited "jumpiness" because of war fears and, without quite saying so, the desire of some persons to seek publicity.

He also said that a trained Air Force pilot, or an experienced radar operator, assigned to chase saucers or define them on his radar screen also was subject to "curiosity stimulus" that would result,

Major General Roger M. Ramey: There have been no radar sightings. One or two reported (inaudible) --

Reporter: There have been no airborne radar sightings, General Ramey? Is that --

Ramey: That's correct.

Actually, as we have seen, there were airborne radar locks. This is based on the testimony of Norman Sykes, one of the interceptor pilots who was involved in some of the attempted intercepts on July 26. He had no visual sighting, but his radar operator did, in fact, detect some of the UFOs that night.

Reporter: On what did they report sightings?

Samford: Lights.

Ramey: In one or two instances, they reported sighting lights. In one instance, they reported locking on an object. It is pretty clear from the discussion of the pattern of two airplanes that went out that one of them was locked on the other one.

Samford: Yes.

Reporter: Back to the ionized cloud. Were the blips picked up recently comparable to the ionized cloud or were they different in maneuvering or motion?

Samford: They were different.

Reporter: General Samford, I understand there were radar experts who saw these sightings Saturday night or early Sunday morning. What was their interpretation of what they saw on the scope?

Samford: They said they saw good returns.

Reporter: Which would indicate that these were solid objects similar to aircraft?

Samford: No, not necessarily. We get good returns from birds.

Reporter: Well, you wouldn't get as large a blip from a bird as

Samford: No, unless it was close.

A point must be interjected here. The radar operators were all trained men who had been working at the nation's capital airport. They would have, in the past, seen birds and temperature inversions on their radar scopes. They would be familiar with these sorts of natural phenomena and wouldn't be easily fooled by them, especially when it is remembered that they had years of experience. This wasn't the situation ten years earlier when radar operators were poorly trained, and the operations of radar were poorly understood.

Reporter: Did they report that these could have been birds?

Samford: No.

Reporter: Can you get a good return from a reflected ground target, General?

James: You can get a very large return from a reflected ground target.

Reporter: Just as good as you might get from an object actually in flight in the air?

James: Actually thicker. It depends on the amount of bending.

Reporter: And just as sharp on the scope?

James: Yes.

Reporter: Can you get a blip from the (inaudible) created by temperature inversion?

James: On the ground target, yes.

Reporter: In other words, something that's on the ground that's reflected off a refracted cloud bank would throw off a blip on the radar screen?

James: Yes, sir. That's true.

Reporter: Would a nearby radar set get that blip at exactly the same speed?

James: Not necessarily; no.

Reporter: In other words, you can have a light and something that lacks substance and material and still have a blip?

James: I don't quite understand the question.

Reporter: You can have a radar image that's created without the necessity of radar striking the solid object or a semi-solid object, such as a cloud.

James: Well, eventually, it does have to strike an object.

Reporter: But you said it can be simply a reflection of something on the ground.

Reporter: I see.

Reporter: In other words, it doesn't have to be in the air.

James: That's correct.

Reporter: In the area covered by the sweep on the radar?

James: It has to be in the area covered by the radar set. It has to be within the range.

Reporter: But not in the air.

James: But not in the air.

Reporter: What sort of ground targets give these reflections?

James: It depends on the amount of temperature inversion and the size and shape of the ground objects.

Reporter: Would this reflection account for simultaneous radar sightings and visual sightings which appear to coincide on the basis of conversations between the radar operator and the observer outside?

James: There is some possibility of that due to the same effects.

Reporter: Why would these temperature inversions change location so rapidly or travel?

James: Well, actually, it can be the appearance or disappearance of different ground targets giving the appearance of something moving when, actually, the different objects are standing still.

Reporter: Would these pseudo-blips cause any difficulties in combat at all?

James: Not to people that understand what's going on. They do cause some difficulty.

Reporter: Then the experienced operators really can tell the difference between --

James: That's correct.

Reporter: How about the CAA men?

James: I don't know.

Temperature Inversion and Reporter Confusion

It is clear from the questions that the reporters understood little about radar operations and temperature inversions. Captain James made it clear with his answers that trained, qualified, experienced men could tell the difference between real targets and those caused by temperature inversions.

It is also clear that the reporters had somehow come to the conclusion that the temperature inversions were responsible for creating the lights reported by both airline and military pilots and the men on the ground. The reporters had begun to think of a temperature inversion as a "cloud." That is, they seemed to think that it was something that could be seen and even glowing, not realizing that a temperature inversion was merely a cold layer of clear air under a warmer layer of clear air.

Reporter: Would the disappearance or reappearance of these blips be accounted for by the movement of a cloud bank that reflected a ground target?

James: Well, actually, it's not a cloud bank. It's a temperature inversion of the atmosphere. You see, if warm air comes in over a cool area, you have a temperature inversion and the atmosphere is perfectly clear, and still the rays will be bent.

The reporters have become confused, believing, for the moment, that the visual sightings were a result of the temperature inversion. They are searching for an explanation for what was seen by the pilots and ground observers, but a temperature inversion is, essentially, invisible to the human eye.

> Reporter: Would that account for the fact that these images disappeared and reappeared on these screens recently?

> James: I'm not positive about that. There's a possibility.

> Reporter: Captain, was there temperature inversion in this area last Saturday night?

> James: There was.

> Reporter: And the Saturday night preceding?

> James: I'm not sure about the one preceding, but there was last Saturday night.

> Reporter: Was there one last night?

> James: I don't know.

> Reporter: Captain, did any two sets in this area get a fix on these so-called saucers around here?

> James: The information we have isn't good enough to determine that.

This statement might be true, but only because the information had yet to reach him or other Air Force organizations. However, it is clear from the documentation in both the Air Force files and from the newspapers that there were multiple reports on multiple radar set at multiple facilities.

> Reporter: You don't know whether Andrews Field and Washington National Airport actually got a triangulation on anything?

> James: You see, the records made and kept aren't accurate enough to tie that in that close.

> Reporter: What is the possibility of these being other than phenomena?

> Samford: Well, I'd like to maybe relieve Captain James just a minute. Your question is what?

Reporter: What is the possibility of these sightings being other than optical or atmospheric phenomena? In other words, what is the possibility of their being guided missiles launched from some other country, for example?

Samford: Well, if you could select out of this mass any particular one or two and start working on them and say, "What is the possibility of them being these things?" Then you come to the point and say this one is reported to have done things which require for it to do those things either one of two conditions, absolute maximum power or no mass. If this is a thing in terms of a guided missile, it does these things if there is theoretically no limit to the power involved and there is theoretically no mass involved. That's one of the conditions that would say, well, if someone solved one of those problems, this could then be explained as one of those things. You find another one and it has -- it just develops into no other purpose or no other pattern that could be associated with them, a missile. Those which we might identify as being missiles will be tracked. They'll have a track to develop, something that people can put a measurement to. I don't know whether that answers the question. It satisfies some of it, but maybe not all of it.

The truth is, that Samford's response didn't answer the question which was simply if the objects spotted could have been missiles launched by another terrestrial government. The answer was a simple, "No." Instead Samford begins to talk of an object that has access to virtually unlimited power and that has no mass. He never did explain what these two conditions had to do with the question that had been asked but is certainly sounded as if he was rendering a scientifically sound answer.

Reporter: Have there been any such instances so far in which you had information that indicated that either of these two conditions were fulfilled?

Samford: Absolute, no mass?

Reporter: No limit to the power.

Samford: You know what "no mass" means is that there's nothing there! (Laughter).

Reporter: How about the power?

Samford: In terms of earthly weights and earthly value.

Reporter: Yes.

Samford: And unlimited power -- that means power of such fantastic higher limits that it is a theoretically unlimited -- it's not anything that we can understand. It's like my trying to understand -- I want to be careful because I was going to say a million dollars, but I can't understand a hundred! It's one of those questions of unlimited power that just gets beyond your comprehension that has to be used to meet this.

Reporter: General, do you have any tentative conclusion or even a trend towards a belief of what these local radar blips are? There's been talk that you did have the heat inversion those nights. Are you all inclined to believe that's what it is?

Samford: I think that we're learning progressively more and more about the radar and that these instances very likely are maybe good observations that the radar can make of something but not likely to be observations of the things the radar was designed to observe (laughter). Now, (laughter) -- all right. Now, let's say -- we don't know much about -- and I'll be getting far afield here technically -- we don't know much about the Northern Lights. We'd like to be able to measure that a little bit better. That is the kind of thought I was trying to express by saying radar was intended to observe aircraft for control of aircraft and to deal with aircraft. Now, you may have scientific advantages for observation that it wasn't intended for.

I wonder if you'd speak to my point on that, Captain James, whether I've gotten too far afield on something I don't know anything about.

James: Yes, sir; that's quite true. We find that sometimes the radar set will be formed in a manner not desirable and due to the fact that it doesn't happen every day everyone isn't familiar with those characteristics, and it sometimes turns out to be a mystery.

Reporter: Well, getting back, if I may follow it up, on these local radar observations, then you come to the tentative conclusion that they're physical phenomena? Would you say that?

Samford: I think so, yes.

Reporter: How is it we haven't had them before?

Reporter: Well, that's what I was going to get to. What's the history of this thing? Radar operators in the past, when you inquire of them, have they seen similar lights in the past and because they never bothered to associate them with flying saucers they've never gotten in the newspapers?

Samford: Oh, they have associated them in the past with things that were thought desirable to intercept. I said a minute ago we've intercepted flocks of ducks and similar things. There's some history of the lack of identification of friendly aircraft which causes a lot of unnecessary interceptions in some parts of the world, being mixed up with a lot of this sort of thing too in which we've had many interceptions that went out and identified a friendly that should have been established by some other method, but mixed up with those there have been many of these attempts to identify an unknown that fizzled out in the same way that the current ones have fizzled out.

Reporter: In other words, it is not a rare phenomenon, this thing that happened Saturday night and the Saturday before that?

Samford: It is not a rare phenomenon.

Reporter: It's not radar, and it occurs often enough so that you do have a history, and radar experts have been trying to find out what causes them; is that right?

Samford: That is correct. Yes, sir.

Reporter: General Samford, has the Air Force conducted any independent research through universities or through radar people, the Gilfillan people or whoever?

Samford: Yes, sir. We have a number of available consultants, some contracts that have been initiated, some of them are being thought of, but, again, I think I'd like to go back to the point of profit in this thing perhaps being a measurement first, an adequate measurement that can do science. Reports of the same kind we've been getting except for this additional mechanical asset or opportunity called the radar have been going on since Bible times. Now, the radar gives an additional opportunity to observe something about that, but it still doesn't measure it with the kind of precision that is needed to put it into analysis.

Reporter: Are you getting something to do that?

Samford: We have some hope with a camera that has on the front of it a -- will you describe what that --

James: It has a de-fraction grid.

Samford: Yes, a de-fraction grid on the front of it that will be useful against lights because through that de-fraction you'll be able to say, from what substance the light was made? What gases were burning? Was it gas? Was it incandescence? And so forth. Now, those cameras -- the lens is about a $15 item, or this grid is, and the camera is about a $15 item. We have on order a small quantity, two hundred plus of those. We hope to be able to distribute those into the hands of people who might have opportunity. Now, with the great diversity of people who report it's not too easy to put your finger on who has the highest opportunity to report, into whose hands such a device should go, but we think we may learn who might be the most optimum reporters. A great volume of these cameras to scatter around to try through the shotgun approach to get reports doesn't look like too valuable a project but that is one way of trying to measure what their lights are.

Reporter: For what purpose -- they have had similar gadgets before, I mean, to measure and to determine the origin of what generates the light. Is this a new type?

James: The grid is.

Samford: It's not new except that it hasn't been aimed specifically at these items or focused on these items as far as we know.

More on the Temperature Inversions

Reporter: General, the Captain mentioned a moment ago or had the thought that when there is temperature inversion the men know who are observing radar. Is it all right to ask if the Air Force thinks that these objects the other night were a result of temperature inversion?

Samford: Well, I'll answer that first, try to, and then ask Captain James for an opinion. I don't think that we are quite sure that the [Dr. Donald] Menzel theory of temperature inversion or that scientists are sure that that is a good theory. It's supported by

88

some people. Other people who have equal competence, it would appear, discredit it. So, the game as to whether that is the cause or not is about a fifty-fifty proposition. It's appealing. It does satisfy certain concerns. Is that a fair statement or answer to that question?

James: Sir, the Menzel theory applies mainly to light rays.

Samford: Yes.

James: In regard to the temperature inversion effect on radar waves that is fairly well established.

Reporter: There's no doubt about the latter, is there?

James: That's right.

Reporter: That's been established.

Reporter: And it was not --

James: We don't have sufficient information to say definitely that that was the cause.

Reporter: You said an experienced radar operator could tell the difference.

James: I would say so.

Reporter: Wasn't there a naval battle during the war in which there was a great engagement fought against an inversion of radar?

This refers to an incident during the summer of 1943 in which a Navy task force fired a thousand rounds at objects that had appeared on radar. Lookouts reported seeing flares from the Japanese navy. Vice Admiral Robert C. Giffen had commanded the American forces in what he described as a battle of the blips. In other words, Giffen was suggesting that the Navy had fired on targets that were a result of temperature inversions and not on something real, that is Japanese, who were attempting to invade one of the Aleutian Islands.

James: I understand that happened.

Reporter: You had two experts over there last Saturday night, Major Fournet and Lieutenant Holcomb, who described themselves as radar technicians and intelligence officers. What was their opinion?

Samford: May I try to make another answer and ask for support or negation, on the quality of the radar operator. I personally don't

89

feel that is necessarily associated with quality of radar operators because radar operators of great quality are going to be confused by the things which now appear and may appear in radar. The ability to use the radar for the thing it was designed for is, I believe, dependent upon the thing that they see doing a normal act. If it does a normal act, then it becomes identified as the thing that they thought it was and then it pulls itself along through this mass of indication and they say, "That one has normal processes." I think that a description of a GCA landing has some bearing on that in which to get associated with the GCA you have to make a certain number of queries and do a certain number of things and then you become identified through the fact that you obey. If you obey, then you have an identity and you can then be followed with precision. So, I wouldn't like to say that this is a function of inadequate radar operations. I think it's a thing that can happen to any radar operator. If he sees something in there and says, "That one is neither behaving nor any other normal pattern." What is it? Curiosity stimulus, any other kind of stimulus can result in overemphasis at any particular time on any radar scope. These recently appear to have been much more solid returns than ordinarily classifiable by the arguments that I have just given.

Would you address yourself to what I've just said?

Reporter: Yes. What do the experts think? That was the question.

Samford: The experts?

Reporter: The ones that saw it last Saturday night. What did they report to you?

Reporter: Two of them saw it in --

Reporter: What did they say?

Samford: They said they made good returns.

Reporter: Did they draw any conclusions as to what they were, whether they were clouds?

Samford: They made good returns, and they think that they ought to be followed up.

Reporter: But now you come to the general belief that it was some either heat inversions or some other phenomena without substance.

Samford: The phrase "without substance" bothers me a little.

Reporter: Well, could you --

Samford: -- say what we do think?

Reporter: Yes.

Samford: I think that the highest probability is that these are phenomena associated with the intellectual and scientific interests that we are on the road to learn more about but that there is nothing in them that is associated with material or vehicles or missiles that are directed against the United States.

Reporter: General, you said that -- can you stop that short of the United States, sir, or the menace to the United States?

Samford: Well, that was the -- I think that is the part that I believed. Now, what was it that I would have said otherwise?

Reporter: Well, you said were not associated with vehicles --

Reporter: Materials.

Reporter: Missiles.

Reporter: Period.

Reporter: Material, vehicles, and missiles directed against the United States.

Reporter: The question whether these are hostile or not makes very little difference. What we're trying to get at is are you eliminating, excluding from consideration a missile, a vehicle, or any other material object that might be flying through the air other than sound or light or some other intangible.

Reporter: Somebody from this planet or some other planet violating our air space. (Laughter)

Samford: The astronomers are our best advisers, of course, in this business of visitors from elsewhere. The astronomers photograph the sky continuously perhaps with the most adequate photography in existence and the complete absence of things which would have to be in their appearance for many days and months to come from somewhere else. It doesn't cause them to have any enthusiasm whatsoever in thinking about this other side of it.

Reporter: Have any astronomical laboratories reported any sightings whatsoever or any astronomers?

Samford: I don't recall. Captain Ruppelt, do you know whether we've had reports from astronomical laboratories or observatories?

Ruppelt: No, sir. None have ever had any real bearing.

The question as posed and the answer as posed, at this point are misleading. Astronomers had made UFO reports on a number of occasions. Dr. Clyde Tombaugh who discovered Pluto, had made a UFO sighting report to the Air Force. He was not at an observatory at the time, but in his backyard, with his wife, but the real point is that here was a scientist, one with impressive credentials, who had made a UFO report to the Air Force.

Dr. J. Allen Hynek

More recently, studies have been conducted using professional astronomers and engineers as the subjects. It was reported that these people reported UFOs at a higher rate than the general population. In other words, it would be expected that astronomers, who watch the sky on a regular basis, would see UFOs more frequently that the general population and they did, according to a scientifically reported study.

In fact, because they are familiar with the sky and the astronomical phenomena in it, they would be able to eliminate many of the mundane answers that confuse and confound the general population. Their sightings, normally of longer duration, are not easily explained by the mundane and are, therefore, more likely to be labeled as unidentified.

But there was another point that is generally overlooked. According to Dr. J. Allen Hynek's survey of his fellow astronomers, most astronomers, in 1952, would not have been inclined to report a UFO sighting. Hynek wrote, "I took the time to talk rather seriously with a few of them, and to acquaint them with the fact that some of the sightings were truly puzzling and not at all easily explainable. Their interest was almost immediately aroused, indicating that their general lethargy is due to lack of information on the subject. And certainly, another contributing factor... is their overwhelming fear of publicity.

One headline in the nation's papers to the effect 'Astronomer Sees Flying Saucer' would be enough to brand the astronomer as questionable among his colleagues."

So, there is a very real possibility, according to the information available, that astronomers do see UFOs, but they don't report them with any frequency. Ruppelt had to know that Hynck was conducting the study, even if it had not been completed, and he had to know that, at least, one astronomer had reported a UFO.

To be fair, it must be noted that General Samford might not have had the information, or that it might not have been reported to the Air Force at the highest level. The general attitude of the Air Force was that if something wasn't reported to them, it simply didn't exist.

> Reporter: General, does that -- the kind of involved explanation you just gave us -- does that apply to the recent Washington sightings or upon your observations over the past years since 1946 based on all your experience with it?

> Samford: Well, our reaction to the recent Washington sightings is related to the past experience in terms of -- we have dealt with radar blips before.

> Reporter: General, if these were vehicles or materials of our own making, they wouldn't be a menace to the United States. Do you exclude that?

> Samford: I'd exclude that, definitely.

> Reporter: General, let's make it clear now you are excluding -- if you'll affirm that -- you are excluding vehicles, missiles, and other tangible objects flying through space, including the subhuman bodies from other planets.

> Samford: In my mind, yes.

> Reporter: Anything material -- would that be a clear statement.

> Samford: When you deal with a scientific man, maybe he might quarrel with you by what is the real meaning of "material." With my limited knowledge of material, I would say yes. In my own view the thing is excluded as being material evidence.

> Reporter: In other words, General, if you remove the EEI [Essential Element of Intelligence] from that statement, it could apply to any

missile, material, or object that is in the air, regardless of whether it's a menace to the United States or not?

Samford: Well, yes.

Reporter: In other words, it just isn't there.

Samford: I believe that, that there is no -- well, now, that is a little bit in error because a minute ago I said birds do these things. Now, a bird has substance, you see. I don't want to go out and say that these things are reflections of nothing. If they're reflections of something. That's why the thought of saying that this thing satisfies us in having no real pattern other than that of phenomena.

Reporter: General, you said there'd never been a simultaneous radar fix on one of these things.

Samford: I don't think I wanted to say that.

Reporter: You didn't mean to say that?

Samford: I meant to say that, when you talk about simultaneously, somebody will say, "was it on 1203 hours, 24 and a half seconds?" and I don't know.

Reporter: Well, I'd like to point out this fact that the officer in charge of the radar station at Andrews Field told me that on the morning of July 20th, which was a week from last Saturday, he picked up an object three miles north of Riverdale and he was in intercom communication with CAA and they exchanged information and the CAA also had a blip three miles north of Riverdale and on both radars the same blip remained for about thirty seconds and simultaneously disappeared from both sets. Now --

Samford: Well, their definition of simultaneous, yes. But some people won't be satisfied that that is simultaneously.

Reporter: Well, it is pretty damned simultaneous (laughter) for all purposes, it is satisfied by the inversion theory, Captain.

Samford: Well, I'm talking about the split-second people who want to say you've got to prove now that this happened at such-and-such a time, and they'll say your observations are delayed by half a second; therefore, you can't say it was simultaneous.

Reporter: And does your inversion theory explain away that situation?

James: It possibly could, yes.

Reporter: It possibly could, but could it?

James: We don't have the details.

Reporter: Is there any reason why it couldn't.

Reporter: General, can we get this clarified?

Samford: I believe -- I'm trying to let this gentleman ask a question. Excuse me.

UFOs and Nukes

Reporter: Isn't it true, sir, that these show a definite grouping, the sightings around atomic bomb plants or areas? Doesn't your map at Wright Field show that?

Samford: I find no pattern in this dispersal of sightings than I do in a radar screen. You can perhaps take distribution of sightings and say that you arrange it this way and you take this group during this period and that gives you a dispersal that may have some significance in it. But I'd like to have Captain Ruppelt develop that because he probably knows more about what has been done to try to plot these things and say, "Does that have any meaning?" I am not satisfied that any effort we've made toward a dispersal pattern has developed one shred of evidence or meaning. Would you correct me or speak to that point?

Ruppelt: We've plotted these things out on a map, and they do come out grouped around some of the atomic installations in the country. However, there's one point, you don't know, maybe people in that area are a little more jumpy and, if they see a meteor, they'll report it into the guards. If some farmer out in the middle of Iowa saw a meteor, he'd just forget about it. Now, that is one possibility that we can't eliminate. A lot of sightings that occurred around these atomic installations have turned out to be balloons, etc., but it may be that the story has gone out that those are vital areas, and more people are reporting. We don't know.

Ruppelt's concluding remark, that "We don't know," is about the only thing said here that is true. Everything else is speculation. The data are incomplete.

The Air Force simply didn't know what percentage of sightings was legitimate, how many sightings had not been reported, or if the explanations offered were real.

While it is not completely fair to Ruppelt to mention that Robert Hastings, in the last few years has been tracking sightings around nuclear facilities, around  military installations in which atom weapons are stored and near missile launch complexes does suggest an interest in UFOs. Ruppelt's remarks are misleading when he suggests that the guards and personnel at these facilities are more likely to report something than a farmer in Iowa, it is also fair that those guards and their chains of command are more likely to be able to identify a strange phenomenon than that farmer in Iowa.

Ruppelt seemed to be suggesting that reporting requirements by military personnel tend to skew the results is misleading. Hasting found and reported in *UFOs and Nukes*, that there seemed to

Robert Hastings

be disproportionate sightings and reporting of UFOs around those facilities, but as I say, Ruppelt wouldn't have had access to the information that Hasting used in his book.

> Reporter: What percentage of your unexplainable ones that you've got are around there?

> Ruppelt: A few of them.

> Reporter: Is it the same pattern?

> Ruppelt: I wouldn't say that every sighting around an atomic installation is unexplained. There's really no -- I don't quite follow you.

> Reporter: His question is what percentage of the unexplainable percentage of the sightings are grouped around atomic energy --

> Ruppelt: We've never broken it down.

> Reporter: Is it uniform to the general percentages?

> Ruppelt: It followed the general percentages. In other words, if twenty per cent of the sightings are unexplained, twenty per cent of the sightings around Los Alamos are --

Reporter: Unexplained.

Ruppelt: -- unexplained; right.

Reporter: What percentage of these have come from technical men in science at these installations?

Ruppelt: It varies with the type of people. In other words, at Los Alamos most of the people are fairly technical people. However, you run the guards in a place like that. Now, that may be another factor. All those installations have guards that stay out twenty-four hours a day and those people are in a better position to observe than other people.

Reporter: Have many of the scientists though, for instance at Los Alamos, the scientists or technical people, reported these things?

Ruppelt: Yes; they have. We have reports from very high technical people.

Reporter: If your reports, some of them, come from these technical people, what type of information would they Air Force like to have?

Ruppelt: The Air Force would like to have - can I answer that, sir?

Samford: Go ahead.

Ruppelt: The Air Force would like to have a size, speed and altitude and what-have-you on these things.

Reporter: Number of men inside it? (Laughter)

Interestingly, the type of information that Ruppelt suggested had already been provided by some of the very best of the sightings available in the Blue Book files. For example, in near Arrey, New Mexico, in 1949, a technical crew, using various scientific equipment available to them, made observations of a high-flying disk. They provided exact measurements, and the sighting was forwarded to Project Blue Book at that time. It was labeled as an "Unidentified," in the Project Blue Book files.

Reporter: In view of practicalities, what would an ordinary citizen do if he saw one? Would you be interested in his information? What can he do to help you?

Ruppelt: Actually, we are very much interested. However, there isn't much we can do with their information. It's possible that you might get a series of sightings. In other words, if you get everybody

97

up and down the East Coast looking, you might be able to plot a ground track from it, but the information we get from the general public or from a scientist -- there's no difference. In other words, well, let's take a meteor-like object, for example. If you're out some night and see a meteor, what can you tell me about that meteor? You don't even know in which direction it was going. Actually, it looked to you may be like it was going across the sky from east to west, but you're not sure. You're just looking at horizontal projection of that meteor. And a scientist the same way. Just because he's a scientist doesn't mean he's got better eyes.

The most impressive series of sightings came from Portland, Oregon, where police officers and civilians in widely separated locations watched as a variety of disks flashed through the sky during the July 4, 1947, weekend. The first was reported by C.J. Bogne and a carload of witnesses north of Redmond, Oregon, when they saw four disk-shaped objects flash past Mount Jefferson. The objects made no noise and performed no maneuvers.

At one o'clock, an Oaks Park employee, Don Metcalfe saw a lone disk fly over the park. A KOIN news reporter in Portland saw twelve, shiny, disks as they danced in the sky-high overhead.

A few minutes after 1:00, Kenneth A. McDowell, a police officer who was near the Portland Police Station, noticed that the pigeons began fluttering as if frightened. Overhead were three disks, one flying east and the other two south. All were moving at high speed and appeared to be oscillating.

About the same time two other police officers, Walter A. Lissy and Robert Ellis saw three disks overhead. They were also moving at high speed.

Just across the Columbia River, in nearby Vancouver, Washington, sheriff's deputies, Sergeant John Sullivan, Clarence McKay, and Fred Krives, watched twenty to thirty disks overhead.

RESTRICTED

GUIDE TO CLASSIFICATION

UNCLASSIFIED   UNIDENTIFIED AERIAL OBJECTS

UNCLASSIFIED   Incident No. 30/

1. Date of Observation 24 April   Date of Interview _____

2. Exact time of observation (local) BETWEEN 1030 - 1035 MST

3. Place of Observation: 32° 53'N   107° 20'W
   (Map Coordinates)

4. Position of observer (air, car, bldg, location of - give details): GROUND, OPERATING A THEODOLITE for off TRACKING a...

5. What attracted attention to object: TURNED TO LOOK AT Balloon WITH NAKED EYE

6. Number of objects and sketch of formation or grouping: ONE

Information about the Arrey, New Mexico sighting. The important point here is that the document was clearly marked as "Secret, before it was downgraded to "Restricted," and later "Unclassified."

Not long after that, three harbor patrolmen on the river saw three to six disks traveling at high speed. According to the witnesses, the objects looked like chrome hubcaps and oscillated as they flew.

About 4:00 P.M., more civilians saw the disks. A woman called police, telling them she watched a single object as "shiny as a new dime, flipping around." An unidentified man called to say that he'd seen three discs, one flying to the east and the other two heading north. They were shiny, shaped like flattened saucers and were traveling at high speed.

Finally, in Milwaukie, Oregon, not far from Portland, Sergeant Claude Cross reported three objects flying to the north. All were disc-shaped and were moving at high speed.

The question that must be asked is why none of the aircraft on alert, in that area, on orders from the Pentagon, responded to this series of sightings. It would seem logical that they would have spotted the disks at some point, but there was never any indication that such is the case. Nothing appears in the Project Blue Book files to suggest that gun camera footage was obtained by the Oregon National Guard, which had been alerted because of the increase in UFO sightings in the area. A few days later, it was announced by the Pentagon that

99

the searches would be discontinued. The lack of concrete results was the suspected reason, though another reason is that they had completed the mission, meaning that the gun camera footage had been obtained.

The point, however, is that here was a series of sightings, in a single location, spread over a single day, that had been reported to the official Air Force project. No real investigation was carried out by military officials. Instead, the case was ignored by the Air Force.

> Reporter: What about a report, for example, about one week ago from an engineer who sighted six or seven who followed a definite pattern and then all turned in the same direction and went straight up at an estimated speed -- I forget what he said it was.

> Ruppelt: I couldn't pick that one out from the mass and size -- I'm not familiar with that one.

> Reporter: Have you investigated these so-called saucers here in Washington.

> Reporter: The ones we've been seeing on radar screens.

> Ruppelt: We've got data on them.

> Reporter: Have you investigated them yourself?

> Ruppelt: Well, what do you mean by that, now -- gone out and personally talked to all these people?

> Reporter: Yes.

> Ruppelt: No; I haven't.

> Reporter: Has anybody from the Air Force talked to Harry Barnes, who's the Senior Controller in the CAA radar?

> Ruppelt: We have a report from the CAA Controller.

> Reporter: But nobody's interviewed him?

> Ruppelt: I couldn't tell you that.

Attempts to Photograph UFOs

> Reporter: General, you started to say you wanted certain means of measuring these things and you mentioned this camera. Were you going to name others or is that the only thing you have in mind as a possible way of identifying and measuring these phenomena?

Samford: Mr. Griffing is here from the Electronics Section. Would you address yourself to that, Mr. Griffing?

Griffing: I didn't hear the question.

Reporter: The question was we'd ask what -- the General had said the greatest need now was to get some way of measuring these reports in terms that you can turn them over to a scientist and I asked him what was he seeking in that way, what he was getting. He mentioned this camera. I connected the question with some way of measuring the gases and lights. I asked him were there other things than that that he might mention that they're now ordering or procuring for that purpose.

Griffing: The refraction camera should tell whether it's an incandescent source or whether it's illuminous (sic) gas. Well, that would immediately tell whether it was a meteor or reflection of a headlight, a mirage theory and it might also identify what kind of gases.

Reporter: What other than this camera? Are there any other tools that you're seeking now?

Griffing: There is another proposal which also uses de-fraction grating, which is a continuously operating Schmidt telescope, and that will give a continuous record over the night.

Reporter: What's this?

Reporter: That's a telescope to photograph the entire heaven in one whole picture?

Griffing: Yes, sir.

Reporter: Would you repeat that? What is this Schmidt telescope?

James: It's a type of telescope.

Reporter: What type of telescope are you talking about, Mr. Griffing?

Griffing: The Schmidt, S-c-h-m-i-d-t, telescope is an optical system that has a wide aperture. That is, you can have a wide range or aperture, in this case, about 150 degrees, or nearer the whole hemisphere can be photographed in one plate and you can have a continual record of what happens in the sky at night, meteor trails or what-have-you and make a photographic record.

Reporter: Where is this being used?

Griffing: This is a new development, this particular one, but there have been ones similar to this in use in many observatories. Palomar has a Schmidt telescope.

Reporter: Are you ordering a number of those for placing around the country?

Griffing: That is a possibility.

Reporter: Is that a movie-camera type?

Griffing: Not exactly. The plate is exposed for ten minutes and then is replaced with another plate and then so on through the night. That is, one can expose a photographic plate for ten minutes without overexposure, in fact, a longer time, but a continual record will be made. Any motion that can be indicated with a time exposure can be found with considerable accuracy.

Reporter: Does the Air Force have access to any of these right now?

Griffing: That particular thing is not in production yet.

Reporter: How much does it cost?

Griffing: Shall I go into it, General?

Samford: Well, go ahead.

Griffing: The cost will be between three and five thousand dollars apiece.

Reporter: General, has there been any indication that any of these radar sightings have been made by electronic countermeasures being used by U.S. Strategic Air Command bombers practicing?

Samford: No; they haven't. We've investigated that and come up negative.

Reporter: Is that Schmidt camera telescope the only one, astronomical telescope that's capable of being used on a project like this?

Samford: Probably not.

Griffing: It's not the only one, but it is the most practical telescopic method. Any telescope can be used but the probability of getting a flying object is very remote. Because it has such a wide aperture it makes it more useful.

Reporter: Well, are you planning any other measurement tools other than this camera and telescope?

Griffing: Well, of course, the difficulty is if we have a high-powered instrument, we can't guarantee that they'll intercept flying objects so there are other simple measurements that can be made with trained personnel. There are measurements of time. One can time the appearance and disappearance with his own watch and then check his watch. Accurate measurements of time are one thing and simple measurements of angle can be made by trained people with very crude apparatus, and they can tell whether an object is one mile or fifty miles high.

Reporter: Haven't we already had some trained personnel, so-called trained personnel, who timed these appearances?

Griffing: There perhaps have -- Captain Ruppelt can answer that. The point is in any of these operations there have to be two simultaneous observers to get altitude. You can't use one observation, and it may be that two simultaneous observations have not been in the reports.

Reporter: General --

Samford: I think that the gentleman here has been waiting quite a while with a question, if you don't mind.

It should be noted here that the question was not answered. Ruppelt was not given an opportunity to answer it and it could be suggested that Samford didn't want it answered. That is why he cut off the discussion at that point.

By the same token, it must be noted that the reporters let him get away with it. They didn't come back to the question which was a very important one. It was not the first time in the press conference that they had let an important answer get away from them.

Reporter: General, you mentioned that eight per cent of the reports come from airline pilots. Some of these men have as much as twenty years' flying time, twenty years' experience flying. What's the reaction of the Air Force to creditable observers like that who give you a detailed description?

Samford: It's very high. We react to them as saying this is an important item.

Reporter: Do you classify that, some of those things, as phenomena?

Samford: Well, what else can we call it? His terms of the statement about it are not placeable in anything else as phenomena. I have one that a friend of mine who is an Air Force officer reported from the Middle East. He said, "I thought that my mental processes were adequate to avoid seeing these things, but I did see something that didn't belong there." He was no more able to put a precise measurement on it although he had competent witnesses. He's a creditable observer. We're not trying to discredit observers. That's the reason that I said that we have many reports from creditable observers of incredible things. They also say they're incredible.

Reporter: Are these phenomena capable of change of direction and speed such as has been reported?

Samford: There is nothing else known in the world that can do those things except phenomena! (Laughter)

Here is an interesting point from the perspective of 2022. We are now engaged in attempts to determine what these strange things are based on their observed capabilities. These are the same sorts of observations to which Samford was referring. This suggests that the Air Force was aware of these things back in 1952 but glossed over them. Now, we come full circle with new suggestions on gathering data of these objects that seem to have extraordinary capabilities. It just shows that little has changed since 1952.

Reporter: General, while we're in this mass of areas for a minute, suppose some super-intelligent creature had come up with a solution to the theoretical problem of levitation, would that not be massless in our observations either by radar or by sight? No gravity.

Reporter: A balloon has no gravity, but its rate of movement is distinctly limited.

Samford: Well, I don't know whether I can give an answer to that, sir, that makes any sense because I'm not a metaphysician. I think, probably, just to return to saying that -- we believe most of this can be understood gradually by the human mind.

Reporter: So far as we know, have any of these manifestations been reported over Russia or any of the satellites?

Samford: Well, we don't know if there have been any reported over there, no.

This seems to be disingenuous. There were, of course, the Ghost Rockets over Scandinavia in 1946, and there were hints that the Soviets were plagued by UFO sightings as well. Information about the Ghost Rockets had been gathered by Colonel Howard McCoy in 1946. Samford should have known this but suggested he didn't know if there had been such reports.

Reporter: General Samford or perhaps General Ramey, you have described fighters over the district here in the last few weeks. Is there any kind of a policy as far as the rest of the country of the Air Defense Command on such sightings?

Samford: I would like General Ramey to speak to that, if he will, please.

Ramey: There's no special policy as a result of these reports. We have a standard operating procedure that would call for an investigation of reports that can be tracked on a reasonable assurance of some sort of intercept or some direction to (inaudible). Those instructions are standard, however, and are not especially caused by this.

Reporter: General, is it true that there was a two-hour delay between the sighting of these objects last Saturday night and the dispatch of the jets from New Castle?

Ramey: Yes; that is true because there was never a track established. As soon as a track was established to tell the airplane the direction to go in and the authenticity of the thing was established, then the pilots got off. As long as there's a sporadic report with no identification, no track established, there's no use sending a very short-range short-field-duration interceptor in the air because he wouldn't know where to go or what to do.

Reporter: In other words, it was the decision of the operations officer that occasioned the delay and not any error in transmission of the alert.

Ramey: That's correct; yes, sir.

The Temperature Inversion Answer is Solidified

Reporter: General, it's been rumored that the Air Force has been picking up blips of this sort for quite a while but waited until civilian radar picked it up. Is that true?

Samford: I think I mentioned earlier our past experience in dealing with these things in many areas where we have had, oh, hundreds of fruitless intercept efforts in response to radar blips. It's not new with us at all.

Reporter: But of those same caliber as recently as the past couple of weeks, I mean, the same caliber blips. I think we've all heard about this blip, but is that the thing that you sighted before in the past by the Air Force? That's what I wanted to ask.

Samford: Well, I can only say that I feel fairly sure that they were the same or reasonably the same. No two blips on radar are alike.

Reporter: Have these been better, clearer, bigger?

Samford: I wouldn't say better or clearer. These are good returns. Other people have said, "There are good returns."

Reporter: General Samford, to clear that point up, I think Captain James indicated earlier in this reference to temperature inversion you now say that these are good returns. Can you get good returns on this temperature inversion reflection?

Samford: Yes.

Reporter: Can you get a return that's as sharp as the ones you get off aircraft.

Reporter: That moves.

Reporter: Captain James said they were sharper, larger, a while ago.

James: I said it depended upon the target.

Reporter: I'm referring to these seen Saturday night. Were those good returns? Could the good returns have been caused by this reflection against heat (inaudible)?

Samford: We think so. We think that that is probable.

106

Reporter: General, do you think that's probably what they were?

Samford: My own mind is satisfied with that, but my obligation to learn more is not. My own mind is satisfied with that explanation.

Ruppelt, in writing his own book about UFOs, suggested that the temperature inversion explanation "had been construed by the press to mean that this was the Air Force's answer..." While it can be suggested that the reporters had not understood what was being said, it was at this point in the press conference that General Samford told them that he, and by extension, the Air Force, was satisfied by the temperature inversion explanation. What were the reporters to believe, given the nature of the information and the answers supplied by Samford?

Reporter: General, if after six years of studying these things, you're now convinced that they do not constitute a threat to the safety of the country, is the Air Force thinking about turning this over to some other scientific investigating body or something?

Samford: Well, I think that we would want to move into it with them rather than to say turn it over.

Reporter: Is there any thought of that, bringing in other governmental scientific bodies perhaps?

Samford: Yes.

Reporter: Have you any program along that line? You spoke in the beginning that you wanted the methods of measuring things. You mentioned two or three little things like the possibility of buying some cameras and telescopes. Is there a program being set up to go about this scientifically, and what other organization are you thinking of bringing in on it?

Samford: I believe that Colonel Bower of the Technical Analysis Division at Dayton is here. Are you here, Bower?

Bower: Yes, sir.

Samford: Would you address yourself to that point, please?

Bower: Our idea on that is to implement our present study with instruments wherever possible, as Mr. Griffing mentioned, the refraction grid camera and other pickups that we might get.

Reporters: How many of these telescopes have been ordered, the Schmidt telescope?

Bower: The Schmidt telescopes are not on order by us. The refraction grid camera is an item which we are --

Reporter: Is the Schmidt telescope project an Air Force project or --

Griffing: Yes. Yes, sir.

Samford: I think the point that the gentleman over here wanted to have answered is can you explain from memory the kind of structure that I know that you have in ATIC for, well, I've seen it somewhere in my memory that you have this step and this step and this step.

Bower: We have several steps in analyses and that might explain to you one reason why we cannot give you an instantaneous answer. I mean this requires a study just like any technical problem. First of all, we need technical data. Our first step is to collect the data and check it against other identified objects such as balloons, if aircraft or missiles or such things as meteors are following that, and it comes back, and we make an analysis of it within our own groups. We have specialists in our own organizations, people on electrodynamics, physics, geophysics, and various other specialties that would fit into this. Following that, if it is necessary, we will send it to consultants or specialists in the field. Your mention of a contractor -- we are considering that with the idea, if we can't come out with an answer, of giving it to a contractor to study it. That won't be a short-time job.

Reporter: Are you taking a new approach in this whole thing?

Bower: I would say implementing the past approach.

Reporter: Going at it more systematically.

Bower: Yes, I think that's the thing to stress. In a lot of these things, you can't get technical data and without technical data you can't get a technical answer very well.

Samford: Maybe I have a thought that might help in answering that problem. When we started to say this is an obligation, we must learn more about, we thought initially that we could learn something from the volume of reports. We say we want all the reports we can get and then see that through that volume maybe we can make a pattern. I think we're beginning to believe now that the things which we can sense from volume are not necessarily the things which we value. In other words, volume can come from many different things. It can come from external stimulus. It can come from an unusual opportunity. It can come from such a variety of meaningless things so that the volume of reports is not going to be our answer. We have thought we'd get thousands and thousands of reports and out of these we will develop something through better reports with equipment or with a trained reporter specifically attempting to report the valuable things about these items are we likely to produce material that is suitable grist for a scientific analysis. The stuff we have now hasn't enough meat on its bones to interest scientific people.

Reporter: Well, General, would you say a qualified observer would be the pilot from New Castle -- I believe his name was Lieutenant Patterson -- who got within what he estimated was two miles of this object last Saturday? Have you questioned him?

Samford: He has no measurement that you can put in scientific hands.

Reporter: Well, other than his eye as a pilot.

Samford: He says -- if the quality of the observer is that of seeing something, he was a qualified observer. If the quality is measuring something, he is not a qualified observer.

Reporter: Well, the reason I'd implied that he'd be qualified is he was probably concentrating with all of his intensity upon this object that he was pursuing. He must have been thinking about it pretty intensely; therefore, can probably give you some pretty good information. Have you questioned him about it?

Samford: Yes. He had motive; he had direction; he had interest; he had opportunity. But he had no measuring devices to measure this thing, or these things that need to have measurement before it can become anything other than a sighting.

Reporter: Well, do you explain his sighting on the basis of this heat inversion theory too, now?

Samford: Not necessarily. That very likely is one that sits apart and says insufficient measurement, insufficient association with other things, insufficient association with other probabilities for it to do any more than to join that group of sightings that we still hold in front of us as saying no.

Reporter: Hasn't he admitted that that might have been a ground light that he was looking at?

Samford: I don't recall that I --

Reporter: Well, have you formed any conclusion as a result of interrogating this pilot?

Samford: None other than that this is another one of the thousand or two thousand sightings.

Reporter: General, this fellow that almost flew into the ground, did he go around a corner as if on a bent return? What were the circumstances of that flight?

Samford: Did I get the information of the ground lock-on from you, James?

James: Yes, sir; you did.

Samford: Would you answer the question?

James: I'm sorry. I didn't hear it.

Reporter: Did he lock on a reflected image, go around the corner, and go down to the ground? Was that the pattern?

James: Yes, that's true. That was the pattern, and he did that three times and each time it led him to the same point on the ground.

Reporter: Captain, what about the man who saw four lights, Saturday night?

James: Well, I'll have to ask Captain Ruppelt to explain the lights.

Reporter: General --

Samford: There's this difficulty. May I make this statement? I was trying to -- let's take any one of these reports and pull it out and say, "Well, what is the meaning of that one report?" None of these things in the period of our entire experience with them has had any validity on its own. The only thing that we hope for is to find enough similarity in sequence of these things so that you can begin to pull something out. There is no validity in them as individual sightings to mean any particular thing.

Reporter: General, did you notice in all of your, say, twenty per cent of the unexplainable (sic) reports a consistency as to color, size, or speed, estimated speed.

Samford: None whatsoever.

Reporter: None whatsoever.

Samford: No.

Reporter: Have you ever tracked the speed by radar of any particular object that you can explain?

Samford: There have been many radar reports giving speed.

Reporter: What did they range from, sir?

Samford: They run from zero to fantastic speed.

Reporter: General, how do you explain this case, now. The CAA, as I understand the story, after picking up these objects on radar, also got this Capital Airlines pilot named Pierman on their radar as he was going out west and, as the Senior Controller told me, he said whenever a blip, one of the unidentified blips, appeared anywhere near Pierman's plane, he could call Pierman on the radio and say, "You have traffic at two o'clock about three miles," and Pierman, in return, would look to the given range and bearing and say, "I see it. I see the light!"

Reporter: Happy New Year! (Laughter)

Reporter: Pierman described it as a light that was zooming and all such things and this was done not once but Barnes told me he instructed him on that target three times and then, Saturday night, this past Saturday night, when they all saw all these blips, Barnes vectored at least half a dozen airline pilots and planes into these things and they all reported seeing lights.

Reporter: Many of them didn't see them, according to Barnes.

Reporter: Yes. Many of them didn't see them, but then some did.

Samford: I can't explain that.

Reporter: Well, how do you explain this directing? Is that autosuggestion or --

Major General John Samford

Samford: I can't explain it at all. I think maybe --

Reporter: Have you investigated that phase of this thing, this vectoring the planes into that?

Samford: You can investigate, but the technique of investigating a process or mind-reading, for example, or the technique of investigating the process of mesmerism. You can say will you investigate those things? I think probably we know no more about mind-reading than the technique of investigating that or the technique of investigating evidence of spiritualism than we do about these fields, but for many years the field of spiritualism had these same things in it in which completely competent creditable observers reported incredible things. I don't mean to say that this is that sort of thing, but it's an explanation of an inability to explain and that is with us.

Reporter: General, I understand that the wavelength of the radar has something to do with what it can pick up in the way of phenomena. Were these relatively low or relatively high wavelength radar?

Samford: I couldn't say, and I don't know whether Captain James can or not, but I'd like him to have him have the opportunity.

James: These were relatively high frequency or short wavelength. However, the same effect can be observed on long wavelength equipment with differing degrees.

Reporter: You say very short wavelength?

James: In this case, yes.

Reporter: They were designed for different purposes?

Samford: Yes, sir.

Reporter: General, why has the Air Force refused to disclose the substance of Captain Mantell's air-ground conversations before he died? Do you remember the case?

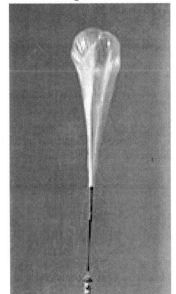

A Skyhook Balloon

The Mantell case took place in January 1948, when an Air National Guard, and former Army Air Forces transport pilot, was killed chasing a UFO near Fort Knox, Kentucky. Although Mantell's fighter well equipped with an oxygen system, it had not been charged before flight was scheduled to fly below 5000 feet. Mantell, in violation of regulations, climbed above 25,000 feet chasing what he thought was a metallic object of tremendous size... He blacked out and his aircraft crashed, killing him. Although the case has been discussed at length in other books, suggesting that UFOs are hostile, the truth, now available is that Mantell had been chasing a Skyhook balloon. These huge balloons, made of polyethylene were classified in 1948. No good explanation, without knowledge of the Skyhook project was possible. There is little doubt today that Mantell was killed in a tragic accident that did not involve an alien spacecraft.

However, in 1952, this explanation was not readily available. There were also rumors of the discussion that Mantell had with ground controllers and tower personnel before his crash. None of the rumors were ever confirmed, and with a good solution to the Mantell incident, the questions about the rumors are now irrelevant.

Samford: Well, I don't know enough about it to say what was said or what some reasons were.

Reporter: Well, a popular book made quite a point of that, that the Air Force was holding back on that because it told the true nature of the saucer, that he had approached it, and --

Samford: Well, I wish that that were true, that he did say something that had enough substance in it for use. I haven't the slightest idea what he said.

Reporter: Are you withholding any information about these so-called --

Samford: Are we now?

Reporter: Yes. Is anything –

Samford: There is one thing that we have asked our -- some of our informers have asked -- I don't like the word "informer" either -- reporters had asked –

Reporter: We don't like that word either.

Samford: I like the word. Reporter is all right. But many people are reticent about reporting these things if their names are mentioned because they are frequently looked on by others as being publicity seekers or maybe people will avoid them and go on the other side of the street for a while (laughter), so they ask us to not say who made this report and sometimes information is received that deals with the credibility of a reporter saying he's drunk all the time or he never did do anything but lie. (Laughter). Well, those things we get are not revealed, but in so far as the statement of what they saw, when and where they saw it, the measurements that they took, such as they were, we are not withholding any of that data.

Of course, it can be shown that this is simply not true. There are any number of sightings that were classified. Two photographic cases, the Montana Movie and the Tremonton, Utah film were not viewed outside of the military for a number of years. As we have seen here, the Arrey, New Mexico sighting file had originally been classified as "Secret." The Air Force was clearly withholding information and Samford knew it.

The question to be asked was if that was justified, given the nature of the work being done and the world situation at the time. A fair answer is, "Yes." Some of the secrecy was justified. Samford, if he answered in the positive, would be giving away one secret and so, he was forced into a position where he said they were not withholding data.

Reporter: How about your interpretation of what they reported?

Samford: Well, we're trying to say as much as we can on that today and admit that the barrier of understanding on all of this is not one that we break.

Reporter: General, have you ever said flatly that these are not machines that the United States has made or is developing?

Samford: What was that?

114

Reporter: Have you said this afternoon these are not machines or weapons that the United States is developing?

Samford: I would say that these that we have been speaking about in this locality are definitely not. However, many reports that we have received, and we've been able to correlate and put in their placc wc havc bccn ablc to do so through association with an activity we had somewhere, a jet aircraft line, a missile, certain balloons. We could say, well, the report probably was associated with this thing which we've done, but in so far as what you are thinking about in his locality --

Reporter: These are not missiles or rockets?

Samford: -- there is nothing.

Reporter: Well, General, could you turn that over a little bit? A lot of people keep saying that all this talk is a cover-up and that saucers are really the result of some experiments the United States, either the Air Force or Atomic Energy, is carrying on. Can you make a flat statement and say that these unexplained flying saucer manifestations are not the result of any American weapons or other experimentation or test?

Samford: I'd say that those that we categorize as unexplained or unidentified have gone through the process of trying to associate them with something we were doing and when we fail to associate them with something we're doing, we say that is one other clue that ran to nothing. Now, to say that sightings everywhere are -- none of them could possibly be associated with what the United States is doing, isn't quite true because we know that a particular jet fighter has been flying in a certain area; somebody has reported thus and thus and thus, and we get those two things together and we say something that we were doing caused this report. As General Ramey said a minute ago, there is a fair degree of probability that two fighters locked on each other and saw and received senses. That was certainly something we were doing that cause those two reports.

Reporter: What I was aiming at was this popular feeling –

Samford: Of mystery?

Reporter: -- of mystery, of something, that it's some very highly secret new weapon that we're working on that's causing all this.

Samford: We have nothing that has no mass and unlimited power! (Laughter)

Reporter: General, somebody asked you before how much money you'd spent on this investigation since the start. How much have you spent on it?

Samford: It's very slight. I don't know.

Reporter: General, in connection with withholding information, I'd like to ask General Ramey a question. That is, how many times have fighter planes been brought down over the Washington area in the last couple of weeks to investigate reports of flying objects?

Ramey: That's a matter of record -- three, I believe. I think two flights one night and one flight Saturday night. I don't remember the night the other two were up. I think there have been six sorties.

Reporter: One flight the first Saturday night and two flights -

Ramey: In this immediate area, yes. We have airplanes that investigate various reports all over the country or places where we have these fighters, but --

Reporters: I thought the Air Force had said that it couldn't send any fighters up because it didn't have them.

Ramey: No. I don't believe it said that.

Reporter: The first night.

Reporter: How about the last night, General?

Ramey: No; there were no fighters up last night.

Reporter: Were there fighters sent in here from New Castle on both those Saturday nights in questions?

Ramey: That's right; yes.

Reporter: Last night, was that because of lack of a track?

Ramey: Lack of a track.

Reporter: General, are sightings from military personnel made public generally, or are they --

Samford: There's no reason why they shouldn't be.

Reporter: Thank you, General. Thank you.

There was much that was wrong here. For one thing, it didn't seem that the reporters followed up on some of the questions. There were points that were overlooked or ignored, and the reporters didn't return to them. The reporters should have stayed on a topic rather than allowing the discussion be diverted to something else.

The problem here is that the curtain of ridicule, that would be completely brought down in January 1953 with the Robertson Panel was in affect here. Reporters didn't want to seem to be unsophisticated so that when something was glossed over or ignored, they didn't come back to it. The whole thing seemed to be a tacit agreement between the military and the reporters to put out a story that was acceptable to the general public. While the flying saucers were, in fact, a matter of national security, that took a backseat to the idea that the air traffic controllers could be distracted by uncorrelated blips on the radar scope.

Questions that should have been asked were not, and in the end, the stories written and reported on the radio was that it was all a big mistake. There were no flying saucers over Washington, D.C., just a temperature inversion that provided the radar returns and a misidentification of stars seen through the haze created by that temperature inversion.

With that, everyone was happy. The military didn't have to answer any more questions. The air traffic controllers could return to their jobs without pressure from the press, and most of the public was satisfied by the answers. Attention could now return to both the upcoming presidential election and to the Olympics.

Chapter Eight: The Air Force Investigation, Part II

With the second round of sightings over Washington, D.C. now a matter of public record, and even after General Samford had "explained" the sightings as nothing more important that temperature inversions, there was the matter of an investigation to prove the case. Air Force records show that such an investigation was conducted and that the sightings were grouped together, so that those who had been involved the Saturday before were not re-interviewed in light of the new sightings. New interviews were conducted with those who had only seen lights, objects or radar returns on the second Saturday night.

This time there were more than just lights seen in the sky. Those who saw

Barnes at radarscope.

something were describing a range of different objects. Much of what was seen was corroborated with radar sightings as well. Harry Barnes again was on duty at the ARTC at Washington National. And, as has been mentioned earlier, representatives of the Air Force, both on the civilian side by Al Chop and on the military side by Major Dewey Fournet, were present that second night. Interestingly, there is no indication in the Project Blue Book files that either Chop or Fournet were interviewed by the Air Force investigators. Apparently, they were considered nothing more than bystanders for the sightings. Of course, neither man had gone outside to see the UFOs for themselves. They had remained in the radar room, watching as the drama unfolded on the screens. Still, it would seem that they would have an interesting perspective of what had gone on in the radar room that night and what they did as the events played out on the radar scopes.

The investigation that did take place was not much, when compared with other such cases and considering that the radars at National Airport and Andrews Air Force base were both involved. It wasn't much considered that President Truman had requested, from the Air Force, some sort of report about the situation. After all, it meant that the UFOs were again over Washington, D.C., they were causing trouble and the President was interested.

(Uncl) Material for Project Blue Book

Chief, Air Technical
Intelligence Center
Wright-Patterson AFB
Dayton, Ohio

Dept of the Air Force
Hq USAF — AFOIN-2A2

11 Aug 52

Maj Fournet/vg/71016

  1. Inclosed are summary reports of observations as telephoned to AFOIN-2A2 during the past two weeks plus a report on radar observations at Washington National Airport on the night of 26/27 July 52. In all cases, the outline specified for electrical messages in paragraph 7c of AFL 200-5 has been utilized for the sake of expediency with appropriate notations as necessary.

  2. No attempt has been made to follow-up on any telephone reports taken by the Estimates Duty Officer nor was any attempt made to obtain great detail in the other telephone reports. Wherever possible, a general statement of weather conditions, usually as reported by observer, has been included. In all cases where pro-forma items are omitted, they are negative.

  3. No further action is contemplated on any of these incidents.

    BY COMMAND OF THE CHIEF OF STAFF:

26 Incls:
 Rpts of U/I Flying Objects
 originated by AFOIN-2A2

JAMES P. BECKETT

WILLIAM W. WILCOX
Colonel, USAF
Chief, Policy and Management Group
Office, Deputy Director for Estimates
Directorate of Intelligence

Air Force communication about Washington Nationals.

James P. Beckett and William W. Wilcox provided a letter to the "Chief, Air Technical Intelligence Center," at Wright-Patterson AFB, dated 11 August 1952. The letter explained that "Enclosed are summary reports of observations as telephoned to AFOIN-2A2 [Air Force Office of Intelligence] during the last two weeks plus a report on radar observations at Washington National Airport on the night of 26/27 July 52.... No attempt has been made to follow-up on any telephone reports taken by the Estimates Duty Officer nor was any attempt made to obtain great detail in the other telephone reports...."

So, what they were saying was that they had made the investigation as required by Air Force regulations, but they were not going to do anything more than what was strictly required by those regulations. While there might have been some good information to be developed by follow-up on some of those visual sightings, the Air Force investigators didn't even bother. Instead, they focused their attention on the reports that came through the proper channels from the military personnel and those who had been at the airport during the sightings.

According to the report found in the Project Blue Book administrative files that can be accessed online:

> This incident involved u/i [unidentified] targets observed on radar scopes at the Air Route Traffic Control Center and the tower, both at Washington National Airport, and the Approach Control Radar at Andrews AFB. In addition, visual observations were reported to Andrews and Bolling AFB and to ARTC Center, the latter by pilots of commercial a/c and CAA a/c. Two flights of interceptors were dispatched from Newcastle, Del., but their official reports have not been received by this office; [nor is there any indication in the Blue Book files that those reports were ever received] comments on their conversations with ARTC Center personnel are included herein.... This report covers the facts obtained from Washington National A/P personnel, the USAF Command Post and the AFOIN Duty Officer log. As yet, the commercial and CAA pilots who reported visuals have not been contacted, nor have other potential sources been investigated. Such action will not be possible by this office.

> Varying numbers (up to 12 simultaneously) of u/i targets... termed by CAA personnel as 'generally, solid returns', similar to a/c return except slower. No definable pattern of maneuver except at very beginning about 2150 EDT, 4 targets in rough line abreast with about 1½ mile spacing moved slowly together (giving about a 1"

trace persistency at an estimated speed of less than 100 mph) on a heading of 110 [degrees, or east southeast] .... ARTC checked Andrews Approach Control by telephone at 2200 EDT and ascertained that they were also picking up u/i targets. U/i returns were picked up intermittently until about 27/0100 EDT [1:00 a.m. on July 27], following which weak and sporadic (unsteady) returns were picked up intermittently for another 3½ hours. Washington National Tower radar crew reports only one target positively u/i. This return was termed a 'very good target' which moved across the scope from West to East at about 30 to 40 mph. However, the radar operators stated that there could have been other u/i targets on their scopes, particularly outside their area of a/c control, which would not have been noticed or would have assumed to be a/c under ARTC Center control, however, they noticed no other unusual (i.e., very slow or erratic) returns.

To this point the report suggested that a few of the returns were solid and mimicked the solid targets presented by aircraft. The difference was the speed. Aircraft do not routinely fly at 30 or 40 miles an hour, especially when on the air routes or close to the airports. They are in the traffic areas and a very slow-moving plane would be in danger of being rundown by a larger and faster aircraft. The unidentified targets were simply not part of the system and were not small, light aircraft, again because of the speed.

There were, however, some visual sightings of the objects. Again, according to the report in the Blue Book files, "ARTC Center controllers also report that a CAA flight instructor, Mr. [named deleted] flying a/c #NC-12 reported at 2246 EDT that he had visually spotted 5 objects giving off a light glow ranging from orange to white; his altitude at the time was 2200'. Some commercial pilots reported visuals ranging from 'cigarette glow' (red-yellow) to 'a light' (as recorded from their conversations with ARTC controllers)."

What this means, simply, is that pilots, both commercial airline pilots, and an instructor for the CAA had seen something strange in the air. There was no attempt, at that point, to correlate these sightings with the blips on the radar. This means that there were lights seen in the sky and blips on the radars, but nothing that tied the two together. To make the case a valuable resource, that should have been one of the missions of the military investigators.

The report continued, "At 2238 EDT the USAF Command Post was notified of ARTC targets. Command Post notified ADC and EADF at 2245, and 2 F-94's were scrambled from Newcastle at 2300 EDT. ARTC controlled F-94's after arrival in area and vectored them to targets with generally negative results (flew through 'a batch of radar returns' without spotting anything). However, one pilot mentioned seeing 4 lights at one time and a second time as seeing a single light ahead but unable to close whereupon light 'went out' (these comments from ARTC controllers)."

This then, was an attempt to correlate the blips with the lights in the sky. The results, as mentioned, were negative, with the pilots seeing nothing solid where the objects were indicated. That could suggest that the objects were not lighted, though the comment about one of the interceptors flying through "a batch of radar returns" would seem to suggest that there was nothing solid in the air where the radar suggested they should be.

According to the documentation available in the Project Blue Book files:

> Maj. Fournet... and Lt. Holcomb... arrived at ARTC Center about 27/0012 EDT [or about fifteen minutes after midnight on July 27]. Lt. Holcomb observed scopes and reported '7 good, solid targets'. He made a quick check with airport Weather Station and determined that there was a slight temperature inversion (about 1 degree) from the surface to about 1000'. However, he felt that the scope targets at that time were not the result of this inversion and so advised the Command Post with the suggestion that a second intercept flight be requested. (2nd intercept flight controlled by ARTC, but no strong returns remained when they arrived. There were vectored on dim targets with negative results.) Maj. Fournet and Lt. Holcomb remained in ARTC Center until 0415, but no additional strong targets were picked up; many dim and unstable targets (assumed due to temperature inversion) were observed throughout the remainder of the period.

The report also rated the reliability of all those civilian radar crews that had observed UFOs that night. All those ARTC radar operators and controllers, including Harry Barnes were considered "...serious, conscientious and sincere although vague about details of their experience on 26/27 July. Considered fairly reliable."

Of the men in the Washington National control tower, they were considered "conscientious and sincere. Direct manner. Appeared sure of themselves. Considered very reliable."

In the remarks section of the report, also available in the Blue Book files, it was noted:

ARTC crew commented that, as compared with u/i returns picked up in early hours of 20 July 52, these returns appeared to be more haphazard in their actions, i.e., they did not follow a/c around nor did they cross the scope consistently on same general heading. Some commented that the returns appeared to be from objects 'capable of dropping out of the pattern at will'. Also, that returns had 'creeping appearance'. One member of the crew commented that one object to which F-94 was vectored just 'disappeared from Scope' shortly after F-94 started pursuing. All crew members emphatic that most u/i returns were 'solid'. Finally, it was mentioned that u/i returns have been picked up from time to time over the past few months but never before had they appeared in such quantities over such a prolonged period and with such definition as was experienced on the nights of 19/20 and 26/27 July 52.

In another report found in the Project Blue Book files, originally classified as "Confidential" and sent on to the Director of Intelligence in Washington, D.C., as well as ATIC at Wright-Patterson Air Force Base, an unidentified pilot's impressions were described. According to the document:

2 F94B acft were scrambled by the 646 ACW Sqdn, Highland, New Jersey ([codename] Dogcatcher) at 270304Z [meaning July 27, 3:04 in the morning, Greenwich Mean Time] against unidentified obj picked up by the GCI Sta. The GCI station was reptg clusters of 5 or 6 obj coming in on their scope. Upon being vectored into the midst of the reptd obj, nothing could be seen by the intcpcws other than lights on the ground. However, one intcp pilot reptd seeing 2 bright lights in the vicinity of Mount Vernon possibly 5 to 10 miles in the distance at 1500 feet. Upon closing with these lights, they disappeared when within approx 2 miles....

One of the pilots had an opinion that "Every time he was vectored into the area of sightings by Dogcatcher [radio call sign of the radar facility], it was noticed that the area was very hazy, dark, turbulent and had a high moisture content.... Lights were sighted on the ground below this haze area and pilot believes at a distance of from 5 to 10 miles out the reflection of these lights appeared on the bottom of the haze but upon approaching they disappeared."

The overall investigation, some of it conducted by intelligence officers at Bolling AFB, but none from Wright-Patterson or from ATIC, included some statements made by Air Force personnel who were at Andrews early on the morning of July

27. The statements were eventually forwarded to Project Blue Book, but there is no evidence in the files that any of the witnesses were questioned carefully, or that follow-up investigations were conducted.

Master Sergeant Harrison, for example, told WOJG (Warrant Officer, junior grade) Clyde Mahaffee, Jr. that:

> While standing in front of GCA unit [at Andrews AFB] I observed a bluish white light move from vicinity of range in a NNE dir at an incredible rate of speed - about 45 sec later I observed another light moving from over the vicinity of the range to the NW. About one min later while walking toward AAPC [Andrews Approach Control] from the GCA unit I saw the same kind of light moving from the NE toward the range station. These lights did not have the characteristics of shooting stars. There was no [sic] trails and seemed to go out rather than disappear and traveled faster than any shooting star I have ever seen.

T/SGT H. Spiewakowski, also at Andrews was also interviewed by WO Mahaffee on the day after the sightings. He said:

> At 2023E [daylight time] Wash Center called requesting info as to whether we were observing many unidentified targets in the immediate area, on our radar equipment. We observed & noted a great many targets some of which later were identified as aircraft (conventional). We continued to maintain a sharp lookout & observed target following very erratic courses, sometimes appearing to stop, then reverse course, accelerating momentarily, & then slowing down. Target sightings were all coordinated with W.A.R.T.C. [Washington Air Route Traffic Control, that is, ARTC] & verified, using radar facilities. Another peculiarity noted was the sudden disappearance of targets then suddenly reappearing 8-10 mi farther along the same course. A couple of aircraft which happened to be in the area were given vectors to targets however I am uncertain of results as this was handled by Wash. Radar. We had targets in vicinity of ADW(R) [Andrews range], the field & the SHZ [location unidentified] vicinity, also NW of us targets were present in great No's. The only area relatively free was the S.W. Andrews tower personnel were advised of positions & were attempting to make visual sightings - results Unkn. The biggest problem appeared to be the large No. of targets present which

made it difficult to have any definite [sic] targets singled out for checking.

Air Force files also reveal that a report was submitted by the 91st Strategic Reconnaissance Wing, Medium, [meaning that the aircraft flown by the wing were considered to have a medium payload] about a sighting by one of their flight crews in a B-29 while they were flying at 9,900 feet. Staff Sergeant David L. Walker was described as having three- and one-half years of experience in the Air Force as an aerial gunner, as well as duty in the Navy. According to the report, "Three (3) different amber edged white flashing objects [were] observed. Travelling (sic) at approximately speed of sound each caused yellowish trail. First object moved across the sky in horseshoe path; second appeared to drop vertically; and the movement of the third not identifiable."

According to the report, "Visual observation from B-29 cruising at speed at altitude of 9,900 feet. Unknown to observer (sic) if radar received return on these objects but believed radar received return from later object."

Another report, coming from the "Vicinity of Wilmington, Delaware," described "A single grey cylindrical object with slightly domed top and bottom [that] was observed with the naked eye moving along a Northwest-Southeast course.... The cylinder appeared moving in an upright position. Just prior to the end of the sighting the object briefly reflected a silver light then entirely disappeared."

Analysis of the sightings continued by the Air Force with several different departments competing to supply the answers. After General Samford's press conference, the temperature inversion answer became the preferred answer. In a letter dated August 29, 1952 and sent to both Ruppelt and James (the radar expert of Samford's conference), it was suggested, "The general trend or tone of the available reports of the subject targets strongly indicates anomalous (bending) propagation (temperature inversion and/or moisture lapse) effect on the radiated electromagnetic waves of the radar sets, thereby allowing the detection of ground targets which are not normally seen."

The author of the letter, Major John E. Libbert, reported up the chain of command:

> There are several factors, given the above [which was the temperature at various altitudes on July 26], which are favorable for concluding that the subject radar targets were actually ground targets which are not normally detected. It is considered that an abnormal propagation condition caused a mild bending of the radar waves so that the detection of ground targets were not giving

'solid' returns every antenna (sic) sweep and could cause a misinterpretation that stationary ground targets were in [the air and moving].

It is now clear, based on the tone of the investigations, such as they were, the statements issued by high-ranking military officers, and belief that all UFO sightings could be explained if there was sufficient data for review, that the Air Force had found an answer that sounded scientific, objective, and fair. The sightings were the result of the mistakes made by the air traffic controllers, the radar operators, and an opinion that the solid returns indicated a "real" object in the air. When all the factors were weighed, it was obvious to the Air Force officers conducting these limited investigations, that the sightings, for the most part could be explained by the temperature inversions.

It should be noted, however, that the pilot reports, and the debriefing reports, were not present in the files. Remember, one of the men who had flown an intercept on the second night said that he had been debriefed by military officers and men dressed in civilian clothing on a number of occasions. This suggests a real, and thorough, investigation, but that is not represented in the documentation presented to Blue Book or found in the microfilm files.

Ruppelt, in his book published in 1956, suggested that the Washington Nationals were still carried on the Blue Book files as "unidentified", meaning, simply, that there was no positive answer for the series of sightings on either night. However, the Blue Book records suggest something else. The sightings are broken down into their various components, and each of those is listed in the Blue Book master index. Although there are a few that are labeled as "unknown," the majority of them have no labels. In other words, no solution is noted, but then, the "unidentified" label has been avoided. Some are listed as insufficient data for a scientific analysis, meaning that not enough information, according to the Air Force investigators, had been forwarded for a proper investigation to be completed.

Interestingly, there was little in the Blue Book files to suggest that the pilots who had reported UFOs, both military and civilian airline pilots, were interviewed. Or, if they were, those interviews were not forwarded to ATIC. Instead, summaries of some of the statements, and letters exchanged between the Air Force and the pilots, are mentioned. Although the Air Force was working to write the sightings off as temperature inversion, the pilots did have some interesting stories to tell.

Chapter Nine: The Pilot Reports from Washington, D.C.

With the Washington National sightings there is a fact that stands out. Pilots saw the lights. Military pilots who flew the interceptors did close on the lights and civilian pilots, both commercial and private, saw the lights. Whatever was being seen on the various radars those nights over Washington were visible to the unaided eye. Lights, or objects, were in the sky where the radars suggested they should be and the pilots who were asked to look for them found them.

General Samford, in his press conference knew some of this, but not all of it. He did mention Captain Pierman's sighting, and that information had been reported in the newspapers. Other pilots, especially those involved in the last round of sightings, had not been properly debriefed at the time of the press conference. No solid investigation had been completed before the press conference and some of this is an outgrowth of investigations held years later.

Flying Objects Near Washington Spotted by Both Pilots and Radar

Air Force Reveals Reports of Something, Perhaps 'Saucers,' Traveling Slowly But Jumping Up and Down

Remember, after the targets began appearing on the radars, first at Washington National's ARTC, the controllers there checked the equipment to make sure that it was functioning properly, and then talked to the men in the tower, located about a quarter mile away, to learn if their radars had similar objects. Later still, in communication with Andrews Air Force Base, those same controllers at the ARTC, learned that something was appearing on the radar there as well.

Not only were objects being seen on the radars, but the men in the tower at Andrews, and some of those on the airfield itself, were reporting that they were seeing objects, or lights, in the night sky. Those lights, for the most part, were small, bright orange lights that maneuvered above Washington. Few, if any, reported anything that resembled a flying saucer, or a manufactured craft, because all they saw were lights. And, according to the Air Force, many of those lights were really stars that were very bright and fooled the men.

Radar Spots Odd Objects

clock. Civilian Defense ground observer operation now under-way.

Preliminary Report

The Air Force said it has received only a preliminary report, and therefore does not know why no attempt at interception was made.

The air traffic control center at Washington National Airport, reported its radar operators picked up eight of the slow-moving objects about midnight last Saturday. They were flying in the vicinity of nearby Andrews Air Force Base.

The center said Capital Airlines Flight 807, southbound from National Airport, reported seeing seven objects between Washington and Martinsburg, W. Va., at 3:15 a.m., the same night.

Capital Airlines said the pilot, Cat. "Casey" Pierman of Detroit, 17 years with the company, described the objects in these words:

"They were like falling stars without tails."

Picked up Blips

Company officials said the airport picked up radar "blips" —contact with aerial objects— and asked Capt. Pierman to keep a watch out for any unusual objects in the sky.

Shortly thereafter, officials said, Pierman reported back to the dispatcher's tower that he had spotted a group of objects.

Pierman, then flying at normal cruising speed of 180 to 200 m.p.h., reported the objects were traveling with "tremendous vertical speed"—moving rapidly up and down—and then suddenly changing pace until they seemed to hang motionless in the sky.

Officials said Pierman made only a routine report of the incident.

The eight objects picked up by Air Force radar were said to be traveling at slightly more than 100 m.p.h.

Pierman story.

In their attempts to learn what was happening, to identify the uncorrelated targets on their scopes, the controllers asked for help of the pilots in the area. At first, before the Air Force arrived with their interceptors, those pilots were airline pilots on commercial flights. One of the first asked for help, and one who saw the lights being described was Captain Casey Pierman of Capital Airlines flight 807. According to Capital Airline officials, the airport had picked up the radar targets and asked Pierman to look for them.

Pierman was described as a seventeen-year veteran with the airline, and that he lived in Detroit. In the early morning of July 20, at about 2:15 a.m. (though some published stories suggested it was an hour later at 3:15), he reported that he eventually saw seven objects between Washington, D.C. and Martinsburg, West Virginia. He had been asked by the ARTC to be on the lookout for something in the sky. He said, "They were like falling stars without tails." This is, of course, a description similar to that given by others such as the Air Force personnel at Andrews.

In an official report found in the Project Blue Book files, Pierman took off from Washington National on a heading of 180 degrees, that is, due south, and climbed to 1200 feet. He slowly changed course to 330 degrees, or north-northwest. According to the report:

CAPTAIN Pierman stated that he switched over from Tower Control to AIRWAY TRAFFIC CONTROL CENTER (ATCC) at WASHINGTON NATIONAL AIRPORT. At this time ATCC informed him that their radar scope indicated two or three objects on the screen traveling at high speeds. ATCC instructed CAPTAIN Pierman to steer 290 degrees so as to intercept the objects which were approximately nine (9) miles ahead of him. At this time CAPTAIN Pierman's rate of climb was approximately 600 feet per minute and his altitude was between 3500 and 4000 feet.

Again, according to the Air Force report, "Immediately after ATCC instructed CAPTAIN Pierman to alter course to 290 degrees he stated that the following events occurred within 5 - 8 minutes in the order in which presented and at the approximate intervals as indicated:

a. 3-5 minutes after take-off - ATCC informed pilot that the objects were five (5) miles distant dead ahead.

b. 3-5 seconds later - ATCC informed pilot that objects were four (4) miles distant.

c. 1-3 seconds later - ATCC informed pilot that objects were at ten (10) o'clock. At this time pilot stated he plainly observed a DC-4 type aircraft at ten (10) o'clock level proceeding in the opposite direction. This information he reported to ATCC.

d. 4-5 minutes later - COPILOT [name deleted] observed one (1) object bluish white in color in a twenty-five-degree dive from northeast to the southwest traveling at a tremendous rate of speed. The copilot told CAPTAIN Pierman that he could neither estimate from what altitude the object began its descent nor at what altitude it faded. CAPTAIN Pierman stated that at this time his altitude was 6000 feet, and he could look down almost vertically and see CHARLES TOWN, WEST VIRGINIA.

e. Immediately upon sighting CHARLES TOWN, CAPTAIN Pierman and his copilot observed a brilliant bluish light flash past from high over his left and disappear level flight ahead travelling (sic) at a tremendous rate of speed and appeared to be outside the earth's atmosphere.

f. Next CAPTAIN Pierman and his copilot observed a brilliant bluish white light reappear where the last light had disappeared and flash past from right to left at approximately 80 degrees about the horizon and travelling (sic) at a tremendous rate of speed. This light also appeared to be outside the earth's atmosphere.

4. CAPTAIN Pierman stated that he may have seen as many as seven (7) objects during as many minutes but due to the fact that things were happening so fast he had no way of keeping an accurate account of the number of objects."

Pierman later told reporters for various newspapers and radio stations, "In my years of flying I've seen a lot of falling or shooting stars - whatever you call them - but these were much faster than anything else that I've ever seen. They couldn't have been aircraft. There were moving too fast for that."

Pierman provided more description, saying, "They were about the same size as the brighter stars. And were much higher than our 6,000-foot altitude. [I] couldn't estimate the speed accurately. Please remember, I didn't speak of them as flying saucers - only very fast-moving lights."

Pierman said that he was flying at about 180 to 200 miles an hour when he saw the lights traveling at a tremendous speed. He said no special attention was paid to these because they could be taken for falling stars. Pierman qualified that, however, saying that the lights were moving up and down and then changed pace until they seemed to hang in the sky.

Later, he said that he had seen three lights, traveling horizontally, and were in sight for three to five seconds. He didn't know what they could be, only that he had seen strange lights.

Howard Dermott, captain of Capital Airlines flight 610, and apparently unaware of the sightings around Washington, told the controllers at the ARTC that while in the vicinity of Herndon, Virginia, a light seemed to be following him. The airfield tower at Washington National found an object on the radar where Dermott suggested it should be. Those at the ARTC also had a target on their scopes.

The light was, Dermott and his crew kept the light under observation, following them in the "eight o'clock" position, or to the rear and left of the aircraft. It stayed with them until they were within four miles of the airfield. When Dermott radioed that the light was leaving them, the two radar scopes, in two separate positions at Washington National, showed the object moving away.

Another pilot, unidentified in various records but apparently flying a commercial airliner, reported an object near Mt. Vernon, Virginia, at about five thousand feet. He said that the object came from his right side, and he had to veer to avoid a collision.

Military Reports

It was a week later when the events repeated themselves. Military pilots, on this Saturday night, were the ones most heavily involved. As had happened the Saturday before, there was a delay between the request for interceptors and the arrival of the jets, but, by midnight, after the targets had been tracked for about an hour or so, two F-94s from New Castle were on the scene. Dewey Fournet later told me that as the jets fighters arrived, all the UFOs disappeared from the radar scope.

The F-94s made a routine search, but the pilots could see nothing. The on-board radars failed to detect anything, suggesting that any inversion layer in the area was extremely weak. And, while the aircraft were in the area, there were no targets on the scopes of the radars at Washington National.

Fred Woods of the Houston UFO Network located one of those military fighter pilots involved in these intercepts. The pilot said that he, as well as his fellow pilots, were aware of the UFOs seen over Washington. They had talked about it, but none of them were very concerned at the time. On the night of July 26, he was on the scramble alert, and just before midnight, they were ordered into the air.

He said that they had lifted off from Dover and were vectored toward Washington. They normally operated at a high altitude, but on this night, they were ordered down, under ten thousand feet. He also said that usually, they were sent after objects out over the Atlantic to identify, but this time they were kept over dry land. It meant, to him, that something unusual was happening.

In a taped interview conducted in front of the HUFON group, he told them:

> This night, however, we quickly figured out that we were not going to get catch or get near this object. Now in the little article passed around the room that it's indicated that this was a short duration and short incident, but we tried for a few minutes to acquire the object. We tried very hard. We gave it our best shot with everything that little airplane had. And that night it was state of the art equipment. But the object we were trying to catch was too elusive. It moved at times above supersonic speeds and other times very slowly. The change of direction was so quick, so erratic that there was no way an aircraft, a manned aircraft, could stay with it or turn, climb or descend. We just couldn't catch it.
>
> My radar operator said that he saw a couple of passes on his scope that was in it was a high-speed object. Like I said, one time it was supersonic. He felt supersonic. So, it didn't take but a few minutes. That was all we did that night. The object disappeared.
>
> There was another jet that went with us, and I don't recall the report he might have given when he got back. But any rate the reason that I know that I was on that mission is because my

logbook will show that I landed at Langley Air Force Base that night. The reason I did we had worked south of Washington, D.C. a little bit and running at low altitudes and at high power settings I didn't want to try to go back to Dover, Delaware, so I set down at Langley to refuel. And then we went back.

During Samford's press conference, he said that one of the interceptors had detected something on his radar, but Samford said it was the other airplane and not a UFO. This pilot, however, who was there, and who knew where the other aircraft was, knew that Samford's off-the-cuff remark did not reflect reality. The object they detected was not the other fighter.

Once the jets had disappeared from the radars, the UFOs returned. With the UFOs back on the scopes, the ARTC again requested interceptors and another two F-94s were dispatched. This time the UFOs didn't disappear, and the situation became, according to what Fournet told me, "The reports that we got from at least one of the fighter pilots was pretty gory."

He wouldn't elaborate on that, telling me, "Let's just say that it was pretty interesting." Al Chop would later fill in the details for me.

This time the pilots were able to see the objects, vectored toward them by the air traffic controllers. But the fighters couldn't close on the lights. The pilots saw no external details, other than lights where the radar suggested that something should be seen.

After several minutes of failure to close on a target, one of them was spotted lopping along. A fighter piloted by Lieutenant William Patterson turned, kicked in the afterburner and tried to catch the object. It disappeared before Patterson could see much of anything.

Interviewed the next day, Patterson said, "I tried to make contact with the bogies below one thousand feet, but they [the controllers] vectored us around. I saw several bright lights. I was at my maximum speed (600 miles an hour or more), but even then, I had no closing speed. I ceased chasing it because I saw no chance of overtaking it. I was vectored into new objects. Later I chased a single bright light which I estimated about ten miles away. I lost visual contact with it..."

Al Chop remembered this intercept, as did Dewey Fournet. Chop said, "The flight controllers had directed him to them [the unknowns]. We had a little cluster of them. Five or six of them and he suddenly reports that he sees some lights... He said they are very brilliant blue-white lights. He was going try to close in to get a better look... he flew into the area where they were clustered, and he reported they were all around him."

Chop said that he, along with the others in the radar room, watched the intercept on the radar scope. What the pilot was telling them, they could see on the radar.

Patterson had to break of the intercept, though there were still lights in the sky and objects on the scope. According to Chop, the pilot radioed that he was running low on fuel. He turned so that he could head back to his base.

Edward Ruppelt

Chop said that the last of the objects disappeared from the scope about the time the sun came up. Ruppelt later quizzed Fournet about the activities that night. According to Ruppelt, Fournet and Holcomb, the radar expert, were convinced the targets were solid, metallic objects. Fournet told Ruppelt that there were weather related targets on the scopes, but the controllers were ignoring them. Everyone was convinced that the targets were real they had been chasing were real and solid.

In fact, Fourney told me, "When you combine radar reports with Holcomb's explanations to me [Fourney] about solid returns with the reports of the pilots, I think you can conclude they were not reflections from the atmosphere or temperature inversions."

This wasn't quite the end, however. The military pilots still had to be debriefed. Remember, Ruppelt had suggested that those military officers and tower personnel at Andrews had been persuaded to alter their stories slightly. Pressure from above suggested explanations about the UFOs those men had reported. The situation with the pilots wasn't any different.

According to the pilot of one of the first intercepts, there was an interrogation about what he had experienced. He said:

> The next day back at Dover some strange things happened. I started getting interviewed by ranking officers. They take the radar officer that was with me into separate rooms and debrief us. Now it wasn't like you were in Vietnam where they pulled your fingernails out and do worse. They threatened you. And they did certain

133

things that I was surprised. It really surprised me. And then when came to an end in a few days, they said, 'you are not to say a word about this to anybody.' They even threatened me with a court martial.

Concerning the interrogation phase that I had right after the attempted interception. We were called in separately, as I said. We were called in several times. It wasn't just one time, but it was several times. It seemed to get a little bit heavier all the time. A little bit more serious all the time. Thinking back on this, the ranking officer was trying to get something out of us. To tell them something. What could I tell him but what I've told you. I told them the same story over and over. Sometimes I felt like maybe they didn't believe me, but they had my radar operator and they had other crews that had been on the same type of incident. We just were frank with them. After a few minutes they just told us that we want you to forget about it, it didn't happen, don't ever talk about it to anybody... I don't remember the exact questions at this time.

We [meaning he and his fellow pilots] just didn't talk about it. I knew there were some others at other bases that had scrambled on such objects.... I was one of those on that particular mission that night.

He did say, however, that he didn't have a visual sighting with the blips detected by his onboard radars. He said that the visibility was very good and that he could see far outside the cockpit. He didn't see anything that might be a UFO.

The pilot was asked about the chances he had made some kind of mistake or that the blips on the radar had been weather related phenomenon. He said:

Chances are that the blips that were seen at the time I was Dover Delaware were some weather... I don't think so. Because there were too many times and because these radar operators who were on the ground both the USAF service ground radar and the air traffic controllers had too much experience. There were too many of them and too much experience to be put off as something that was a temperature inversion or something they mistook. I don't believe that.

What all this suggests is that there was something in the air over Washington, D.C. and it wasn't just a temperature inversion. Yes, it is certainly possible that the men in the various radar facilities at Washington National and at Andrews could have been fooled. That does not explain the visual sightings from all those other locations, nor does it explain the interceptor pilots or airline pilots' experiences.

Chapter Ten: The Pilots Reports from The Rest of the Country

Other fighter pilots in other parts of the country were having the same problems as those flying over the Washington, D.C. area. In those other locations fighters were scrambled as the radar operators tried to vector them toward the UFOs. Early on the morning of July 29, the scene shifted from Washington, D.C. to Osceola, Wisconsin.

According to the reports from Wisconsin, all are available in the Project Blue Book files:

> Numerous unidentified flying objects of undetermined size and shape were sighted by ground electronic means between 0130 and 0230 (lasting 1 hour) ... by members of a radar unit located near Osceola, Wisconsin, who were on duty. Size of blips which constituted the sightings were normal with the exception of one large well-defined target, speed of this target was 600 knots as computed on the radar scope set on the fifty nautical mile range. The remainder of the sightings were individual sightings having multiple targets, up to ten, appearing in a loose cluster on the radar scope, speed of these targets was fifty to sixty knots as computed on the radar scope set on the fifty nautical mile range. The only possible formation noted during the entire sighting period was during one or two of the sightings which consisted of multiple targets when two or three of these targets might possibly have been moving in a loose formation. All targets suddenly appeared on the radar scope and after having traveled between thirty and seventy nautical miles would just as suddenly disappear. Targets did not appear on the height indicator due to anomalous propagation. Targets followed a general pattern of appearing on the radar scope SW of the sighting station and proceeding E[ast] until disappearing. There was a continual overlapping of patterns on the radar scope; a new pattern would have appeared before the old pattern would have disappeared. In the sightings which consisted of multiple targets, with the exception of possible formation movement, targets progressed across the radar scope, until disappearing, independently of each other in regard to track and heading with some targets making a turning course. There was some correlation between these electronic sightings and visual

136

sightings made by a pilot scrambled in conjunction with the radar sightings. This correlation placed both types of sightings in the same area at the same time. Pilot estimated height of objects he visually saw at 125,000 feet. Sighting station was specifically searching for possible unidentified flying objects at time of first sighting due to a GOC [Ground Observers Corps] report of visual sighting of unidentified flying objects.

One F-51 [known as the P-51 Mustang during the Second World War] aircraft was sent to sighting area for purpose of intercepting and/or identifying unknown targets. Pilot did report visually sighting unidentified flying object but interception and/or identification was not possible. This action occurred between 0130 and 0255.

Appended at the end of the document were the ATIC comments. According to them, "Report indicates that anomalous propagation was affecting the radar performance. This condition would allow detection of ground targets which are not normally detected. This would explain movement of targets unless weather conditions were such that every target (ground) was not detected in each sweep of the antenna thereby causing an apparent movement of stationary targets. A firm analysis cannot be made." The final conclusion, according to the report was "Unknown."

In another document in the file, prepared by an intelligence officer, there was a description of the objects. The description, however, was based on the "electronic" detection of the UFOs rather than any of the visual sightings. The report said, "Size of the blips which constituted the sightings were normal with the exception of one (1) large well-defined target... speed of this target was 600 knots as computed on the radar scope... The remainder of the sightings were individual..."

One of the points that is important, but that is almost ignored in the official documentation, is that the search for the UFOs was initiated by sightings from the Ground Observers Corps. These trained men and women were on duty to watch the skies for possible sneak attack from a more terrestrially based enemy.

Recruiting for the Ground Observers Corps.

138

At the time that enemy would have been the Soviet Union. Without the Ground Observers Corps visual, ground-based sightings, the radar operators would not have been searching for anything unusual and the UFOs might have gone unnoticed.

The ground based visual sightings were all rather vague and seemed to match the descriptions given in Washington, D.C. a few days earlier. According to the handwritten report from an airman second class (A/2c) "The object seemed to be a shooting star at first but appeared and disappeared (sic) in an arc starting about over the pump room and extending to about the boiler shack [which were, obviously, ground based reference points that provide no modern clues as to size]. I was located on top of the operations building, over this arc it appeared and disappeared (sic) about three times."

In another, like statement, another of the airman [name redacted by Air Force officers in 1976] wrote, "I [name redacted], being of sound mind do hereby state that I saw following occurrence (sic)... Standing on top of operations roof and saw flashes of light at different intervals that appeared as if they were in one same cycle. These flashes of light that were seen by me appeared to be between 15 and 30 degrees above the horizon and seemed to leave a trace for a second."

A very interesting note in the file revealed that "16 mm film, July 29, 1952, Osceola, Wisc. Multiple observers. In custody of Audio-Visual archives." This might refer to the radar scope photographs taken during the sightings because there is no suggestion of analysis of any sort of movie footage, nor is there any suggestion that this might be gun camera film from the lone fighter scrambled. Air Force records provide no clue about the movie footage.

The file also lacks a statement given by the fighter pilot. He was apparently dispatched from another unit and the investigation centered on the radar operators and observers stationed in the Osceola area. The investigating officer was more impressed with the electronic sightings, believing them to be more reliable than the visual sightings made by the low-ranking enlisted men. Lt. Col. Willard L. Worden wrote, "The significance of this report lies in the fact that these sightings are electronic sightings made and recorded by competent personnel."

The following evening, at about 9:40 p.m., another radar site, this one in central Michigan, began to detect a solid target as it flew south across the Saginaw Bay in the area of Port Huron. It was traveling at 625 miles an hour and wasn't a jet according to the local radar operators and observers.

They checked the flight plans from around the local area and found no explanation among them for the UFO.

There were three F94s in the local area on various training missions and one was diverted to identify the UFO. When he reached an altitude of about 20,000 feet, the ground controller told him to turn. As he did, both he and his radar operator in the backseat saw a bright blue light that was quite a bit larger than a star. As they watched, it turned reddish and then began to shrink as if it was flying away from them. The ground radar controller said that he had both the UFO and the jet on his scope and that the UFO had made a 180-degree turn.

The F-94 couldn't match the turn, and the speed of the UFO suggested that it had to be some kind of a jet. The pilot rolled around, leveled, and then began a high-speed pursuit using the afterburners. The F-94s radar operator was able to get a lock on, using the onboard radar. He said that the object was as big as those made on the largest military bombers.

The chase had lasted for about thirty seconds or so as the jet began to slowly close the distance between the it and the unidentified object. The ground controller said that the distance, according to his calculations, was about four miles. At about that time the object brightened considerably and the distance between the jet and the object doubled in a single sweep of the radar antenna.

The chase lasted another ten minutes with the jet periodically closing the distance to the UFO, and then having the object flash far ahead. No one was sure what the top speed of the UFO was because the sudden bursts were too short for anyone to get an accurate reading. Estimates, however, suggested that the UFO could fly as fast as 1400 miles an hour, much faster than any aircraft in the then known inventory.

With the F-94 getting low on fuel, the intercept ended. As the jet turned away, the ground-based radar suggested the UFO had slowed to about 200 to 300 miles an hour. These plots weren't too accurate because the UFO was at the outer range of the radar's capability.

This case is important because, once again, it involves military pilots, a visual observation, and a radar track. The UFO seemed to respond to the presence of the jet, speeding ahead and then slowing enough to let the F-94 close the distance before flashing ahead again. The visual sighting, of a bright blue light, is not much of a description, but it does show that something was in the sky over the radar station. And the UFO's maneuvering seemed, to many, to rule the possibility of a weather-related target that had been offered as an

140

explanation for the Washington Nationals only a couple of hours earlier by General Samford and his staff.

On August 1, 1952, over a small town in Ohio named Bellefontaine, radar contact was made with something moving very fast. Movie footage was taken, but this time the photographer was an Air Force pilot and the camera he used was the gun camera on the wing of his F-86 interceptor. Later Air Force analysis suggested that the object photographed was nothing more extraordinary than a weather balloon at a very high altitude that had been misidentified.

According to the Air Force records available in the Project Blue Book files, "At 1551Z [or just before 10 a.m. in the local area], a radar track appeared 20 miles NNW of W-P [Wright-Patterson] AFB. The course was 240 degrees at 400 knots. Two F-86's under GCI control were then located ten miles SW of that position. The fighters were vectored and made visual contact at 1555Z. Fighters stayed with the object until 1613Z [or about eighteen minutes]."

According to one of the documents, the pilots of the two aircraft, a major, identified later as James B. Smith, and a lieutenant, identified as Donald J. Hemmer [or Hemer, depending on the source] showed that:

> The F-86's climbed to 48,000 feet. The major made a camera run the second time and received a weak return on his radar gunsight. The lieutenant's sight was "caged" [meaning that it was turned off and locked down] so he received no return. The major estimated the object at 12,000 – 20,000 feet above his altitude of 48,000 feet. This estimate was substantiated by the range capability of the radar gunsight [meaning that if the object was much farther away, there would be no return]. The object's size, accepting the source's estimate of distance, was 24 – 40 feet in diameter and source said his optical sight just covered the object. The films were not sufficiently clear. The object appeared as a fuzzy, small image in the upper right corner with discernable motion to the lower left.

The investigating officer made a couple of notes that are quite important. First, he wrote, "re-affirmation that the UFO moved at 400 knots and indication that the two F-86's and the UFO appeared simultaneously on the GCI scope." Second, he suggested, "It is obvious that all eyes and antennas were fixed on the same object."

In the comments section, the officer wrote:

The object as not a balloon, since the speed was too fast [winds aloft data suggest the winds at altitude were blowing between 25 and 32 knots]. A rawinsonde was released at 1500Z and moved off to the east. The object moved against the wind. The blip size was that of a normal aircraft. The object was not a known aircraft because the altitude was too high. The object was not astronomical as dual radar returns eliminate this. Electronic or visual mirage of meteorological phenomenon is out of the question as the radar set was on high beam, and both would not occur simultaneously the same place…. [The Conclusion was] Unknown.

It should be noted here that this case was another that contradicted Samford's claim about radar returns. Again, in fairness, it should also be noted that this sighting was made days after the press conference.

And there was gun camera film of the object. True, the object was not clearly resolved on the film, but there was film. This case had the observation of the pilot corroborated by the radar and by the film. The evidence might not be as clear as might be desired, but in the end, there were three chains of evidence involved.

Dr. Donald Menzel

The final conclusion, after investigation, according to the Project Blue Book files was that the radar sighting was an aircraft and the visual sighting, as well as the gun camera films, were of a balloon. The Air Force files said, "[T]he radar did not, however, have a height finder…. When they reached the area, the controller requested them to get a visual. At approximately this time the ground radar failed… The original object painted by the radar was an aircraft flying out of Cleveland. The object sighted by the pilots later was positively identified as an upper air research balloon."

Donald Menzel reviewed the case in one of his UFO debunking books, *The World of Flying Saucers*. He wrote, "[T]he radar operator at the Air Defense command post picked up an unidentified target north of Dayton, moving southwest at a speed of about 525miles an hour. Two jets from Wright-Patterson Air Force Base were scrambled for an intercept."

Menzel noted, correctly, that there was no height finding capability on the radar, so the operator could only direct them toward the target but could not tell them if it was above or below them. Menzel wrote:

A few seconds later, the returned from the jects and the UFO blended on the radarscope and the operator advised the pilots that they would have to continue the search visually... Soon after the communication between ground and air had ended, the lead pilot observed a silver-colored sphere several thousand feet above him. Both jets went after it but although they climbed to their maximum altitude, 40,000 feet, neither could get close enough to identify the object, which was still some 30,000 feet above them. One pilot, however, managed to expose several feet of film with his gun camera. At the same moment the warning light of his gunsight blinked on to indicate a solid object...

Menzel added, "Both pilots then realized that, although they had been chasing an unknown for some ten minutes, they were still northwest of the base in almost the same area where they had started the intercept. This surprising fact seemed to indicate that the unknown had slowed down from its original speed of 525 miles an hour, to hover in the sky nearly motionless."

Menzel, the Air Force and "Flying-saucer addicts [as Menzel described them]" realized the importance of the case. Menzel noted that one of those flying saucer addicts had commented, "For the first time a saucer had been photographed during simultaneous radar and visual sightings, with the camera plane [sic] also locked on by radar. It was absolute proof that this saucer was a solid object, a controlled disc-shaped machine."

While it isn't true that anyone had described a "disc-shaped" machine, this is one UFO sighting that had multiple chains of evidence. There was the radar sighting that started it, the visual sighting by the pilots, corroborated by the on-board radar, and finally the motion picture film taken by the gun camera. Three different types of evidence, each corroborating one another. Clearly there was no hoax here in the sighting report and certainly no faking of motion picture film. Just as clearly, there was no mirage because the radar sightings established that a solid object was in the sky. Finally, the visual sighting by the pilots provided another perspective for investigators. The only element that could be added would have been additional witnesses on the ground or in the air. This truly was a very important case, one that could go a long way to establishing the reality of the flying saucers.

According to Menzel, the Air Force investigators eventually found "the more prosaic though complicated solution to the puzzle..." The object picked up by radar was, according to Menzel and the Air Force, a jet plane flying out of Cleveland, Ohio. At the time the radar return was discovered, the low flying jet was "on a southwest heading, at a speed of around 525 miles an hour - the exact time, position, and speed of the radar unknown." Of course, the speed, as outlined in the file was only 400 miles an hour, hardly the "exact" speed of the jet.

The pilots, according to this explanation, didn't see the jet which was below them and far away. What they had seen was a twenty-foot in diameter radiosonde balloon that had been released about an hour earlier. The ground radar did not "see" the balloon because the operator was concentrating on the fast-moving UFO.

A reason for the confusion was that the ground radar did not have height-finding equipment. Without that, the jet, tracked by the ground was confused with the balloon seen by the pilots. According to Menzel, "At 30,000 feet the pilots were too high to see the Cleveland jet far below them."

Had the radar not failed at this point, the operator would have seen the jet continuing on its path while the pilots continued to watch the sphere above them. The radar operator would have been able to redirect the pilot's attention to the object that had fooled him in the beginning, and they would have then been able to identify the jet.

According to Menzel, "The photographs [taken by the gun camera] confirmed this reconstruction of a complicated series of events. The pictures obtained by the gun camera displayed a round, indistinct blur. Analysis showed that the size of the object was that of a twenty-foot sphere - a balloon - photographed from a distance of 30,000 feet."

Ruppelt, in his book, *The Report on Unidentified Flying Objects,* also wrote about this case. He noted that "At exactly ten forty-five on the morning of August 1, 1952, an ADC [Air Defense Command] radar near Bellefontaine, Ohio, picked up a high-speed unidentified target" and continued, suggesting that the object "continued on its southwesterly course at about 525 miles an hour." Ruppelt also wrote that the lead pilot interceptor pilot knew that he wasn't chasing a hallucination, mirage, sundog or reflected light.

The Air Force investigator on this case, Lieutenant Andy Flues, interviewed the interceptor pilots and obtained a copy of the gun camera film which he took to the base photo lab at Wright-Patterson. There he asked them a very basic question. He wanted to know what a twenty foot in diameter weather balloon would look like on 16 mm movie film if it was about 30,000 feet [around six miles] away. The lab, according to Ruppelt said that it would look pretty much like the object photographed by the major's [that is, the interceptor pilot's] gun camera.

There is, in the official file, a one page "Air Intelligence Information Report" that appears to be a carbon copy of something else. It is badly smeared in places, and nearly indistinct in others. It contains some information that tends to corroborate the story as reported by Menzel but contradicts other reports also in that file.

The document begins by noting, "Observed by 1/Lt. James Lott" and provides both his home address and his telephone number. Then, in a single paragraph, the story is told again. According to the document:

> At 1551Z [3:51 in the afternoon, Greenwich Mean Time] a track appeared on the scope 20 miles north northeast of Wright-Patterson field. Two F-86's under control were then located 10 miles southeast of that position. Major Smith of the 97th Fighter Interceptor Squadron [unreadable] flight leader. The track was making a ground speed of 450 knots so a cut off vector was given. The flight leader immediately tally hoed at 1055Z [clearly a mistake, the time should read "L" or local] on the track and the heading was changed 30 degrees to cut the track off more. [Unreadable] clock position was affirmed by flight leader. Track was on scope for 15 miles heading 240 degrees from time of pickup. Flight leader reported object as silver in color round in shape. Flight leader climbed to 40,000 feet, and estimated object at 70,000 feet. Flight of F-86's stayed with object until 1113L [local time] returning to base low on fuel. At the time it was dropped object was 5 miles northwest of Springfield, Ohio. Attempt had been made to get gun camera film.

There is one other fact that is interesting. On a copy of the original report, in which the unidentified officer reported that the case was unknown, someone else made notes. Over the comment about the speed of the object, he had scribbled, "but speed relative!" And, near the suggestion the case was "Unknown," he had written "unless backend of jet exhaust photographed."

That about covers all the information in the Blue Book file, with the exception of the radar report form. Of interest on the form is the name of Lt. Lott, who apparently was the radar officer during the intercept, and a note that the speed of the object was constant at 400 knots.

Here is an important case that seems to have been lost in the publicity that the Washington Nationals generated. In Washington, there were only radar tracks and attempted intercepts, but no photographs. Here, there is no indication temperature inversion that could cause the radar returns and the mysterious object, there are visual sightings, and the all-important gun camera film.

Like the Washington Nationals, the explanation has been distorted. There is nothing in the file to suggest that the track of the object 525 knots as claimed by Menzel. Given the on-board radar indication, and the estimate of the pilot, the object was not 30,000 feet above him, but 12,000 to 20,000 feet. The analysis of the film, if the distances are changed, eliminates the balloon explanation. The Air Force, however, has a thing about balloons. They blame them for nearly everything.

Ignoring Menzel's analysis because it simply does not square with any of the facts in the file, ignoring the Air Force claim that this has been absolutely identified as a balloon, there is one other fact to consider. The pilots were interviewed by a newspaper. One of them said, "I don't think the light was reflected. I deliberately maneuvered around it at several angles to make sure it wasn't a reflection."

The article also reported that the officers had reported that the object disappeared at a high rate of speed. This is not suggestive of a balloon, or any sort of natural phenomena. It does suggest, however, that something unusual was seen.

These were the last comments reported because, according to the story, the pilots had been ordered to stop commenting on the sighting. It just wasn't good form to have Air Force interceptor pilots reporting they had seen something that they couldn't catch, that it had disappeared, and that they had photographs of it. There was simply too much information about it. Besides, what did it say about the Air Force if their pilots couldn't identify a balloon when they saw one.

Although the lion's share of the publicity about UFOs on radar went to the Washington Nationals these other intercepts provide important clues about what was happening in July 1952. They provide a glimpse into the attitudes of the men investigating UFOs, and at those who are explaining UFOs. It also tells us something about human attitudes at the time.

But attempted intercepts weren't the only cases being reported in 1952. There were dozens of cases being reported from around the country after the last sightings were made in the Washington, D.C. area. Those sightings suggested that UFOs were overlying all of the United States. Those sightings suggested that the UFO sightings were not limited to Washington, D.C. or the east coast. A great deal of information was gathered, suggesting some interesting things about the 1952 summer wave of UFO reports.

Chapter Eleven: The End of July

The UFO sightings throughout the country did not end with the last of the Washington National reports on July 26. More military installations, more military officers, and more military pilots were making official reports of UFOs during the end of the month. These sightings seemed to mirror those in the Washington, D.C. area, but they did not involve the numbers of witnesses or pilots, nor did they receive the national attention that the sightings did in Washington, D.C.

On July 26, 1952, Airman 1/C J.M. Donaldson, while walking near the service club on Kirtland Air Force Base in Albuquerque, New Mexico, reported that he saw eight orange balls, in a triangular formation, cross the sky from west to east without making a sound. He only saw the objects for three or four seconds. In his short report, filed with Project Blue Book, he wrote, "I did not observe any exhaust or trail from these objects... I observed these objects for approximately 3 or 4 seconds. They seemed to be traveling west to east and were north of my position."

The Air Force investigation was conducted by a local intelligence officer, 1st. Lt. Glen D. Parrish. He noted that the statement by Donaldson was "sworn and subscribed (sic) before me," and that he believed "the reliability of the observer is considered excellent."

Of course, the problem with Donaldson's sighting is that he was the only witness to make any sort of statement, and given the nature of the observation, as well as the length of it, there was little chance that a plausible explanation would be found. The Air Force, with uncharacteristic candor, labeled the sighting as "unidentified," though, in this case, in might have been more accurate to suggest that it was "insufficient" for a proper and scientific analysis.

AF FORM 112—PART I
APPROVED 1 JUNE 1948

COUNTRY	REPORT NO.	(LEAVE BLANK)
UNITED STATES	NOT APPLICABLE	

AIR INTELLIGENCE INFORMATION REPORT

SUBJECT:
FLYOBRPT

AREA REPORTED ON		FROM (Agency)
ALBUQUERQUE, NEW MEXICO		34th AIR DIVISION (DEF)

DATE OF REPORT	DATE OF INFORMATION	
29 July 1952	26 July 1952	

PREPARED BY (Officer)	SOURCE
GLEN D. PARRISH, 1st Lt., USAF	Visual Observer

REFERENCES (Control number, directive, previous report, etc., as applicable)
None

SUMMARY: (Enter concise summary of report. Give significance in final one-sentence paragraph. List inclosures at lower left. Begin text of report on AF Form 112—Part II.)

SUBJECT: FLYOBRPT

In accordance with AFL 200-5, dated 29 April 1952, Subject: Unidentified Flying Objects Reporting (Short Title: FLYOBRPT), the following report of unidentified flying objects is submitted:

On 26 July 1952 at 0005 MST, ██████████████████ 34th Air Division (Def), Kirtland Air Force Base, New Mexico, saw 8 or more bright orange objects in the sky. From ground level these objects were approximately 30° and were traveling at a very rapid speed. They were moving in a triangular formation with the wedge of the triangle appearing to be open. These objects were observed for 3 or 4 seconds. They seemed to be traveling from west to east and were located north of the observer. The observer was located at approximately 35°38' latitude and 106°36' longitude. At the time of this observation, ceiling was unlimited and visibility was approximately 50 miles. The winds at this time were north 16 MPH.

The reliability of the observer is considered excellent.

DOWNGRADED AT 3 YEAR INTERVALS
DECLASSIFIED AFTER 12 YEARS
DOD DIR 5200.10

7-3719-1-1

INCLS.

DISTRIBUTION BY ORIGINATOR

RESTRICTED
SECURITY INFORMATION

UNCLASSIFIED

(CLASSIFICATION)

16-55488-1   U. S. GOVERNMENT PRINTING OFFICE

Air Intelligence Report form from the Kirtland sighting.

A day later, from Selfridge Air Force Base in Michigan, three bomber crewman, Captain Cyril H. Rogers, Jr., 1st Lt. Malvin W. Samuel, and S/Sgt Kenneth E. Kling, while on the ground, watched five silvery-white objects flying in a loose trail formation. The first two UFOs were close together, but the last three were not at any sort of regularly spaced interval. They just seemed to follow the path of the first.

There were jet fighters in the area at the time of the sighting, and one was seen crossing the sky after the last of the UFOs had disappeared. The witnesses suggested that the UFOs were faster than the jet, having just seen them. It is also apparent that the jets were not attempting to intercept the UFOs, and there is no evidence that the objects were seen on radar by any of the base facilities.

Again, the Air Force believed that the witnesses were all very reliable, were familiar with aircraft, and were all members of a combat flying crew. The Air Force was unable to explain the sighting and it is carried as an "unidentified" in the Blue Book files.

About ten hours later, that is, about 8:30 that evening, Adrian Ellis and his wife, in Wichita Falls, Texas, reported they watched two glowing, circular objects fly by at about a thousand miles an hour. The UFOs came to a complete stop, flew in a half circle, and then flew off in a straight line. The objects had no exhaust and left no trail. They were in sight for about fifteen seconds so that the witnesses had enough time to identify them as conventional objects had they been airplanes, weather balloons, or atmospheric phenomena.

The following day, July 28, at McGuire Air Force Base, the ground radar operators reported that they had detected UFOs at various points within thirty miles of the base. Master Sergeant William F. Dees provided drawings of the objects as they appeared on the radar, and told the investigator, S/Sgt. Dennis G. Washburn, that the objects remained in the area for about fifty-five minutes. Dees said that he had contacted the control tower to tell them about the UFOs and that two of the men there said they had seen the UFO through binoculars.

Dees supplied a statement to the Project Blue Book investigators that said:

> Turned on scans [radar] at 0600 and observed scopes... Contacted Dog Catcher [code name of the unit at McGuire]. In a period of time about two sweeps or so the blips move about and change their pattern... until at 0620 they lined up... All returns were clearly defined radar targets... At 0652 and 0655 the returns... lined up in

perfect echelon... Four (4) clear blips lined up and then several more moved from the big cluster 20 to 25 miles out down to the line and made about eight (8) in a perfect spaced row.

Dees' statement isn't very exciting. It refers to blips on a radar screen, and frankly, they could be just about anything. However, S/Sgt Thomas R. Dunn and A/2c Albert M. Holmes, in the control tower saw the objects. According to the statement they gave the Air Force investigator:

At 0600 D.S.T. [daylight saving time], G.C.A. advised of various targets to the southeast... Then they advised one target had left the bunch and proceeded north and then turned west. We sighted this aircraft passing seven to eight miles north of the station... It was a B-25 or B-26.

Then approximately 3 to 5 minutes later at 0610 D.S.T. we sighted another object northeast of the field... There was a sound at the same time that was similar to a foghorn or a boat whistle. The object at first appeared to be a bomber type aircraft, but as it was about 10 miles northeast at an altitude of 8000 or 9000 feet, it was hard to determine any silhouette.

The object was moving at conventional speed directly inbound to the field. The two of us on duty were observing this object through sets of binoculars by this time. It was a steep turn, or an abrupt turn, with no noticeable increase in speed. When inbound the object seemed to be reflecting the sun's rays off the left side, the sun being to the object's left, but in turn what seemed to be the reflection remained on the same spot on the object and two more bright yellowish-orange reflections appeared after completing the turn, leaving one light on either side and one light at the rear of the object moving away. It was at this time we noted that it was not reflection but some other cause for the light on the object.

The object had no known silhouette. It appeared sort of oblong with no visible tail or wing sections. Then the object flew northeast at the same rate of speed until it was out of sight.

The investigating officer then reviewed, in detail, the statements made by Dees, Dunn and Holmes. He found nothing to suggest that the object seen from the tower, which neither Dunn nor Holmes could identify was any kind of a conventional craft. That one sighting was left as an "unidentified."

Nor was any good explanation offered for what Dees had watched on the radar scope. There were multiple targets, all looked to be solid and although there were some weather-related targets present, Dees had spotted them quickly and marked them. The question that could not be answered was if the single object seen by the men in the tower was one of the objects that Dees was watching on radar.

One other important point comes out of this sighting. Air Force investigators had often suggested that the longer the UFO was in sight, and the better trained the witnesses, the less likely that the sighting would remain unidentified. In this case, the observers were well trained, at least in aircraft recognition because that was part of their job. They had the object in sight long enough to get a very good look at it, and they observed it through binoculars. In other words, the criterion the Air Force suggested would help solve UFO sightings prohibited the solution here. There was just too much information available for them to suggest on of the possible solutions.

In stark contrast to the work done by the Air Force investigator at McGuire, is the report that comes from McChord Air Force Base in Washington. The only investigative work here seems to be the message sent by teletype to the various Air Force agencies that received UFO sighting reports.

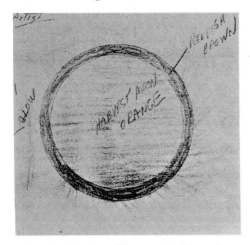

According to the teletype, the witnesses, identified only by their military ranks and last names, were T/Sgt Walstead and S/Sgt Calkins. They watched a dull, bluish green, glowing ball of light that they believed was at about 20,000 feet. They said that it was traveling as fast, or faster than meteorites. They said that it wasn't a meteorite, and that they had an unobscured [sic] view of the sky.

Illustration of McChord UFO.

A second sighting was made by Mrs. Leidy of the Ground Observer Corps, at about the same time. She reported that it moved "sporadically (sic)" back and forth, and that it had no propulsion, no sound and no trails. The object disappeared straight up.

The sightings continued to pour into the Air Force. One of the better such reports came on July 29 near Merced, California. According to the Air Force investigative report:

Late in the afternoon on 29 July 1952, Mr. [name redacted by the Air Force] and an employee of his, [name deleted] were standing in front of his house waiting for some friends of the family to arrive. Mr. [name redacted] and [name redacted] had just returned from their job... At approximately 1544 PDT they heard a noise which sounded like a jet fighter passing over and they both looked up to see it. After scanning the sky for a moment, they spotted a dark object in the sky... to the Southeast. At first glance they both thought it was a buzzard however they immediately changed their minds for this object was perfectly round... he estimated its actual size as slightly larger than a B-29 and all thru (sic) the interview continued to emphasize the impression he received of its large size. When the object first appeared it seemed to be just below the clouds which more or less covered the sky, which was estimated to be about 12,000 feet. Right after they spotted the object it tipped on edge into a steep dive towards them, diving about two or three thousand feet. During this dive they got a good end view of the object which [name redacted] described as "like a discus from the side" ... At the end of the dive the object did not round out like an airplane but righted itself smoothly and stopped momentarily before beginning a slow circle to the left. It was at this time that they noticed a translucent silvery light behind the object a distance equal to two diameters of the object itself and apparently not connected. At first sighting the object appeared to be black however now its color seemed be a dark blue "similar to the color Navy planes are painted". The object circled slowly to the left completing the circle, then made a second circle, and finally took off at high speed to the North Northeast towards Castle AF Base and also towards a large hole in the clouds about eight miles away where blue sky was showing through... The object passed out of sight thru this hole. Mr. [name redacted] who claims to be able to estimate distances quite will (sic) due to experience in chasing brush and forest fires by estimating the distance of the smoke stated that the object traveled about 10 miles in 10 seconds on its departure. He further stated that its speed appeared to be very much faster than that of two B-29's which were in the area at the time, one to the Northwest and the other to the South.

Aside from the noise which attracted their attention initially no other sound was heard which could be attributed to the object. All of its movements were extremely smooth as was its acceleration (sic) on departure. The object was in view for a full 2 minutes and was viewed against a background of clouds until it passed thru the hole.

The report contained in the Blue Book files is incomplete. There is no record card, and no additional information, other than the case is considered "unidentified." Major William H. Timlin, the 93rd Bomb Wing Intelligence officer prepared the report based on a detailed interview conducted by Captain Gerald S. Chapman.

Chapman did note that the witness was "...self-employed in a small but thriving business... He enlisted in the Air Force in 1942 and was enrolled as a navigation student but 'washed out' for physical reasons. He served the rest of his time with a ground radar unit at Boca Baton [obviously Raton], Florida, and was discharged in 1945. He impressed me as being very sincere, and one not readily excited. He said he was reluctant to tell anyone about what he saw because of their probably reaction, but he is positive that what he saw was no ordinary object and was real."

At this point, that is July 29, 1952, the Blue Books files become confusing. The project cards, which give the location, time, date, conclusions, and a brief description of the sighting are missing. File after file is thrown together so that it becomes difficult to tell which report goes with which file. The master index is some help in sorting through the mess, and that does, for the most part, provide conclusions to the various reports made during July 29 to the end of the month, but it does not solve all the problems.

One of the most comprehensive of the files, which includes numerous military and civilian witnesses was listed in the master index as taking place at Ennis, Montana. Without the card to separate the file from other reports, and with a master report that was generated at Kelly Air Force Base near San Antonio, Texas, it would be easy to overlook this report. Given the length of time over which the objects were seen, and given the number of witnesses involved, it is too important to ignore.

The case began, apparently, in Seattle, Washington. Someone there called the Air Force base at Great Falls, Montana, alerting them that UFOs were on the way, or at least heading in their direction. One of the statements, written by a captain whose name was redacted, reported, "A little background of this incident will clarify the statements that I, Captain [name redacted] have to make. The question was asked by myself to the [names redacted]. 'How did they know to go outside and look for these flying saucers?' The statement she (Mrs. [name redacted]) made was that they had heard a transmission over the squawk box that flying saucers had been reported and that they were headed toward Great Falls. I asked her where the transmission came from, and she did not know as it came through the squawk box."

The captain said that he was outside one of the hangars and looking to the east when he saw two objects, hovering. The captain noted, "The altitude which these objects were cannot be estimated due to the fact of not knowing size or conception of these objects I was unable to determine the altitude."

Although it is clear from his report that he was not happy about seeing the objects, he wrote:

> The appearance of the objects did actually have the size of a cup's saucer and appeared to have a flat aluminum base... These two objects were stationary when I first saw them, for approximately 3 or 4 minutes. Suddenly one came in at about a 45 -degree angle, between the two stationary objects. It appeared to be of a dusty color without any shiny appearance to it. This object continued to travel past these objects and off into a southernly direction. By this time the object on the right... started with a backward motion which appeared to be with tremendous speed. The one on my left darted off to the south and all three were lost from sight at this time.

A major, assigned to the same unit, about 20 minutes later, watched circular objects at very high altitude. He reported to Project Blue Book that they were disk shaped and silver in color. He wrote, "They appeared to travel from west to east at approximately 2,000 miles per hour. There were no vapor trails visible. One larger disc shaped object hovered... It hovered for about 20 seconds and immediately darted off at a high rate of acceleration and disappeared to the southeast."

About that same time, a 1st Lt. said that he arrived at work and saw fifteen or twenty people watching the sky. He was told that they had seen flying saucers but was quite skeptical about it. He reported, "After watching approximately five (5) minutes I was able to see what appeared to be a disc, white or metal in color approaching from the west. As it moved directly overhead it turned generally north at a 90 degree turn then slowing down and made approximately four (4) more 90 degree turns and the proceeded east."

He continued the report. "After seeing this I knew what I was looking for and was able to pick up at least five (5) more of these objects... However, after keeping them in my sight long enough (sic) to study their appearance they definitely seemed to be very high.... All of these appeared in the west and proceeded east what appeared to be an extreme high rate of speed."

Others were still inside and overhearing conversations. A master sergeant reported that he had been in the Transport Control Center and:

> heard a transmission over the PLAN 113, stating that 'flying saucers' were sighted over Seattle, Washington at approximately 1515 MST and were headed toward Great Falls. They were immediately cut off in the middle of a sentence, as though someone threw a switch. Just for fun I figured that if they were over Seattle at 1515 MST they should arrived at Great Falls around 1520 MST due to reported speed from various sources in the past of these flying objects. I walked out the front door of the Control Section at 1520 MST and looked into the south quadrant of the sky... and sighted three (3) objects. One appeared to be larger than the others. The larger object was stationary with the two smaller objects circling around it counter-clockwise. When the first object reached the western side of the stationary object it immediately darted off to the southwest, behind a group of small clouds and it was lost from view. The other smaller object darted off due west and when I looked back at the larger object it had disappeared.

In all, there were seventeen separate statements taken and appended to the report by Lt. Col. George S. Geanetos, the wing intelligence officer. His report seemed to be straight forward, providing copies of all the statements, and additional information about other sightings that had taken place some two years earlier. He drew no conclusions about the validity of what he had been told, or the reliability of the witnesses.

There is one disturbing aspect to this case. According to a partial report in the file, "At 1200 hours MST Thursday, 31 July 1952, the local radio station KMON broadcast an interview with Mr. [name redacted]... who claims he saw and took pictures of unidentified flying objects and that he had turned the undeveloped films (sic) over to the Air Force. We contacted the manager of the radio station

KMON, who informed us that Mr. [name redacted] turned the undeveloped film over to the Commanding Officer..."

At that point the report ended. There is no indication, elsewhere in the file about who the commanding officer was, where the film was, or if anyone ever heard anything else about it. With seventeen other witnesses, such photographs could be very important, but they seem to have disappeared. In fairness to the Air Force, it must be noted that there is no evidence that the man on the radio had taken pictures of anything. It could be just someone attempting to gain his fifteen minutes of fame.

Later in the file, however, is another report, labeled that it was "Submitted in accordance with AF LTR [Letter] No. 200-5, dated 20 April 1952, Sub: Unidentified Flying Objects Reporting. At the bottom of that report it said, "Observer took 8mm motion pictures (Bell & Howell camera) with colored film, and still shots with Kodak Retina black-and-white. Films turned over to Major [name redacted] Air Division Defense, Great Falls AFB, who dispatched the films to WADF, Hamilton AFB, Calif. Later WADF advised to ship films immediately to ATIC."

This, since it was in the report written by Major Joseph M. Penny at Great Falls, seems to prove that both motion picture and still photographs were taken by someone during the sightings. There are no indications in the master index or in the file itself as to what happened to this valuable evidence once the Air Force took it, other than it was forwarded first to Hamilton in California and then ordered on to Wright-Patterson.

In the end, the sightings are labeled as unidentified. There are seventeen witnesses who were interviewed and a possibility of many more. There are indications that sightings were made over Seattle, Washington, and that reports were made to Great Falls because some of the witnesses went outside to look for the UFOs. There are indications of both motion picture and still photography, which could make the sighting unique in UFO history.

Unfortunately, there is nothing else in the files. There are no indications of what happened to the photographic evidence. It just disappears. There are no indications of who had alerted the people at Great Falls about the approaching UFOs. The case, though fairly well documented, is left hanging. It is important to learn if the film, either motion picture or still, revealed anything, and how those objects looked compared to what the witnesses had claimed to have seen.

Think about this. On July 2, a Navy officer passing through Tremonton, Utah, filmed a number of objects soaring in the afternoon sky. They were too far away when he began to film for them to be any sort of valuable proof, based solely on what can be seen on the film. Less than a month later, someone else took more footage of objects over Great Falls, but there seems to be no record that the Great Falls films ever reached Project Blue Book. Ruppelt made no mention of them in his book, and no one else has brought up anything about them. They aren't mentioned in any of the surveys of the Blue Book material. The films are just gone.

It is interesting that the films and cases that have survived in Project Blue Book fall just short of providing the evidence that is needed. Now we have another case that seems to provide the clues, but it has disappeared.

Although the Washington National sightings are quite important, they might not be the most important of the July 1952 sightings. While there were radar sites involved, and that provided a type of physical evidence, the important case might have been the Montana sighting that came just days after the last of the Washington Nationals. Unfortunately, the Montana sightings seemed to be confined to the Air Force base and there was little in the way of local publicity. There certainly was nothing on a national level.

As July drew to a close, the number of UFO sightings did not diminish by much. People were still seeing the UFOs, still reporting them, but the important cases had already happened. Other, interesting cases would be reported, including one of the first occupant sightings to gain any sort of national attention, but the good, solid cases, with physical evidence, radar, interceptors, and photographs, had happened. Now it was just a question of picking up the debris.

Chapter Twelve: Blue Book and the Aliens

Throughout its twenty-two-year history, first as Project Sign, then as Project Grudge and finally as Project Blue Book, there were very few reports of alien creatures. Blue Book's attitude seemed to be that UFOs in the sky were fine. UFOs close to the ground, and even landed, were fine. But they drew the line at a UFO which had not only landed, but from which came the pilots or crew. Blue Book avoided, as much as possible, reports of alien creatures, possibly believing them to be too weird.

That is not to say that no one ever reported alien beings to the Air Force. There were several such reports, but only three were marked as "unidentified. The best known of these cases happened in Socorro, New Mexico, in April 1964. The Air Force seemed impressed with Lonnie Zamora's sincerity, the physical marks left by the egg-shaped UFO, and the fact that Zamora had only seen the creatures in the distance. He had not interacted with them, he claimed no telepathic communications with them, and he didn't suggest they had been there to abduct him. He only reported seeing the craft, briefly on the ground, and only reported a quick look at the two, small, humanoid creatures that scurried back into it.

The Air Force file on the Flatwoods, West Virginia sighting of September 12, 1952, however, is quite different. Like the Zamora case, it contains a project card, a form created at ATIC that holds a brief summary of the sighting, what the solution is, if one has been offered, and other such easily condensed data. Unlike the Zamora case, the Air Force found a solution. According to the project card for the Flatwoods sighting there is the notation that the case was solved by the meteor that had been reported over the east coast of the United States on September 12.

The file contains one other piece of important information. It is just a single sheet of paper with some information about the object seen and a notation that it was a meteor. There is nothing in the file to suggest that anyone saw creatures, that the Air Force attempted to learn more about those sightings, or that any sort of official investigation was made.

In fact, the only reference to anything suggesting a creature was on the Project Card where there is the note about the "West Virginia monster, so called." All other notes suggest that the case was inspired by a meteor.

This presents a curious problem. Clearly the Air Force had heard of the case, and just as clearly, they had written it off as a very bright meteor that had been reported over the eastern seaboard on September 12. There is also a note that the meteor (or meteorite for those of a precise and technical nature) landed somewhere in West Virginia. Apparently, the Air Force believed that the "landing" of the meteorite was enough to inspire local residents to imagine a creature on the ground. And, apparently, they believed that the meteorite would account for the reports of physical evidence.

The Flatwoods Monster

Ufologist and biologist Ivan T. Sanderson, writing in his UFO book, *Uninvited Visitors,* was aware of both the Air Force explanation and the meteorite that had been reported. Sanderson wrote:

Ivan T. Sanderson

...we met two people who had seen a slow-moving reddish object pass over from the east to west. This was later described and 'explained' by a Mr. P.M. Reese of the Maryland Academy of Sciences staff, as a 'fireball meteor.' He concluded - incorrectly we believe - that it was 'traveling at a height of from 60 to 70 miles' and was about the 'size of your fist.'... However, a similar, if not the same object was seen over both Frederick and Hagerstown. Also, something comparable was reported about the same time from Kingsport, Tennessee, and from Wheeling and Parkersburg, West Virginia.

The whole story, as it is usually told, begins with several boys playing on a football field in Flatwoods, West Virginia. About 7:15 p.m., a bright red light, described as large as an outhouse, "rounded the corner of a hill" crossed the valley, seemed to hover above a hilltop and then fell behind the hill. One of the boys, Neal Nunley, said that he thought the glowing object might have been a meteorite. He knew that fragments of meteorites were collected by scientists, so he suggested they all go look for it.

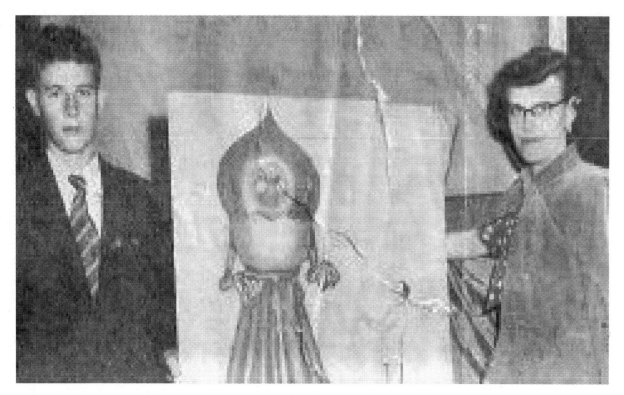
Gene Lemon and Kathleen May with drawing of the monster.

As they watched, there was a bright orange flare that faded to a dull cherry glow near where the object had disappeared. As three of the boys started up the hill, toward the lights, they saw them cycle through the sequence a couple of times. The lights provided a beacon for them, showing them where the object was.

They ran up the main street, crossed a set of railroad tracks and came to a point where there were three houses, one of them belonging to the May family. Kathleen May came out of the house to learn what was happening and where the boys were going. Told about the lights on the hill, and that "A flying saucer has landed," she said that she wanted to go with them. Before they left, May suggested that Eugene Lemon, a seventeen-year-old member of the National Guard (which has no real relevance to the story, but is a fact that is always carefully reported) went to look for a flashlight.

They found the path that led up the hill, opened, and then closed a gate, and continued along the winding path. Lemon and Nunley were in the lead with May, her son Eddie, following, and they were trailed by others including Ronald Shaver and Ted Neal. Tommy Hyer was in the rear, not far behind the others.

161

As they approached the final bend in the path, Lemon's large dog, which had been running ahead, began barking and howling, and then reappeared, running down the hill, obviously frightened. Lemon noticed, as the dog passed him, that a mist was spreading around them. As they got closer to the top of the hill, they all smelled a foul odor. Their eyes began to water.

Kathleen May spotted something in a nearby tree. She thought they were the eyes of an owl or other animal. Nunley, who was carrying the flashlight, turned it toward the eyes. What they saw was not an animal, but some sort of creature. The being was large, described as about the size of a full-grown man to the waist. They could see no arms or legs but did see a head that was shaped like an ace of spades. No one was sure if there were eyes on the creature, or if there was a clear space on the head, resembling a window, and that the eyes were somehow behind the that window and behind the face.

Lemon reacted most violently of the small party when he saw the object. He passed out. There was confusion, they were all scared, and no one sure what to do. The boys grabbed the unconscious Lemon and then ran.

They finally reached May's house. Inside, they managed to bring Lemon back to full consciousness. They called others, and a number of adults arrived at the May house. The group, armed with rifles and flashlights, headed back up the hill, to search for the strange creature. None of the men seemed to be too excited about going up the hill, and in less than a half an hour, they were back, claiming they had found nothing at all.

Still others, including the sheriff, eventually arrived. Most of them didn't bother to mount any sort of search, and the sheriff, who was clearly skeptical, refused to investigate further than talking to May and the boys. Two newspaper reporters did, at least, walk up the hill, but they saw nothing. They did, however, note the heavy, metallic odor that had been described by the May and her group.

The next day, there were some follow-up investigations. Some people reported that they had found an area where the grass had been crushed in a circular pattern. Sanderson, who visited the scene a week later, said that he and his fellow investigators, were able to see the crushed grass and a slight depression in the ground.

Sanderson pointed out that the other physical evidence that had been reported, skid marks on the ground, an oily substance on the grass, and the foul odor, might have been part of the environment. The type of grass growing wild in that area gave off a similar odor and the grass seemed to be the source of the oil.

Sanderson said that he couldn't find the skid marks and knew of no one who had photographed them.

When this story is reported, it always seems to end here, with the one group, led by May and Lemon, seeing the strange creature or entity. The investigations, carried out by various civilian agencies always fails to find any proof. Many believe that if there was some corroboration, if someone else, not associated with May and her group, had seen the creature, it would strengthen the report. Several years later, a men's magazine carried another report about the Flatwoods monster. Paul Lieb wrote that George Snitowski, who was driving in the Flatwoods area that night with his wife, Edith, saw something on the ground.

Corroboration for Flatwoods?

Snitowski didn't tell his story until two or three years after the fact. He then told it to an officer of the Flying Saucer Research Institute who published the account in the magazine. Looking at it from that point of view, that is, a tale told long after the national publicity that was provided for May and the others, there certainly is the hint that Snitowski was influenced by those tales. There is no proof he was, only the very real possibility.

Snitowski was, according to his story, returning home with his wife and their baby when, near Sutton, West Virginia, which is not far from Flatwoods, his car engine stalled. He tried but couldn't get it to start and because it was getting dark, he didn't want to leave his wife and baby alone on the semi-deserted highway. He thought they would wait for morning, and then he would walk the ten or twelve miles to the closest town, if someone didn't come along to give them a hand before then.

Snitowski said that a foul odor began to seep into the car's interior making the baby cry. Snitowski didn't know what this odor was but suspected it might be a sulfur plant nearby burning waste. It was then that a bright light flashed overhead and both Snitowski and his wife were confused by it. He said later, that looking down, into the woods, he could see what he thought of as some kind of dimly lighted sphere.

Snitowski finally got out of the car and started walking toward some nearby woods where he believed the earlier light flash had originated. Inside the tree line sat the sphere. As he moved deeper into the woods, closer to the sphere, he said that his legs began to tingle, almost as if they had gone to sleep. Slightly sickened by a foul odor, barely able to walk, he began to retreat, heading toward the car.

His wife screamed, and Snitowski yelled, "Edith, for God's sake. What's the matter?"

She was unable to speak and Snitowski saw, leaning against the hood of the car, a strange creature. He couldn't see it well because of the lack of lighting around the area, but he thought it was eight or nine feet tall, was generally shaped like a human, with arms and a head attached to a bloated body.

Snitowski reached the car, climbed in, and grabbed a kitchen knife that he had in the glove box. He forced his wife down, to the floor and begged her to silence the crying, and frightened, baby. He didn't know what to do and said that the odor was now overpowering. But then, out of the corner of his eye, he saw the object, the sphere, beginning to climb erratically into the sky. It stopped to hover several times, suddenly it swooped downward, climbed upward in a bright, dazzling light, and vanished. When he looked outside the car, the creature was gone too.

Not knowing why, Snitowski tried to start the car now that the object was gone. Without trouble the engine started. They drove away, found a motel and checked in. The next morning, they heard about the sighting from Flatwoods, but neither wanted to tell authorities what they had seen. Snitowski said that he didn't want his friends and neighbors to think that he was crazy. Besides, he didn't have any evidence about the creature or the UFO. There was only his story, corroborated by his wife, which wouldn't help all that much.

If his story is true, and there is no way, today, to learn if it is, then it makes a nice corroboration for the Flatwoods case. The problem, however, and as outlined earlier, is that the Flatwoods report was national news the day after it happened. At that point, the case was contaminated because an investigator could never be sure that Snitowski, or anyone else who came forward with a report, hadn't been primed by the story as published in the newspapers or was seen on television.

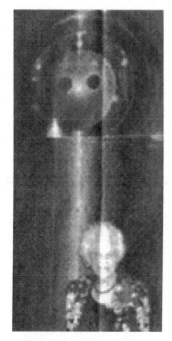

Older Kathleen May and monster drawing.

These two reports, by May and those with her and Snitowski were not the only ones made about that strange, tall, smelly, creature. About a week earlier, according to an investigation conducted by two Californians, William and Donna Smith, a twenty-one-year-old woman, who lived about eleven miles from Flatwoods, said that she had seen the creature that gave off the horrible odor. She was so upset by the encounter, that she was hospitalized for three weeks. Like Snitowski, she wasn't interested in publicity at the time, so when the report from Flatwoods made the news, she elected to remain silent.

Years later, in the mid-1990s, Kathleen May Horner, was interviewed about the sighting. She told investigators that the two men that everyone thought where newspaper reporters were, in fact, government agents. She also remembered that a local reporter received a letter from some unidentified government agency that revealed the creature was some sort of rocket experiment that had gone wrong that day. There had been four such "rockets" and all of them fell back to earth. The government agents were able to recover all but one, and that one, had been seen in Flatwoods. It must be noted here that there is no corroboration for this story of government intervention and that it did not surface until forty years later.

The Kelly-Hopkinsville Encounter

A somewhat similar event, involving strange lights and alien creatures, took place about three years later. Again, a group of people in a small town were confronted by very strange, alien creatures. Again, the Air Force would be aware of the sighting and again, they wouldn't bother to investigate. They would create an "information" only file at Project Blue Book. Two years later, as questions began to be asked and the case began to receive some national publicity, the Air Force would initiate a short investigation but apparently only so they would be able to answer questions, rather than actually attempt to learn anything about the sighting.

It was in August 1955, that the Sutton family, in the Kelly-Hopkinsville area of southern Kentucky, reported that their farmhouse had been assaulted by small alien creatures. The siege lasted through the night with the men shooting at the small beings with a number of weapons. Eventually the family deserted the farmhouse and drove the sheriff's office to tell the tale. Because a UFO had been seen, and because the creatures were apparently alien, there were those who believed that Project Blue Book would be involved in the investigation.

But, according to the case file, such as it is, Project Blue Book did not investigate. They had no real interest in the sighting, or in alien creatures, especially in 1955, although the Blue Book files do contain documents that suggest one active-duty officer, and possibly more, did some sort of investigation right after the event was reported on the radio. This investigation, however, was "unofficial," which allowed the Air Force to deny that they had initiated some sort of investigation.

Without any sort of physical evidence, or proof that the tale was true, most of the people who made their way into the area to interview the witnesses were quite skeptical. The media reflected that attitude. The Air Force, though still claiming there was no investigation, issued two statements. The Air Force told all that they were not investigating the case and that there was no basis for investigating it. In other words, the case was so unimportant that the Air Force wasn't going to waste its time or limited resources on a wild goose chase for alien creatures.

The story officially began early on the evening of August 21, 1955, when Billy Ray Taylor, a young friend of Elmer "Lucky" Sutton, had gone to the well behind the farmhouse, and came running back telling all that he had seen a flying saucer. The object, described as bright with an exhaust that contained all the colors of the rainbow, passed above the house. It continued over of the fields, finally came to a hover, and then descended, disappearing into a gully.

No one in the Sutton house, including Glennie Lanford, Lucky Sutton, Vera Sutton, John Charley (J.C) Sutton, Alene Sutton, three Sutton children, June Taylor and O.P. Baker, believed the story of the flying saucer. None of them considered walking out to the gully to see if something might be down there. The whole idea was preposterous.

Not long after Taylor told his tale, the dog began to bark. Taylor and Lucky Sutton went to investigate that, but the dog ran under the house, not to reappear that night.

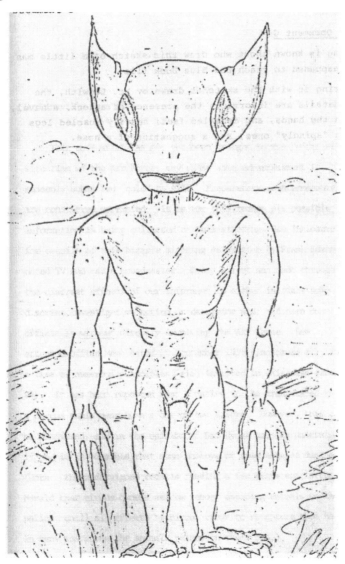

Alien as described by the witnesses.

Out in the fields, away from the house, was a strange, hovering glow. As it approached, they could see a "small man" inside it. He was about three and a half feet tall, with a large head that looked to be round, and long, thin arms that extended almost to the ground. The creature's hands were large and out of proportion with the body and were shaped more like a bird's talons than a human hand. The two eyes were large and seemed to glow with a yellow fire.

As the creature continued to move toward the house, the two men retreated, found a rifle and a shotgun inside, and then waited. When the creature was within twenty feet of the back door, both men fired at it. The creature flipped back, regained its feet and fled into the darkness.

The two men watched for a few minutes, searching for the creature and then walked into the living room where the others waited. The creature, or one just like it, appeared in front of one of the windows and the men shot at it, hitting it. This one also did a back flip and disappeared.

Now the men decided it was time to go out to learn if they had injured or killed the creature, or animal, or whatever it was. Taylor was the first out but stopped on the porch under a small overhang. A claw-like hand reached down and touched his hair. Alene Taylor grabbed him to pull him back into the house. Lucky, pushed past him, turned and fired up, at the creature on the roof. It was knocked from its perch.

Someone, probably Taylor, shouted, "There's one up in the tree."

Both Taylor and Lucky shot at it, knocking if from the limb. But it didn't fall to the ground. Instead, it seemed to float. They shot again, and it ran off.

At the same moment, another of the creatures appeared around the corner of the house. It might have been the one that had been on the roof or one of those seen in the backyard. Lucky whirled and fired. The buckshot sounded as if it hit something metallic like an empty bucket. Just as had the others, the little creature flipped over, scrambled to its feet and fled, running into the darkness.

Having failed to stop the creatures with either the shotguns or the .22 caliber rifle, Lucky decided to leave them alone. Someone noticed that the creatures only approached from darkened areas. It seemed that they were repelled by the light.

At some point they heard noises on the roof and went out the back door to investigate. One of the creatures was back on the roof. They shot at it, knocked it off the roof, but it floated to a fence some forty feet away rather than falling to the ground. Hit by another shot, it fell from the fence and ran away, seeming to use its arms to aid its locomotion.

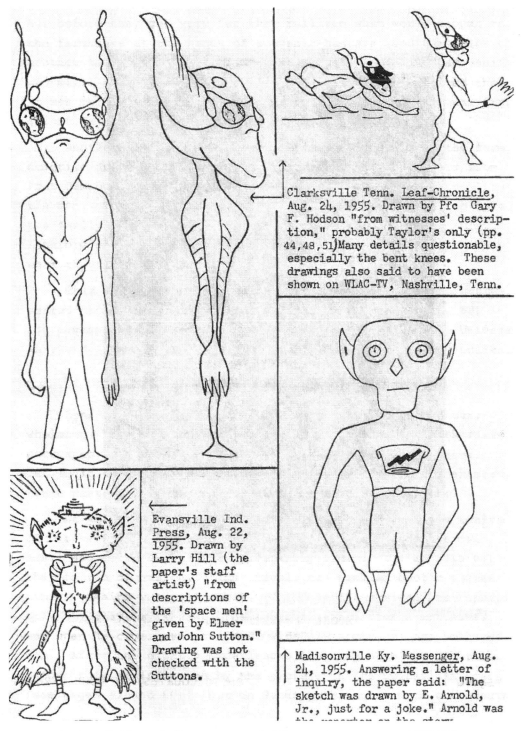

Clarksville Tenn. Leaf-Chronicle, Aug. 24, 1955. Drawn by Pfc Gary F. Hodson "from witnesses' description," probably Taylor's only (pp. 44,48,51)Many details questionable, especially the bent knees. These drawings also said to have been shown on WLAC-TV, Nashville, Tenn.

Evansville Ind. Press, Aug. 22, 1955. Drawn by Larry Hill (the paper's staff artist) "from descriptions of the 'space men' given by Elmer and John Sutton." Drawing was not checked with the Suttons.

Madisonville Ky. Messenger, Aug. 24, 1955. Answering a letter of inquiry, the paper said: "The sketch was drawn by E. Arnold, Jr., just for a joke." Arnold was

A compilation of aliens reported. Illustration courtesy CUFOS.

169

Some of the others in the house were still unconvinced that there were real creatures outside, believing instead, that the boys were playing some sort of a prank on them. With the lights in the house turned out, they had taken up a position close to one of the windows. Taylor told Lankford to wait, and she would see for herself.

After twenty minutes or so, one of the creatures approached the front of the house. According to Lankford, it looked like a five-gallon gasoline can with a head on top of two thin, spindly legs. It shimmered as if made of bright metal.

Lankford, who had been crouching quietly near the window for a long time, tried to stand, but fell with a thud. She shrieked in surprise and the creature jumped to the rear. Taylor fired at it through the screen door.

About three hours after the first creature had been seen about 11:00 that night, they decided it was time to get out. Everybody ran to the cars. One of the kids was screaming and had to be carried. They all raced to the Hopkinsville police station for help.

At the police station, there was no doubt that the people had been frightened by something. Police officers, and the chief, interviewed after the events, made it clear they believed the people had been scared. That doesn't mean they were "attacked" by strange little metallic men but does mean they were relating what they believed to be the truth to the assembled police officials.

Within minutes, the police were on their way back to the house, with some of the Sutton men in the cars. The police also called the Madisonville headquarters of the Kentucky State Police. A call was even made to the chief, Russell Greenwell, at home. He was told that a spaceship had landed at Kelly. Greenwell then told the desk sergeant that it had better not be a joke.

There were now Kentucky State Police, local police, the Chief, and a sheriff's deputy either heading out to the Sutton house, or already there. One of the state troopers, who was only a few miles from Hopkinsville, on the road to Kelly, said that he saw what he called several meteors flash over his car. They moved with a sound like artillery, and he looked up in time to see two of them. They were traveling in a slightly descending arc, heading toward the Sutton house.

The yard around the Sutton house was suddenly filled with cars, and more importantly light. The men tried to point out where the various events had taken place. The chief searched for signs that anyone or everyone had been drinking but found nothing to indicate that anyone had even a beer. Glennie Lankford later said that she didn't allow alcohol in the house.

Once the police arrived, the situation changed radically. Although the atmosphere seemed electrically charged, and some of the police were nervous, they began to search for signs of the invasion from outer space. There were apparent bullet and shotgun blast holes in the screens over the windows, and there was evidence that weapons had been fired, but there were no traces of the alien creatures. The hard packed ground did not take footprints.

The search of the yard and fields around the house revealed little, except a luminous patch where one of the creatures had fallen earlier and was only visible from one angle. The chief said that he saw it himself and there was definitely some kind of stain on the grass. There is no evidence that anyone bother to take samples for later analysis.

But with no real evidence to be found, with no alien creatures running around, and with no spacecraft hidden in the gully, the police began to return to their regular, mundane duties. By two in the morning, only the Suttons were left at the house.

A half an hour or so after the last of the police left, and with the lights in the house down, Glennie Lankford saw one of the creatures looking in the window. She alerted her son, Lucky, who wanted to shoot at it, but she told him not to. She didn't want a repeat of the situation earlier in the night. Besides, the creatures had done nothing to harm anyone during the first episode. They seemed harmless enough.

But Lucky didn't listen to her. He shot at the creature, but the shot was no more effective than those fired earlier in the night. Other shots were fired with no apparent affect. The little creatures bounced up each time they were hit and then ran away.

The little beings kept reappearing throughout the night, the last sighting occurring just a half an hour before sunrise. That was the last time that any of the beings were seen by any of the Suttons or their friends.

The Air Force Investigation

Although it seems that military personnel, from Fort Campbell, Kentucky, did visit the Sutton house, and interviews with the witnesses were conducted in 1955, an investigation by the Air Force didn't take place until two years later. According to Project Blue Book files, apparently, in August 1957, prior to the publication of a magazine article that would review the case, someone in the Air Force decided they should "investigate."

Campbell AFB, now Campbell Army Airfield is located at Fort Campbell.

In a letter from ATIC at Wright-Patterson, to the commander of Campbell Air Force Base, near Fort Campbell, Kentucky, Wallace W. Elwood wrote, "1. This Center requests any factual data, together with pertinent comments regarding an unusual incident reported to have taken place six miles north of Hopkinsville, Kentucky on subject date [21 August 1955]. Briefly, the incident involved an all-night attack on a family named Sutton by goblin-like creatures reported to have emerged from a so-called 'flying saucer.'"

Later in the letter, Elwood wrote, "3. Lacking factual, confirming data, no credence can be given this almost fantastic report. As the incident has never been officially reported to the Air Force, it has not taken official cognizance of the matter." Here, once again is the Air Force attitude that if the case has not been reported to them, no matter how widely it had been reported, then it simply didn't exist.

The matter was apparently assigned to First Lieutenant Charles N. Kirk, an Air Force officer at Campbell Air Force Base. He apparently spent about six weeks investigating the case before sending the material on to ATIC on October 1, 1957. He researched the story using the Hopkinsville newspaper from August 22, 1955, and September 11, 1955. He also had a letter from Captain Robert J. Hertell, a statement from Glennie Lankford, one of the witnesses, and a statement given to Kirk by Major John E. Albert about his involvement in the case, and a copy of an article written by Glennie Lankford.

Albert's statement provides some interesting information. Remember, the Air Force was claiming that the case had not been officially reported and therefore the Air Force had not investigated. It seems that here we get lost in the semantics of the situation and the question that begs to asked is, "What the hell does all that mean?"

It sounds like a police officer who, seeing a robbery in progress, then ignores it because it hadn't been reported to the station and he wasn't dispatched by headquarters. A police officer can't ignore the crime and it seems reasonable to assume that the Air Force shouldn't have ignored the story. The sighting was outlined in the media including the radio broadcasts, and newspapers from various locations around the country were reporting what had happened. Although the Air Force officers at Blue Book or ATIC must have known that the sighting had been made, they chose to ignore it. If the sighting wasn't reported through official channels, directly to them, then it simply didn't exist. Since no one reported this case through official channels, the sighting could be ignored.

Or was it? Lieutenant Kirk, in his report in 1957, sent a copy of the statement made by Major John E. Albert on September 26, 1957, to ATIC. The very first paragraph seems to suggest that notification was made to Campbell Air Force Base which should have, according to regulations in effect at that time (1955), reported it in official channels, to ATIC and therefore Blue Book. The regulation is quite clear on the point, and it doesn't matter if everyone in the military believed the sighting to be a hoax, or if they thought the sighting too outrageous, it should have been investigated because the regulations required it.

That investigation would not have been conducted by ATIC and Project Blue Book but by the 4602d Air Intelligence Service Squadron. AFR 200-2 tells us exactly what should have happened to the report. It went on to the 4602d and apparently disappeared into some bureaucratic limbo there.

In the statement found by Kirk, Albert said, "On about August 22, 1955, about 8 A.M., I heard a news broadcast concerning an incident at Kelly Station, approximately six miles North of Hopkinsville. At the time I heard this news broadcast, I was at Gracey, Kentucky, on my way to Campbell Air Force Base, where I am assigned for reserve training. I called the Air Base and asked them if they had heard anything about an alleged flying saucer report. They stated that they had not, and it was suggested that as long as I was close to the area, that I should determine if there was anything to this report. I immediately drove to the scene at Kelly [for some reason the word was redacted, but it seems reasonable to assume the word is Kelly] Station and located the home belonging to a Mrs. Glennie Lankford [again the name is redacted], who is the one who first reported the incident. (A copy of Mrs. Lankford's statement is attached to this report)."

Albert's statement continued:

> Deputy Sheriff Batts was at the scene where this supposedly flying saucer had landed and he could not show any evidence that any object had landed in the vicinity. There was nothing to show that there was anything to prove this incident.

> Mrs. Lankford was an impoverished widow woman who had grown up in this small community just outside of Hopkinsville, with very little education. She belonged to the Holly Roller Church and the night and evening of this occurrence, had gone to a religious meeting and she indicated that the members of the congregation and her two sons and their wives and some friends of her sons', were also at this religious meeting and were worked up into a frenzy, becoming emotionally unbalanced and that after the religious meeting, they had discussed this article which she had heard about over the radio and had sent for them from the Kingdom Publishers, Fort Worth 1, Texas and they had sent her this article with a picture which appeared to be a little man when it actually was a monkey, painted silver. This article had to be returned to Mrs. Lankford as she stated it was her property. However, a copy of the writing is attack to this statement and if it is necessary, a photograph can be obtained from the above-mentioned publishers.

There are a number of problems with the first couple of paragraphs of Albert's statement, but those are trivial. As an example, it wasn't Glennie Lankford who first reported the incident, but the whole family who had traveled into town to alert the police.

It is the third paragraph, however, that is filled with things that bear no resemblance to reality. Lankford was not a member of the Holly Rollers, but was, in fact a member of the Trinity Pentecostal. Neither she, nor any of the family had been to any religious services the night of the "attack." This unsubstantiated allegation was made in a recent book, suggesting, once again, that the religious tone of the family had somehow contributed to the attack on their house. Or rather, that they were "hysterical" people who would see things that simply were not there.

And, Lankford couldn't have heard about any "article" from the newspapers or magazines as it was read on the radio because there was no radio in the farmhouse. And there was no evidence that Lankford ever sent anywhere for any kind of article about flying saucers and little creatures, those painted silver or any other color. In other words, Albert had written the case off as a hoax, almost before he began his "investigation" because of his false impressions. Apparently, he was only interested in facts that would allow him to debunk the case and not learning what had actually happened.

Further evidence of this is provided in the next paragraph of Albert's statement:

> It is my opinion that the report Mrs. Lankford or her son, Elmer Sutton [name redacted but it is reasonable to assume it was Elmer Sutton], was caused by one of two reasons. Either they actually did see what they thought was a little man and at the time, there was a circus in the area and a monkey might have escaped, giving the appearance of a small man. Two, being emotionally upset, and discussing the article and showing pictures of this little monkey, that appeared like a man, their imaginations ran away with them, and they really did believe what they saw, which they thought was a little man.

It is interesting to note that Albert is not suggesting that Lankford, the Suttons, and the Taylors (other members of the family present that night) were engaged in inventing a hoax. Instead, with absolutely no evidence, Albert invented the tale of an escaped monkey that fooled the people. That does not explain how the monkey was able to survive the shots fired at it, especially if it was as close to the house as the witnesses suggested. In other words, with shotguns and rifles being fired, someone should have hit it and there should have been broken bits of monkey all over the farmland. And remember, the various witnesses talked of a number of little men, not a single individual.

But Albert wasn't through with the little monkey theory. "The home that Mrs. Lankford lived in was in a very run-down condition and there were about eight people sleeping in two rooms. The window that was pointed out to be the one that she saw the small silver shining object about two and a half feet tall, that had its hands on the screen looking in, was a very low window and a small monkey could put his hands on the top of it while standing on the ground."

The final sentence said, "It is felt that the report cannot be substantiated as far as any actual object appearing in the vicinity at that time." It was then signed by Kirk.

What is interesting is that Albert, and then Kirk, were willing to ignore the report of the object because there was nothing to substantiate it, other than the witness testimony that there had been an object. Both Albert and Kirk were willing to buy the monkey theory, though there was nothing to substantiate it either. They needed a little man, or at the very least, a little humanoid creature for the family to see and they created one because a "monkey might have escaped."

Glennie Lankford might have inspired the little monkey story with her own words. In a handwritten statement signed on August 22, 1955, said, "My name is Glennie Lankford age 50 and I live at Kelly Station, Hopkinsville Route 6, Kentucky. She continued:

> On Sunday night Aug 21, 55 about 10:30 P.M. I was walking through the hallway which is located in the middle of my house, and I looked out the back door (south) and saw a bright silver object about two and a half feet tall appearing round. I became excited and did not look at it long enough to see if it had any eyes or move. I was about 15 or 20 feet from it. I fell backward, and then was carried into the bedroom.

> My two sons, Elmer Sutton aged 25 and his wife Vera age 29, J.C. Sutton age 21 and his wife Aline aged 27 and their friends Billy Taylor age 21 and his wife June 18 were all in the house and saw this little man that looked like a monkey.

So, the Air Force, which, of course, didn't investigate sightings of creatures, seized on her description and turned it into a possible solution, suggesting, with no justification that the Suttons had been attacked by a horde of monkeys which were immune to shotguns. They overlooked the evidence of the case, or ignored the testimony, dispatched someone to look into it unofficially at the time, and then denied that they had ever investigated.

That was the pattern they would follow with almost every case in which alien beings were reported. If the witness said that he or she saw the alien creatures, then clearly there were psychological problems with that witness. They attempted to avoid investigations into those tales of alien beings, pretending, when they could, that such reports didn't exist especially if they could claim that had not been officially reported.

The Pittsburg, Kansas Sighting

On September 24, 1952, a "confidential" Report of Investigation was forwarded by the Office of Special Investigation concerning UFO landing on August 25, near Pittsburg, Kansas. Although there was a single witness to the landing and sighting of an occupant, there were landing traces seen by others during the investigation. Soil samples were taken and forwarded to Wright-Patterson AFB for analysis. When the investigation was closed by Lieutenant Colonel Leon F. Bugh, there was no explanation for the sighting.

According to the Project Blue Book files, the witness left home about 5:30 in the morning, driving on a rough gravel road. William Squyers was on his way to work along Highway 160 about 8 miles from Pittsburg when he "noted the unknown object off to the right side of the road... at a distance of about two hundred fifty (250) yards."

He could see the UFO thought the passenger's door window. He slowed and stopped the car, attempting to keep the UFO in sight. As he got out of his car, the UFO began a rapid ascent, disappearing in about thirty seconds. Squyers said that when the object reached a height "about as high as an airplanes flies" the object accelerated suddenly at a fantastic speed and disappeared up, into the clouds. At the time it took off, Squyers thought he was about a hundred yards from the craft.

According to the report, "Squyers described the object as platter shaped; by this he said it looked like two (2) platters or bowls had been put together by reversing one platter and placing it over the first one. He estimated it was about seventy-five (75) feet long and forty (40) feet wide and about fifteen (15) feet through the mid-section."

Squyers said that the UFO was hovering, about ten feet off the ground when he first saw it. He then, according to the report, offered more details about the craft, telling the investigator:

> "It was a dull aluminum color; smooth surface; one window in front section with head and shoulders visible of one man sitting

motionless facing forward edge of the object, clear glass, light in forward section, medium blue continuous light. In the mid-section of object were several windows extending from top to near edge of object; mid-section of ship had a blue light which gradually changed to different shades. There was a large amount of activity and movement in mid-section which could not be identified as being human as it did not have a regular pattern of movement such as mechanical object would make in the bule light. There were no windows doors, portholes, vents, seams, etc., visible to observer in ear section of object or under the object (viewed at time of ascent). Another identifiable feature was that along the outer edge of object, there were a series of propellers about six (6) to seven (7) inches in diameter, spaced closely together, these propellers were mounted on a bracket, so they revolved in a horizontal plane along the edge of the object. The propellers were revolving at a high rate.

This seems to be the type of sighting the Air Force would dismiss as "psychological" which would be a nice way of saying that it was a hoax or there was something wrong with the witness. However, there was some physical evidence left behind. According to the Project Blue Book report:

Object reported as hovering over an open field used for cattle grazing. General area under the exact location was pressed down and formed a round 60' diameter impression, with the grass in a recognizable concentric pattern. Loose grass lay over the top of the impression as if drawn in by suction when the object ascended vertically at a high speed. Vegetation and grass approximately 3 to 4' high. Area us extremely dry at present. Grass showed where Squyers had walked into a fence and stopped. L. V. Baxter and D. Widner, local employees of KOMA, went to the place of sighting at 1135CST with Squyers and confirmed his path to the fence and the 60' diameter impression in the tall grass. Robert E. Greene visited the site at 1600, 25 Aug 52, with source and reports that the vegetation was laid down in concentric circles but with the impression less distinct than reported by Widner and Baxter. Greene obtained grass and soil samples of the immediate area where the impression was made and also gathered control samples

200 yards removed from the site. He is sending some to the Air Technical Intelligence Center, Air Mail, Special Delivery.

What is probably the strangest aspect of this case is the fact that there seemed to be little interest in the pilot of the craft. Although there is another point where he was discussed, there is no real addition to the information. Clearly, based on these descriptions, that alien was human, or human enough to be indistinguishable from a human. Squyers did suggest that the occupant seemed to be frenzied in his activities inside the craft while he was in view.

Although this case is essentially single witness, there was the physical evidence left by the craft. Others, Baxter, Widner and Greene did see the impressions in the ground left by the UFO. Eventually this sort of evidence would become known as a saucer nest, meaning simply, that the crushed vegetation left by a UFO on the ground had somewhat similar features in common with some sorts of nests built by animals or birds. The ultimate description, in the world today, would be of a crop circle. Here, rather than an elaborate design it was a simple circle of crushed or flattened grass.

The soil samples taken by Greene were analyzed by the Air Force. In a short report of a single paragraph, the technicians said they had found no radiation, burning or stress of any kind. In other words, there was nothing in the samples to distinguish those taken from the landing area from those taken 200 yards away.

There is one final aspect to the case that it mildly interesting. In a couple of the letters from the government files there is a notation that reminds all of paragraph seven which is a paragraph in regulations that requires unidentified cases to be classified. Those who have information about the case are not allowed to discuss it with those who do not have the proper clearances and certainly not with members of the news media or the general public.

J. Allen Hynek, writing in *The Hynek UFO Report*, provides a glimpse into the thinking at Blue Book at the time of this sighting. He wrote, "My skepticism was so great at that time that I was quite willing to dismiss it as a hallucination."

Or, in other words, he was willing to reject the physical evidence that something had landed, he was willing to reject the observations of the three other men who had seen the depressions left in the grass because he didn't believe that such things were possible. In the 1970s he modified that belief, suggesting that he was willing to believe that the witnesses to such events, meaning UFO landings, sincerely believed they had a real experience, which, of course, is not to say that a UFO had landed.

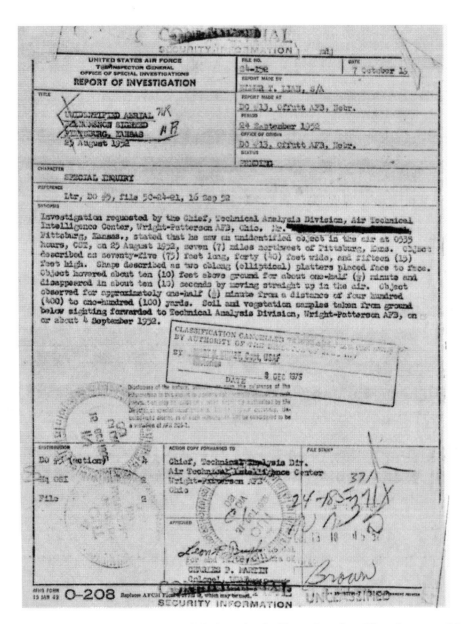

Blue Book document about the sighting, including the classification markings.

Even with that admitted bias against, the case, which never received wide exposure, is another in which the witness said that he had seen the pilot of an unidentified craft and that was left as unidentified by the Air Force. In their zeal to label cases, this seems to be another that they missed. They could have easily labeled it as "psychological" if not for those darned landing traces.

And the problem here, in Flatwoods, as well as in Kentucky, was that there was no corroborating physical evidence. The tales, told by multiple witnesses were interesting, even sensational, but were without any sort of corroborating proof.

Oddly, with the Pittsburg case, there was corroborating physical evidence, but no additional witnesses. There were those who saw the flatten grass, but the soil samples didn't reveal anything of an extraordinary nature. The physical evidence suggested that Squyers had seen something strange, but that didn't prove it was of alien origin, especially with the very human looking crew member.

We are left here, as we so often are, with cases that had potential but just didn't quite make it. Multiple witnesses but no physical evidence. Physical evidence but only one witness. If it all could come together in a single package, then we might change to course of the conversation.

Chapter Thirteen: The Pictures

During the month of July 1952, there were many reports that citizens had taken pictures of flying saucers and a few suggesting that military officers had taken motion picture footage including gun camera film made during attempted intercepts. The most spectacular of that movie footage was taken on July 2 by Delbert C. Newhouse, but the objects in the short film were little more than blobs of bright, white light seen in the distance. Four weeks later an Air Force major would use the gun cameras on his interceptor to take a short film of a sphere high above him, but again, that footage was less than spectacular.

Although there would be rumors about the movie footage, they would not be available to the general public for years. The still pictures made in 1952, however, would be printed almost the moment they were taken and developed. These still photographs, offered by a wide variety of people, both in the United States and in other parts of the world, suggested that the 1952 wave was not localized. People from around the world were seeing flying saucers, and a large number of them were taking photographs.

The Brazilian Disk

Among the first of the 1952 still photographs offered as physical evidence that UFOs were real and here was a series of five pictures taken on May 7, on a cliff near Barra De Tijuca, outside Rio de Janeiro, Brazil. Ed Keffel, along with another man, sometimes identified as his assistant, were taking pictures of the landscape when Keffel thought he saw an airplane in the distance. His friend, however, realizing that the object was not any kind of airplane he had ever seen, shouted, "Shoot! Shoot!"

According to Keffel, during the next sixty seconds he took five pictures of the object. In the first, the UFO, resembled an airplane coming directly toward them over a large group of trees. The second was taken showing that the object was disk shaped and proving that it was not a conventional aircraft. The third photo was taken as the object tilted slightly, showing both the top with a slight dome and the now obvious disk shape. More trees, including a very tall palm can be seen in the photograph. In the fourth picture, taken as the object tilted the other way, a raised ring on the bottom could be seen. Again, the disk shape is obvious.

The last picture was taken as the object was nearly vertical, seen over part of the ocean and some distant hills. The UFO disappeared shortly after this last picture was snapped.

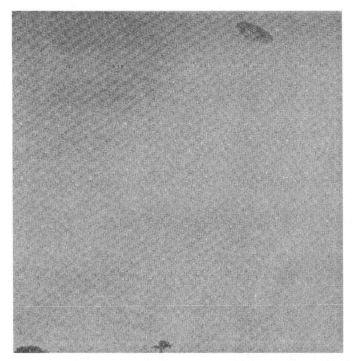

The most dramatic of the Keffel photographs. The tree at the bottom is important to understanding the picture.

According to the story that came out of Brazil and reported later by the Aerial Phenomena Research Organization (APRO), a civilian group interested in UFOs and based in the United States, the Brazilian Air Force became very interested in the report and the pictures. They interviewed the photographer, allegedly tracked down many of the estimated forty additional witnesses who were standing near Keffel and tried to learn something about the object based on measurements made from the pictures. For weeks Brazilian Air Force investigators tried to duplicate the images using trick photography. They made diagrams of the sighting, the location and the position of each of the witnesses. They searched for evidence of a hoax but in the end, according to the reports from Brazil, were unable to find it. They concluded, based partially on the corroboration of the forty witnesses, that this was not a hoax. Keffel had photographed something that was unknown and probably unearthly.

The APRO representative in Brazil, Dr. Olavo Fontes, forwarded a copy of his report, including the pictures and witness statements to the APRO headquarters. There, again, the photographs and statements were subjected to renewed scrutiny. The Brazilian Air Force claim of authenticity was seconded by APRO. APRO found no evidence of a hoax, but then, their pro-UFO stance might have colored their thinking.

The National Investigations Committee on Aerial Phenomena (NICAP) noted that the pictures had been taken by magazine writers Ed Keffel and Joao Martins. NICAP never received negatives for their scientific analysis but did exam prints provided to them. NICAP reported that "Critics have pointed out that in main photograph shadows on object do not coincide with shadows on the ground below." NICAP was suggesting here that there were internal inconsistencies in the photographs and such a finding was suggestive of a hoax. The NICAP representatives were not impressed with the pictures.

The bottom of the UFO.

That is the way the case stood for years. Upon the formation of the Condon Committee, those scientists on the project who wished to review the photographic form of physical evidence asked for copies of the Keffel pictures. All the information that APRO had collected was sent on to Colorado. In the end, the Condon Committee decided, as had NICAP, that there was a "glaring internal inconsistency." According to the committee, in the picture in which the top of the object is tilted toward the camera, the UFO is illuminated from one direction and the trees, specifically a very tall palm, is illuminated from another. According to the Condon scientists, "This is evidence of a hoax unless there were two suns in the sky." They dismissed the case as a hoax and therefore irrelevant.

Both APRO and Dr. Fontes had been aware of the problem. According to them,

\The tree with the improper shadows.

enlargements of the picture that showed the tree and the surrounding area revealed that a shadow cast by a damaged palm caused the problem. They reported that the palm tree's trunk appeared to be in the shade, meaning the sun was behind it and the shadows on the UFO showed the sun should have been in front of the tree. The trunk should be brightly illuminated by the sun. The enlargement, however, suggested that two branches on that tree had been broken and were hanging in such a way that they shaded the trunk. APRO researchers suggested the shadow was, more or less, an optical illusion.

According to the APRO analysis, enlargements of the surrounding area showed a dead tree without any branches on it. They suggested that the sunlight on the trunk of that tree was in the proper place. They suggested that this showed that the photographs were not faked.

184

Or rather, it showed that there were no internal inconsistencies, so the authenticity of the photographs could not be questioned for that reason.

That wasn't the end of the controversy, however. People living in the area reported they had seen a number of men with models of a flying saucer taking pictures. APRO said that the Brazilian Air Force had explained that easily. The men with the models were Air Force officers trying to duplicate the photographs. According to the report issued by APRO, they had failed.

Today, the best evidence seems to suggest the case is a hoax, perpetrated by two magazine writers who wanted an interesting story. By themselves, even if authentic, the pictures do not prove that UFOs are extraterrestrial. The pictures merely suggest that something unusual was seen flying above Brazil. The conclusion of hoax is not surprising, given both the attitudes of the investigators and the mission of the Condon Committee.

The New York Color Pictures

Oddly, with the Air Force attitude about UFO sightings, and their attempts to explain everything as conventional and mundane, the pictures taken some time between July 6 and 12, 1952, were labeled as unidentified rather than simply insufficient data for a scientific analysis. This is odd because there was no visual sighting, either by the photographer or by the millions of other residents of the New York City area. There were just the objects, or more accurately, the blobs of light, that appeared on the time exposures taken by an amateur photographer, identified only as Neff in the Project Blue Book files, in Elizabeth, New Jersey.

According to the report in the Project Blue Book files, the co-owner of the Mel-Art Photo, reported, "While scanning through the pictures which belonged to one of his customers, a group of four pictures came to his attention because of unusual unidentified objects which appeared in the sky. Since he was associated with the Air Technical Intelligence during World War II, he felt that the pictures may be of some interest to G-2... The pictures were taken by an amateur photographer by the name of Mr. [name redacted, but the last name is probably Neff] ..."

The pictures were taken about 11:00 p.m. sometime during the week of July 6-12. According to the report:

> His purpose in taking the pictures was to obtain photos of the moon and it was not until after the film was developed that he became aware of the objects. The initial picture, identified by three spots with trailing lines, was taken with the shutter open for ten

minutes. The second picture, identified by three spots, was taken with the shutter open for fifteen minutes. The third picture, identified by the presence of the moon with a spot mid-way between the moon and the treetops, was taken with the shutter open for twenty minutes. The last and final picture, identified by the presence of the moon with a spot appearing directly under and near the moon, was taken with the shutter open for twenty-three to twenty-five minutes.... The camera was mounted a tripod and the pictures were taken from the roof of his residence with the camera pointed in the general direction of Staten Island.

The project card listed the sighting as "unidentified." However, the picture showing the objects in motion, seem to be akin to something affecting the camera rather than the lights moving. In other words, it looks as if the tripod was bumped during the time exposure.

The pictures themselves reveal little, if anything, that is recognizable or of importance. Without a visual sighting, to help understand the circumstances of the report, it is surprising that the Air Force would label this case as an "unidentified." It would seem to be more properly placed into the "insufficient data" category.

Another photographic case, labeled as "unidentified" came into Project Blue Book. According to the letter that accompanied the pictures, the photographer [name redacted] "I have taken photos that I feel should be of great interest to your Dept.... I have taken these photos on July 9th and since that time I have tried to sell them to *Life* Magazine but to this date I have never heard from them. They [the photographs] have been run in the *Evening Chronicle*... Two of the photos show the object broadside and the other one shows it as though it was standing on end. It came right out of the sky and headed east. At that time, it stood on end and disappeared. Actually, it went so far out into space that I didn't see it anymore. It did not make any noise... and it had no propellor (sic) or other means of visible locomotive. It looked as though it was of an aluminum color."

The Coast Guard Photograph

The next photographic case of importance was the Utah movie shot by Newhouse and discussed elsewhere. It is important simply because it is a film and was shot by a Naval officer. The Coast Guard, not wanting to be left out, was involved in another of the important photographic cases of 1952.

The photographer, Shell Albert, was at work in a building at the Coast Guard installation in Salem, MA. According to the report filed with the Air Force, Shell said, "I turned slightly in the direction of the window and noticed something bright outside. I observed the sky and saw what appeared to be several bright - almost brilliant - lights slightly on the starboard side of the power plant smokestacks."

Full frame of the photograph.

He told the Air Force investigators that "I could not determine the size of the lights, number of lights, the altitude of the lights, the sound, if any, the speed of the lights, if any, direction of lateral or vertical motion [or the] shape of the lights. The temperature of the lights was a high number of Kelvin degrees - extremely brilliant and white. They seemed to be wavering, but I am not certain of this. I observed these lights for possibly 5 or 6 seconds and then turned [grab the] camera."

He moved toward the window. As he prepared to pull the slide from the camera, he noticed that the "lights were considerably dimmed down. I assumed at that what I had seen was merely some sort of reflection, but I rushed out of the lab into the Sick Bay and got [name redacted, but apparently it was Thomas Flaherty], to come back to the window with me. As I entered the office, I noticed the lights were again burning brightly and without saying anything to [name redacted] I dived for the camera and hit the shutter, after which I told him to look out and as he did there was a momentary flash, and we could no longer see the lights."

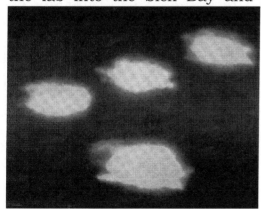

Enhanced version of the four lights.

Alpert suggested that "It was an extremely hot day and I think that perhaps some sort of refraction of ground reflections could possibly have accounted for the lights, but in my estimation, this is an improbable explanation. The lens was quite dirty and so was the window screen. I cannot in all honesty say that I saw objects or aircraft, merely some manner of lights."

Investigation by the Air Force, based on the stories told by the photographs and the hospital man, suggested that the lights were reflections of internal lights on the dirty windows. The Air Force investigation deemed the following points pertinent. The camera was set on infinity, and the cars in the parking lot are sharply focused but the lights are blurry and out of focus. All four lights have the same general configuration and outline in spite of the blurring. Of course, the cars in the parking lot were stationary and if the lights moved during the exposure, that would account for the blurry nature of the images on the film.

The Air Force also set up a number of bright spotlights so that they would be visible from the window where the photos were taken. Whenever they could be seen from the window, they produced reflections on the cars in the parking lot. Since the photograph of the objects showed no such reflections, the conclusion was that the lights were between the photographer and the lot, meaning that they almost had to be reflections on the dirty glass windows.

The Air Force, however, had another explanation. Colonel Delwin B. Avery, in a report to Ed Ruppelt at Blue Book wrote:

> Series D [pictures that the Air Force staged in their attempt to duplicate the photo] prints show how easy it is to construct a hoax by means of double exposure.... The film was multiply exposed at night, with a dark field surrounding the lamp. The daytime exposure of the building was carefully oriented to produce the aerial hovering effect. However, fraud is indicated because no highlights may be seen in the auto roofs.... It is therefore concluded that the authenticity of the picture, taken by the Coast Guard photographer, is open to serious doubt.

The Coast Guard, however, in response to an inquiry from NICAP reported, "...it never has been determined what caused the phenomenal lights shown [in the photograph]." In other words, the Coast Guard was not convinced that the Air Force had solved the sighting with their claim of dirty windows or a suggestion of fraud.

The George Stock Photographs

George Stock UFO photograph.

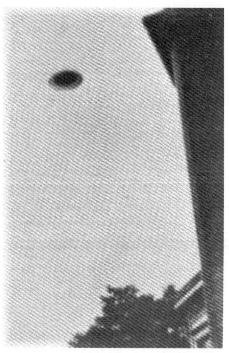

The most spectacular of the July 1952 pictures are probably those taken by George Stock in New Jersey. Because of the number of sightings reported during the summer, the official Air Force investigation began in late November 1952, when the officers assigned to Project Blue Book finally had the opportunity to look into the case. According to Charles Gregg, a staff writer for the *Herald-News* in Passaic, a man came into the office on the afternoon of July 31, 1952, with a series of pictures of a domed disc he had taken earlier in the day. The man, identified by some only as Riley, claimed he was visiting a friend and was talking to him in front of the house when the object appeared traveling "southwest at a leisurely speed. As it drew nearer it came to a stop overhead for a few minutes, about two hundred feet above the ground."

He described the disc as about thirty feet in diameter and greyish in color. It made no sound. Before taking off again, it tilted, "as to observe the ground. An antenna, or something like that darted out of the dome's top for a moment and was withdrawn." The saucer then disappeared.

Gregg, in a letter to the Air Force, said that Riley claimed there were other witnesses, but he hadn't the time to look for them. Riley wouldn't leave the negatives, and Gregg believed that he was taking them to other newspapers to sell.

Later that night, Riley appeared at another newspaper and a man named Dixon called the Air Technical Intelligence Center at Wright-Patterson AFB, Ohio, to let the Air Force know about the sighting.

Major Herman called Dixon back and asked about "the photograph of an aerial phenomena." Dixon responded:

That's about your way of putting it." He then went on to say, "Briefly, the story is this. A commercial photographer came in with the story that he was visiting a friend when the two of them saw the saucer overhead. The guy grabbed the friend's fixed focus camera and grabbed a half a dozen shots before the saucer moved away. He wanted to sell us the pictures. The pictures are phenomenally clear for anything of the sort... What it looks like, off-hand, is something very close to the camera because it is fairly sharp considering the type of camera used. On the other hand, the man swears, and he has one witness who will back him up, that it is a legitimate photograph... we have threatened him with jail and all that and he still insists that it was correct.

Dixon and Herman discussed the photographs for a few minutes more. Dixon reported that no one really knew the man so that he couldn't say whether or not he was credible. Dixon did say that he thought the pictures were too good to be true and was inclined to believe that they were a hoax, but he didn't seem to have any evidence.

After several minutes, Ed Ruppelt entered the conversation. All three of them, although neither Herman nor Ruppelt had seen the pictures, were afraid they were being duped. Ruppelt decided that it would be a waste of time to pursue it any further, based on what Dixon told him.

Even though they felt it was a poor case, they did initiate an investigation into the background of Riley. They learned that he ran a small commercial film processing business and that he didn't take pictures for a living. The people interviewed had nothing derogatory to say about Riley. The case was closed.

And then re-opened. It was learned that the man who had sold the pictures was not, in fact, the man who had taken them. On November 19, 1952, an Air Force investigator interviewed George Stock, after it was confirmed that he,

The best domed disk pictures

Stock was the real photographer. The story told by Stock was quite similar to the one told

by Riley. Stock had been outside about 10:15 on the morning of July 31, 1952, when he saw the object overhead. He ran into the house for a camera, shouting to his father, "I think I see a flying saucer."

Both men rushed into the backyard. Stock noticed the saucer was closer and he began taking pictures of it. He managed to get seven before the object disappeared in the southeast.

Air Force investigators learned that the sighting lasted between five and seven minutes. The sky was clear, and the temperature was in the mid-eighties. There were only two witnesses, Stock and his father. Riley, the man who had tried to capitalize on the photographs hadn't been there when the saucer was overhead, and only had the facts as Stock related them. He had seen nothing himself.

Late that afternoon, Stock took the pictures to Riley for processing. Stock stood by while Riley developed the film and then took the pictures and negatives, but not before Riley had made an extra set of prints, which he had tried to sell.

Subsequent investigation by the Air Force Office of Special Investigation reports showed that both Stock and his father were considered to be reliable men. The neighbors said that neither had ever participated in any type of a hoax. They were, for the most part, quiet men who caused no one any trouble.

Air Force investigation eventually led to the Federal Telephone and Radio Corporation in Clifton, New Jersey, which makes radar and microwave equipment. A check with the corporation president showed that no experiments were being conducted on the day of the sighting that could account for the strange pictures Stock took.

In the end, the Air Force could find nothing in Stock's background to suggest that he might have engineered the sighting or that he was inclined to invent tall tales. The AFOSI agent's report claimed that both Stock and his father were "honest, trustworthy and loyal American citizens."

The sighting, while questioned at first because of the clarity of the pictures, was unsolved. The Stocks were honest, and the negatives, five of which were examined by the Air Force, showed no signs of tampering. Without corroborating evidence, investigators were left with a sighting that was very good, but without the body of proof needed to make it a great sighting.

Late investigations, however, suggested that the case was, in fact, a hoax. The newspapers for July had been filled with stories of UFOs, and a few of the pictures taken elsewhere had been published. Stock's photos came out a period when everyone was talking about UFOs. The Air Force, because they had no other explanation for the pictures, labeled them as a hoax.

So, pictures supplied another form of evidence, but those offered in July 1952 left a great deal to be desired. They were either wrapped in controversy because of inconsistencies in them, or in the stories surrounding them, or they were of little real value because they failed to show any detail. In some cases, the photos could be of practically anything.

Chapter Fourteen: Aftermath

A panel of scientists, chaired by Dr. H.P. Robertson was the outgrowth of the summer wave of flying saucers sightings around the country and specifically over Washington in 1952. In fact, before the wave of sightings began to taper in late August, the CIA, aware of a potential intelligence problem involved with the UFO sighting reports began a series of informal discussions about them. These meetings were chaired by H. Marshall Chadwell, Assistant Director of Scientific Intelligence at the CIA. Chadwell, in fact, with Frederick Durant, apparently traveled to Wright-Patterson Air Force Base for a series of briefings about UFOs from the officers of Project Blue Book.

The CIA sponsored Robertson Panel in January 1953

In late September 1952, Chadwell sent a memo to General Walter Bedell Smith, at that time, the Director of Central Intelligence (DCI). Chadwell wrote, "Recently an inquiry was conducted by the Office of Scientific Intelligence to determine whether there are national security implications in the problem of 'unidentified flying objects,' i.e., flying saucers; whether adequate study and research is currently being directed to this problem in its relation to such national security implications; and what further investigation and research should be instituted, by whom, and under what aegis."

> It was found that the only unit of government currently studying the problem is the Directorate of Intelligence, USAF, which has charged the Air Technical Intelligence Center (ATIC) with the responsibility for investigating the reports of sightings... and major Air Force bases have been ordered to make interceptions of unidentified flying objects...

> [P]ublic concern with the phenomena indicates that a fair proportion of our population is mentally conditioned to the acceptance of the incredible. In this fact lies the potential for the touching-off of mass hysteria... In order to minimize risk of panic, a national policy should be established as to what should be told to the public regarding the phenomena.

It is easy to suspect that the CIA was suggesting that a cover up of the truth be implemented here. However, it can also be suggested that the CIA was concerned about intelligence matters that had little to do with UFOs. In other words, hysteria over the approach of an alleged UFO could set up a situation in which attention was diverted from a real threat, possibly of Soviet manufacture, to a threat that was illusionary. The CIA might be suggesting that public attention be diverted here, from the alleged problems of UFOs to the more real problems facing the United States in 1952.

Fred Durant

These meeting and discussions, about the potential problems, carried into the late fall of 1952, when Major Dewey Fournet, received a call from Frederick Durant, who would eventually be one of the lower ranking members of the panel. According what Fournet told me, "[He, Durant] asked me to make a presentation {about UFOs] to the CIA which I did. I gave them a few of my own opinions based on what I had observed [on July 26, 1952, and from the reports he had seen that had been forwarded to Project Blue Book] ... from that the idea of the Robertson Panel spawned. And Fred, through his superiors, convened it."

The meetings then, were a direct result of the summer's sightings, and the problems they had created in a number of arenas including the use of military fighters for the interceptions and the use of military communications channels for reporting of the hundreds of sightings. The major magazines including all the news magazines had carried stories about UFOs, not all of them suggesting that those who saw UFOs were fooled by the mundane seen under unusual conditions. To add to the pressure on the CIA, and the Air Force, was the fact that UFOs had played games in the skies over Washington, D.C. and that had caught the attention of President Truman. He had asked his military advisors for a few answers especially when Air Force interceptors had been unable to catch, or to identify the UFOs. The public, and the President, were well aware of that failure.

In December of 1952, just weeks before the group actually met, Chadwell decided the form the scientific advisory panel would take so they could study the ramifications of UFO sightings. Dr. Michael Swords, who carefully reviewed the history of the Robertson Panel, said that H.P. Robertson, who would eventually occupy the chair, had apparently accompanied Chadwell and Durant to Wright-Patterson Air Force Base. According to Swords, Robertson accepted the assignment of chairman against his will, but Chadwell had insisted. Chadwell wanted someone with scientific stature and Robertson fit that bill. Robertson, after accepting the chair, then had to "strong-arm" four others to join him in their so-called scientific evaluation of flying saucers, according to Swords' analysis of the situation.

Swords, having interviewed Dr. J. Allen Hynek, a participant in part of the panel's discussions as well as serving as the scientific consultant to Project Blue Book for nearly its entire existence, said:

> As far as Allen Hynek is concerned [these guys] have an immediate aura about the committee room that this thing is going to be debunked from the absolute beginning... [Committeemen Luis] Alverez and [Samuel] Goudsmit are saying nothing but hostile things [about flying saucers] and Goudsmit is also saying wiseass things... [Thorton] Page is more open minded. [Lloyd] Berkner is not there [having failed to arrive on time] ... Hynek had the feeling  that the panel members had already studied the cases that were going to be presented to them, or they simply had their minds made up before they sat down for the first meeting. In other words, the Panel was not designed to review the situation, as it had developed over the summer, but to end the public interest in UFOs and the complications that UFO sightings were causing the CIA and the Air Force.

Samuel Goudsmit

So, under the auspices of the CIA, and headed by Dr. H.P. Robertson, the panel convened on January 14, 1953, just a little over six months after the sightings at Washington National. According to Ruppelt, the first two days of meetings had been set aside for his review of the cases in the Blue Book files, and for the scientists to be briefed on the findings of Projects Sign, Grudge and Blue Book and the situation, as it existed currently at ATIC. Confidence in the explanations offered for some of the sightings studied by the panel ranged from known to possible, meaning that Ruppelt and his staff sometimes felt they had an answer but weren't positive about it.

The briefings to the panel included the intelligence security concerns and a brief history of the UFO project, though it would seem that Ruppelt could have provided a more comprehensive analysis of the situation at Wright-Patterson. Instead, that briefing was left to someone else. Ruppelt, as well as other members of Blue Book team did not attend the first days of the meetings. Once those areas, that is, the sighting reports and the investigations of them, had been discussed, Ruppelt and Hynek, and other observers were finally allowed into the meeting room, on Wednesday, all day Thursday and Friday.

Ruppelt, during his presentation, made it clear that much of the data was observational. These reports relied on the abilities of the witness to accurately estimate the size and speed of the object and provided other, sometimes complex data. Ruppelt wrote, "We could say only that some of the UFO's had been traveling pretty fast."

Objective data, such as that from radar sites, was available, but again, it was open to the interpretation of the radar operators. Ruppelt mentioned that the best cases from their files were those in which radar had tracked the objects at seven to eight hundred miles an hour. All those on the panel were aware that

Frame of the objects over Great Falls in 1950.

UFOs had been seen on radar over Washington, D.C., and given the situation at the time, would surely have been aware of the Air Force explanations offered for those sightings in General Samford's press conference at the end of July.

There was another motivation for the panel to meet, and something else that had to be considered. The word that impressive movie footage of UFOs had been taken had leaked into the public arena. One of the films had been taken about three years earlier, over Great Falls, Montana. It slowed two very bright objects, flying over some low buildings and then behind a water tower. No real shape could be seen in the lights as they silently crossed the sky.

The second film was that taken by Newhouse in July. This one was special, if only because it had been taken by a Naval officer who had been trained as a photographer. Swords has said that these UFO movies was one of the reasons that the panel was formed. The scientists wanted to see the movies. They were all very interested in the movies. Swords said, "As soon as they get finished with all the preliminary briefings, that's the only thing they want to do is look at the movies."

According to Ruppelt, the last day of meetings was reserved for a showing the films. That may not have been the best evidence that Blue Book had, but it was certainly the most spectacular. No one on the panel suggested that either the Newhouse film or the Montana movie were faked. But, in and of themselves, they proved nothing conclusively. Fournet said, "But you can knock out the sea gulls [as the explanation for the Tremonton film] and then where are you?"

It meant simply that one more mundane explanation for the film had been eliminated but that didn't lead directly to the extraterrestrial hypothesis. There was nothing on that film, or that shot in Montana, that allowed the extraterrestrial explanation to be positively put forward. The films might be interesting and might not be explained to the satisfaction of investigators, but that was all. Interesting, spectacular, unexplained, but not proof that Earth was being visited.

Swords said that the last afternoon, Friday, with Hynek invited to stay, was when Robinson was given, or took, the task of writing the final report. Swords said:

> I can't imagine that H.P. Robertson, a guy like him is going to sit down late into the evening and bang out a draft of the report on his own that somehow, mysteriously the next morning is already read by Lloyd Berkner and has already been taken by Marshal Chadwell to the Air Force directorate of intelligence and been approved. So, when they show up on Saturday, Robertson presents this draft to the rest of the committee and the rest of the committee does minor revisions... There are some remarks that are out of line that they decided are not going to be included.

According to Swords, "It seems an amazingly cut and dried deal that by the time Saturday shows up, here's this mildly to be revised draft that has already been seen by one of the other committee members who wasn't even there for the first two and a half days. It's already been seen by Chadwell and the U.S. Air Force."

Over the years, there are those who have claimed the Robertson Panel was a whitewash, but a thorough examination of the record suggests that Panel scientists did the best they could within the framework of their orders. They were not experts in the UFO phenomenon and there is no evidence that those forming the panel, that is, the CIA, wanted UFO experts to be offered a seat at the conference table. Those who joined the panel had not spent months or years investigating and reviewing the sighting reports. They spoke to no witnesses and the only evidence they saw were films that showed bright lights moving through the sky that could, unfortunately, be interpreted as almost anything. And, most importantly, they seemed to ignore the sightings that had been the motivation for the formation of the panel in the first place, meaning the series of radar reports and Air Force attempts at interception over Washington.

One other thing must be understood to keep the Robertson Panel in perspective. Their first concern was to determine if UFOs posed a threat to national security and not what had caused the sightings over Washington, D.C. The question of national security was one that they could answer. They decided, based on the number of UFO reports made inside official intelligence channels through the years, that UFOs did, after a fashion, pose a national security threat.

Dr. H. P. Robertson

Fournet mentioned it in his interview with me and Ruppelt mentioned it in his analysis of the whole UFO question. Too many reports at the wrong time could mask a Soviet attack on the United States. Although hindsight shows us this threat was of little importance, especially when the sorry state of Soviet missile research in 1952 is considered, it was a major concern to those men in the intelligence field in the early 1950s using the best intelligence they had. A sudden flood of UFO reports, not unlike what had happened during the summer of 1952, could create havoc in the message traffic so that critical messages of an imminent attack would be hidden or lost in the clutter.

With that as a concern, the Robertson Panel members, who had seen nothing to suggest that UFOs were anything other than misidentifications, hoaxes, and weather and astronomical phenomena, needed to address that concern. That was the motivation behind some of the panel's recommendations. These recommendations then, were born of a need to clear the intelligence reporting channels, and not of a need to answer the questions about the reality of the UFO phenomena or alien visitation.

The panel report stated:

> ...although evidence of any direct threat from these sightings was wholly lacking, related dangers might well exist resulting from: a. Misidentification of actual enemy artifacts by defense personnel. b. Overloading of emergency reporting channels with 'false'

information ('noise to signal ratio' analogy - Berkner). c. Subjectivity of public to mass hysteria and greater vulnerability to possible enemy psychological warfare...

Although not the concern of the CIA, the first two of these problems may seriously affect the Air Defense intelligence system, and should be studied by experts, possibly under ADC. It U.F.O.'s become discredited in a reaction to the 'flying saucer' scare, or if reporting channels are saturated with false and poorly documented reports, our capability of detecting hostile activity will be reduced. Dr. Page noted that more competent screening or filtering of reported sightings at or near the source is required, and that this can best be accomplished by an educational program.

Of all the suggestions in the panel report, this is the area that has caused the most trouble with interpretation. The panel was suggesting that if people were more familiar with what was in the sky around them, if they were familiar with natural phenomena that were rare but spectacular, then many sighting reports could be eliminated. How many UFO sightings are explained by Venus, meteors, or bright stars that seemed to hover for hours? In today's environment, with video cameras everywhere, how many times has Venus been taped and offered by witnesses as proof they saw something?

Under the subheading of "Educational Program," the panel recommended, "The Panel's concept of a broad educational program integrating efforts of all concerned agencies was that it should have two major aims: training and 'debunking.'"

The panel explained their thoughts, writing, "The training aim would result in proper recognition of unusually illuminated objects (e.g., balloons, aircraft reflections) as well as natural phenomena (meteors, fireballs, mirages, noctilucent clouds). Both visual and radar recognition are concerned. There would be many levels in such education...This training should result in a marked reduction in reports caused by misidentified cases and resultant confusion."

The problem with the next paragraph came from the use of the word "debunking." Many read something nefarious into it, while the use of it, and the tone of the paragraph suggest something that was, at the time, fairly innocuous, at least according to Condon sixteen years later:

The 'debunking' aim would result in reduction in public interest in 'flying saucers' which today evokes a strong psychological reaction.

This education could be accomplished by mass media such as television, motion pictures, and popular articles. Basis of such education would be actual case histories which had been puzzling at first but later explained. As in the case of conjuring tricks, there is much less stimulation if the 'secret' is known. Such a program should tend to reduce the current gullibility of the public and consequently their susceptibility to clever hostile propaganda. The Panel noted that the general absence of Russian propaganda based on a subject with so many obvious possibilities for exploitation might indicate a possible Russian official policy.

They then discussed the planning of the educational program. Some have seen that as a "disinformation" program designed to explain UFOs as mundane. The real reason behind it, however, seems to be to end sighting reports made by those who are unfamiliar with the sky above them. The educational program was suggested as a teaching tool.

Seventeen years later, Edward Condon would address a similar concern. He wanted an educational program that would discourage interest in UFOs. Again, he wasn't addressing the problem of the reality of the situation but was concerned with a symptom of it. The code words were education, but the result would be the same. They could hide the truth about UFOs behind the cloak of superior education, convincing the unenlightened that flying saucers were the realm of the unschooled, the ignorant, and the drunk. It is a policy that seems to have worked, based on public stereotypes of those who see UFOs.

Analysis

The UFO information presented, according to those who were at some or all of the panel's sessions, was stage managed and had little to do with the situation that had developed over the summer of 1952. They had a limited time and were unable to examine all aspects of the UFO field in the time they had. It can be suggested that a careful management of the data supplied would provide a biased picture and that the conclusions drawn from that specific data would be accurate, but those conclusions would be skewed. It could be argued that the panel was designed specifically so that time would not allow those embarrassing questions to be asked. And it can be suggested that panel was loaded with scientists who had already made up their minds about the reality of UFOs and wouldn't be asking those embarrassing questions.

It could also be suggested that the panel, whose formation might have been the result of President Truman's desire for answers, would be presented, instead to President Eisenhower. Truman's administration ended in January 1953, replaced by that of Eisenhower. The panel was not reporting for the man who had asked for answers from the White House, but one who had been campaigning during the critical time of July 1952.

The question then becomes, was someone in the government confident enough in his own abilities to micromanage the data that he could influence the conclusions. Could he be sure that there wouldn't be a wild card on the table that might jerk his carefully prepared plan off the rails? The study was going to be classified so the potential damage was limited to those high up in the government for a time. But what would happen if the study concluded that UFOs were from other planets and that information leaked into the public arena?

It seems to be a very big risk to undertake. It also implies that there was someone at the top managing these things who was smart beyond description. If someone conceived of this plan as a way of convincing the vast majority of the people in the intelligence and scientific communities that UFOs were little more than illusion, misidentification and hoax, it worked brilliantly. And, according to Swords, Robertson, Chadwell, and the others at CIA were just the sort of men who could design such a plan, especially when a new set of managers would be appointed by the new President. Besides, they were the ones who selected the panel members. The only one who seemed unbiased was Thorton Page, and he was overwhelmed by the prestige of the other, high-powered panel members. He was the low man on the totem pole.

It must be pointed out there is some interesting evidence to support this scenario. The evidence suggests that the panel was empowered as a fact-finding commission and because the evidence for the extraterrestrial given to them was weak to nonexistent, it concluded that UFOs posed no threat to national security, and not that they were not extraterrestrial. It is a fine hair to split and there were many would split it anyway.

It would seem that if, as many have suggested, the Robertson Panel was just another in a long line of manipulated investigations with foregone conclusions, that the recommendations would be to cease the operations. If the members of the Panel knew the truth and were hiding it, they were recommending the path that could expose that data for all to see. But the reality of the situation seems to be that only one or two of the top men knew the truth. The others just thought they did. And although they recommended that Blue Book be open to public scrutiny, Blue Book was about to become little more than a shell of its former self. Air Defense Command regulations were already written that would move UFO investigation from Blue Book and ATIC, to another, classified unit. The public would not know the difference.

Dewey Fournet, who was present during some of the Robertson Panel meetings, who briefed them on the sighting reports, and who answered their questions about the investigation said that it was a legitimate effort. They were searching for answers. But Fournet had not been present for all the sessions, and he thought that Durant had authored the report at the conclusion of the discussions late on Friday. Fournet did not know that the report, in draft form, existed before Friday and possibly before the panel was even convened on Wednesday.

But the question that seemed to be foremost in the minds of those on the panel was if there was a threat to national security. That is the angle that has been overlooked too often. Robertson might have wanted to answer the question about the nature of the phenomenon, but that's doubtful. Instead, he answered the one he had to. UFOs, at that point, posed no threat to national security, other than their ability to clog reporting channels. After more than five years of UFO sighting reports, no hostile intent had been observed. The key word here is intent. There had been some tragic results but those were born of the mistakes made by the humans and not direct actions of any alien flight crew.

The emerging documentation, the minutes of the meetings, diaries and notes kept by the participants, and discussions held with them in later years, and discussions with some of the participants and observers provides us with several important clues. It was scripted from the very beginning without those who made presentations aware that the final conclusions were drawn before they even sat down.

The final irony here is that the panel, originated under the Truman administration, partially because of the sightings made over Washington, didn't have to report to Truman. By the time the panel was formed, and by the time they had finished their report, a new administration had taken over the reins of the government. Eisenhower wasn't interested in UFO sightings in July 1952 and that might be because he already had the answers to the questions.

Chapter Fifteen: Radar and Weather

To fully understand the significance of the Washington Nationals, it is necessary to understand something about radar, its history, and anomalous propagation which can render it useless. Radar is a wonderful tool, but to believe that because some object was seen on radar proves that it was a physical object and therefore real, is to misunderstand radar.

Many people also believe that if we can find a good radar case, that is, one without obvious explanation, then we move closer to proving something about the reality of UFOs. There are good cases, involving multiple witnesses including interceptor pilots, multiple radars and gun camera films of the object. The explanations for those sightings offered by officials are less than plausible in some respects, but equally plausible in others. These sorts of cases do, however, supply one aspect of physical evidence about the reality of UFOs and they add a dimension of corroboration by instrumentality, but we must be aware of the pitfalls that dot such a landscape.

Throughout the history of the development of radar, the capabilities of the various sets and designs have been underestimated and misunderstood by those using them. During the Second World War, for example, radar operators and specialists in London were surprised and puzzled by a radar return that would appear quickly, expand and then just vanish. It happened each morning as the sun began to rise, which, had they been paying closer attention, would have provided them with a good clue about what they were watching.

To discover what was happening, observers were posted near the scene where the radar suggested that the blip originated. As dawn broke, hundreds, if not thousands of birds emerged from nesting, and took off in all directions searching for food. The cloud of birds, expanding outward as they left the area of the trees was responsible for the early morning radar return. No one expected the radars to be sensitive enough to pick up and track something as small as the birds. And no one thought about a large flock being responsible for the radar return.

The Fort Monmouth Radar Sightings

In September 1951, technicians at Fort Monmouth, New Jersey, were demonstrating their latest radar and how it could automatically track anything up to and including the fastest of the jet fighters. Using the scope in front of a crowd of visiting dignitaries and generals, a technician tried to lock onto a target about twelve thousand yards away. The target broke the lock and the embarrassed operator tried to re-establish it suggesting that the object, whatever it was, had to be flying faster than a jet otherwise he would have been able to establish the lock.

The equipment, the weather, and the operator were all checked carefully, and no one could find a plausible solution for what had now become a UFO sighting. There were no inversion layers to confound the operator, no unidentified jet traffic in the area according to all the available flight records, and no outside influences that could account for the experiences of the technician as he tried to lock onto the rapidly moving object.

PROJECT 10073 RECORD CARD

1. DATE 10-11 September 1951	LOCATION Monmouth, New Jersey	1.	12. CONCLUSIONS ☒ Was Balloon ☐ Probably Balloon ☐ Possibly Balloon
3. DATE-TIME GROUP Local ___ GMT ___ - - -	4. TYPE OF OBSERVATION ☐ Ground-Visual ☒ Ground-Radar ☐ Air-Visual ☐ Air-Intercept Radar		☐ Was Aircraft ☐ Probably Aircraft ☐ Possibly Aircraft
5. PHOTOS ☐ Yes ☐ No	6. SOURCE Military		☐ Was Astronomical ☐ Probably Astronomical ☐ Possibly Astronomical
7. LENGTH OF OBSERVATION Varied	8. NUMBER OF OBJECTS Single Track	9. COURSE 2. - - -	☐ Other Anomalous Propagation ☐ Insufficient Data for Evaluation ☐ Unknown
10. BRIEF SUMMARY OF SIGHTING See Case Folder Case associated with case from Sandy Hook, N.J.		11. COMMENTS Extensive investigation revealed that the target on 10 Sept was caused by a Balloon. Targets on 11 September were attributed to Anomalous Propagation by Radar analists.	

ATIC FORM 329 (REV 26 SEP 52)

The next day, again at Fort Monmouth, there was a telephone call from post headquarters to the radar facility to find out if they had anything on radar south of the base. The officers at headquarters, who had spotted a spherical shape high overhead, wanted to know how high the object was. According to the information available to the radar operator, who did, in fact find a return on the scope, the sphere was at 93,000 feet, far above the service ceilings of any military or civilian aircraft at that time. Rockets were being fired that could reach those sorts of altitudes, but none were being fired in New Jersey.

It confused those at the radar facility, suggesting that something very unusual had been flying over their base at 93,000 feet.

More unidentified objects were spotted around Fort Monmouth later that day and into the next. Again, the automatic tracking of the radars failed because it seemed that the erratically flying craft were faster than the modern jets. Radar attempts to lock on just wouldn't hold. And finally, a much slower moving object was spotted and tracked for several minutes before it was lost in the distance proving to the puzzled operators that the radar was working just as it was designed to work.

Here were a number of highly credible radar sightings that suggested some unusual objects were being spotted by the technicians at Fort Monmouth. With visual sightings corroborating the radar returns, it was clear that the answer was not some kind of malfunction. The high flying and fast UFOs certainly weren't illusions, and no one thought about suggesting any kind of a hoax because of the equipment involved, the integrity of the officers making the reports, and impossibility of creating that sort of an illusion to fool others.

But there were plausible explanations that made sense to the Air Force officers assigned as investigators as they reviewed the accumulated radar and visual data. The officers suggested the object that was faster than a jet wasn't an aircraft at all. The operator had made a mechanical error as he attempted to lock on the target. It was considerably slower than a jet fighter and was identified, based on the time, location, and direction of movement, as a commercial airliner on a routine flight. The problem was a miscalculation of the range to the target. The operator thought that it was much farther away than it was.

The radar search for the object in the sky that had been precipitated by the telephone call, the object that was flying at an altitude of 93,000 feet, turned out to be a balloon which the officers who called already knew. There was a discussion, at the base headquarters, about how high the balloon was, and they had asked that the radar be used to determine the altitude. Those who had received the telephone call overreacted to it thinking that the officers at headquarters were attempting to identify some sort of UFO. They had not seen the UFO and had not been told what the officers were talking about a balloon. They had just been asked about the altitude of the object.

The last of the Fort Monmouth sightings were identified, again, as a balloon, and as weather related phenomena. The excitement of the day before, that is the belief that they had seen some sort of flying saucer, had influenced those who were involved in the second day's activities. They were primed to accept the stories of flying saucers because of the reaction of the others and their belief that the equipment would not make a mistake. They were right, the equipment didn't make a mistake, the operator did. He had made some assumptions that had not been warranted by the information he had.

These were good sightings, confirmed by radar. Something real was in the sky. But there was also a good explanation for the sightings that was found by proper scientific investigation. It told us something about the capabilities of radar. It also demonstrated that just because something was seen on radar, it didn't mean that the object was unidentifiable or of extraterrestrial origin.

In fact, what we learn about radar is that just because there is something in the sky, it doesn't mean that what the eyewitnesses are observing is the same as the object located by the radar. There are many cases in which an unidentified blip is located and observers outside are alerted. Looking into the sky, they eventually see something that they believe is related to the blip on the scope. Sometimes this simply isn't the case.

More Explanations

Philip Klass, in *UFOs Explained*, noted that just such a case was reported on September 14, 1972. The West Palm Beach, Florida airport control tower began to receive telephone calls about a very bright object seen out over the Atlantic Ocean an hour or so before dawn. The controller looked out and saw what he described as a "glowing circular object" that was, according to his estimate, about two miles from the tower. To him, it was clearly something very strange.

He then turned his attention to an old surveillance radar that had been reconditioned. After studying the scope, he did find an object that was ten miles east of the airport. It was larger than the blips of aircraft displayed on the scope, moving far too slow to be an airplane and was flying toward the coast.

The controller made a number of telephone calls and found that the radars at Miami International Airport also showed the object, as did the Air Defense Command radars at nearby Homestead Air Force Base. The controller also talked to the crew of an Eastern Air Lines jet flying in the area who said that they, too, could see the bright light in the east.

Two F-106 fighters were scrambled into the brightening sky. Although equipped with onboard radars, neither pilot could see the UFO. The controller said that he could still see the object and agreed to help the fighter pilots find the UFO. Vectored by the controller, and after a series of back-and-forth maneuvers, including flying over the top of the tower, the pilots identified the light as Venus.

We could take that as typical Air Force explanation, but the local sheriff, William Heidtman, using a county helicopter, and in response to many calls he received about the bright light, tried to intercept and identify the object. He believed that he was attempting to intercept Venus. His identification was independent of the Air Force, but did corroborate their conclusion, proving that Venus can fool even the most experienced observer.

There seems to be little question as to what the light in the eastern sky was. Venus, at its brightest, when the conditions are proper, can look more like an oval object flying in our atmosphere than a planet some thirty million miles away.

The case also demonstrates that when a light is seen in the sky, it is often possible to find "uncorrelated" targets on the radar scope. These sorts of cases must be investigated carefully, and it must be remembered that the light in the sky might not be responsible for the image on the radar.

It should also be noted that in this case, though the control tower operator was fooled by Venus, as were hundreds of others, the object was properly identified. The report was solved by the men on the scene and the fighter pilot attempts to intercept the object. That identification was corroborated by the local sheriff. While it could be said that the Air Force pilots, because they were Air Force pilots, might have had a hidden agenda, that cannot be said for the local sheriff.

It does seem that when Venus is at its closest to Earth, and when the atmospheric conditions are right, can appear to be something that it is not. I have had people call me about a hovering, blue-white oval shining lights down into pastures or forests, as if searching for something. It is true that Venus, at its closest and brightest will spark UFO reports.

Radar Reliability

This leads us into a discussion of radar itself and the reliability of it. Roy H. Blackmer, Jr., along with R.J. Allen, R.T.H. Collis, C. Herold, and R.I. Presnell, wrote about the workings of radar in the Condon Committee report. The first point they made in that study is one of the most important. According to them:

> At first consideration, radar might appear to offer a positive, non-subjective method of observing UFOs. Radar seems to reduce data to ranges, altitudes, velocities, and such characteristics as radar reflectivity. On closer examination however, the radar method of looking at an object, although mechanical and electronically precise, is in many aspects substantially less comprehensive than

the visual approach. In addition, the very techniques that provide the objective measurements are themselves susceptible to errors and anomalies that can be misleading.

That certainly is true. But it is also true that there are very few cases in which there were only radar contacts and no corresponding visual sightings. To be useful, in a scientific arena, both chains of evidence are necessary. And, as demonstrated by Klass, as well as many others, it is necessary to make sure that the object in the sky that has been located by the radar is the same one being observed on the ground or by the pilots who are asked to identify it.

The Condon Committee report makes it clear that one of the weak links in the radar cases are the radar operators. They wrote, "The radar operator himself is an important part of the radar systems. He must be well trained and familiar with all of the interacting factors affecting the operation and performance of the equipment. When an experienced operator is moved to a new location, an important part of his retraining is learning pertinent factors related to expected anomalies due to local geographical and meteorological factors."

Klass, in his analysis of the West Palm Beach case pointed out that the radar used in the control tower was a "twenty-year-old ASR-3 that had originally been installed at a larger airport that had since been given a more modern radar, while the old ASR-3 had been reconditioned for use at West Palm Beach." He mentioned nothing about the radar training of the control tower operator, but it seems likely that it was more of an "on the job" training than a complete course in radar operations of that particular type of equipment.

I should point out here that this is often the course taken by writers of the UFO phenomenon. We speculate about a condition rather than ask the questions. Klass should have found out the level of training of the control tower operator, as should I. The message is that in science, we can't accept, as fact, our speculations. We must verify the facts of the case ourselves because, sometimes, there are distortions in the reported facts.

A Case on Point

Years ago, I was searching for flying saucer reports that pre-dated the Kenneth Arnold sighting of June 24, 1947. The allegation by the skeptical community was that Arnold, in describing the event, talked about the motion being like saucers skipping across a pond. It wasn't a description of the craft but a description of motion, because Arnold, himself, suggested something that was crescent shaped rather than saucer shaped.

The theory was that this error in reporting created the flying saucers. Many of the sightings made after Arnold were of saucer-shaped craft because that was what the witnesses thought the object should look like. While it can be pointed out that there a multitude of shapes reported after Arnold, I was looking for sightings of saucers documented prior to Arnold.

According to a number of sources, there had been a sighting of a formation of saucer-shaped objects made by a railroad engineer walking to work in Cedar Rapids, Iowa. Richard Hall, in his *The UFO Evidence*, reported that the information was published on June 23, or a day before Arnold. If true, then this was enough to refute the skeptical theory.

The origin of the listing could be traced back to a speech given by Frank Edwards in 1956. But that wasn't the first mention of it. I was able to trace the story to the *Cedar Rapids Gazette*. I searched the newspaper on June 23, but there was no listing of the sighting. I searched on June 24, thinking that a sighting in the afternoon might not have made it into the evening paper, but there was nothing. I continued to search and found an article in the *Gazette*, but it was four days after the Arnold sighting. According to the article, Charles Kastl, had seen "about nine spinning discs speeding through the sky last Tuesday, the same day an Idaho flyer said he some flashing objects in the air."

Kastl wasn't in Cedar Rapids, but in Joliet, Illinois at the time of his sighting but said nothing about it until after the information about Arnold had been reported. I had chased the story to its roots, found that it wasn't reported prior to Arnold, wasn't from Cedar Rapids, and did nothing to refute the theory the skeptics had proposed. But it did demonstrate the necessity to rely on the original source rather than stories that had been published long after the facts.

Radar Operators and Experience in West Palm Beach

The operator's lack of experience in radar systems, on that specific system, or in the local geological conditions might have led to his false conclusion that the target on the scope was related to the object in the sky. It was a question that should have been asked at the time, though by the time UFO investigators arrived, a viable solution had been found and all other considerations had been rendered moot.

There are, according to the Condon Committee experts, "Five possible relationships between radar echoes and targets. These are:

  a) no echo – no target
  b) no echo – when a visual object appears to be in a position to be detected
  c) echo – unrelated target

d) echo – from a target in a position other than that indicated

e) echo – from a target at the indicated location

They point out that both the first and last possibility are indicative of the normal operation of the radar. Of the others, they wrote, "Possibility b) becomes of importance where there is an object that is seen visually. Then, from knowledge of the types of targets that are detectable by the radar, some knowledge of the characteristics of the visual object could be obtained."

They continued, "The situations c) where there is an apparent echo but no target are those when the manifestation on the PPI [plan position indicator] is due to a signal that is not reradiated portion of the transmitted pulse but is from another source."

Situation d), according to the Condon Committee report, "First, abnormal bending of the radar beam may take place due to atmospheric conditions. Second, a detectable target may be present beyond the designed range of the radar and be presented on the display as if it were within the designed range.... Third, stray energy from the antenna may be reflected from an obstacle to a target in a direction quite different from that in which the antenna is pointed.... Finally, targets could be detected by radiation inside lobes and would be presented on the display as if there were detected by the main beam."

The last situation, d), that is an echo and a target located where it is indicated by the radar, is of primary interest to our discussion. In this case, the primary task is the identification of the target. The authors noted:

> The possible relationships listed above show that radar scope interpretation is not simple. To attempt to identify targets, the operator must know the characteristics of his radar; whether it is operating properly; and the type of targets it is capable of detecting. He must be very aware of the conditions or events by which echoes will be presented on the radar in a position that is different from the true target location (of in the case of interference no target). Finally, the operator must acquire collateral information weather data, transponder, voice communication, visual observations or handover information from another radar before he can be absolutely sure he has identified an unusual echo.

During the Washington Nationals, there was a complicating factor. This was the weather in the area. It provided the Air Force, and later the Condon Committee, with a built-in excuse for the sightings. To them, this clearly, was a case of temperature inversion.

The weather data, available from various records, show that there were high temperatures and high humidity, both conditions that create the temperature inversions over Washington at the time. What happens is that a layer of air, at one temperature is trapped between two layers of another temperature. The air, then, acts like a lens, bending the rays of light, and in the case of the Washington Nationals, the radar waves. The electronic beams, then reflected downward, begin to pick up objects on the ground, bouncing off them, and returning to the radar scope. If the object reflecting the wave is a vehicle, a car or truck, it will have motion.

This phenomenon is now well understood by everyone who has ever looked at weather radar. How many times has the radar screen displayed what is called "ground clutter." The one thing that must be remembered is that weather radar is attempting to "see" precipitation. Radars at airports, defense radars, and antiaircraft radar operate on different frequencies so that some of the weather-related problems are eliminated.

The question that must be addressed was the inversion layer strong enough to create the problems and should the controllers at Washington National been able to tell the difference between the solid targets and those created by the weather.

First, as for the strength of the inversion layer, it seems to come down to which expert you want to believe. Some say that it was, others say that it wasn't. All agree that there was an inversion, and all agree that the weather was conducive to the formation of inversion layers which will produce the weather-related targets.

Second, all the controllers, as well as the military experts who were in the radar room on the second night, said they were familiar with weather created targets and the targets over Washington, D.C. were not weather related. At least the ones they were watching. Fournet, and Ruppelt, both said that the controllers were ignoring those targets that were most likely the result of the weather.

Al Chop, who was there, said that the targets seemed to respond to the presence of the interceptors. At one point, as the jet fighters arrived, all the UFOs disappeared. When the jets returned to base, the UFOs reappeared on the scopes. That suggests that some of the targets were reacting to the jets, and that would tend to eliminate weather.

What all this means is that the evidence developed through a radar case is more complicated than just a blip on the screen and a corresponding light in the sky. The evidence has to be assembled carefully and the expertise of the operator, or operators, becomes a critical factor. Without an operator who is good at the job, the case is weakened considerably and the conclusions they draw may be skewed.

But when all is said and done, the radar return adds a dimension of reliability to the case. When the target is spotted visually, right where it is supposed to be, it means that we are no longer dealing with illusion or imagination. We are dealing with something that is real and solid.

Chapter Sixteen: The Condon Committee

To fully understand the Washington National sightings, it is necessary to understand the investigations that took place outside of the official Air Force project, as well as the attitudes of various government officials during this time. Although the Air Force had explained the sightings to their satisfaction and the satisfaction of the press and science, there were still questions to be asked and answers to be sought. Many didn't believe the Air Force suggestion that the trained, professional radar operators at Washington National Airport could be so completely fooled by a weather-related phenomenon that they had to have witnessed dozens of times in the past.

When those sightings were coupled to the reports from both military interceptor pilots and civilian airline pilots asked to look for the lights, many were of the opinion that something solid and real was being seen over the city. The Air Force seemed to ignore too much of the eyewitness testimony, especially that from its own personnel. The Air Force had an answer, and they didn't want inconvenient testimony cluttering up the landscape. Pressure was applied carefully so that all testimony would conform and there would be no loose ends to cause trouble.

One-time Blue Book chief, Robert Friend

The Air Force seems to have understood their real problem very well. To the high-ranking officers of the Air Force, it was no longer so much a problem of national security as it was one of public relations. Given that, the Air Force, not long after the Washington Nationals, began to attempt to move Project Blue Book out of ATIC and into public relations offices of the Secretary of the Air Force in Washington, D.C. Then, on April 1, 1960, in a letter to Major General Dougher at the Pentagon, A. Francis Archer, a scientific advisor to Project Blue Book, commented on a memo written by Colonel Evans, a ranking officer at ATIC, about Blue Book. Archer wrote, "...[I] have tried to get Blue Book out of ATIC for 10 years... and do not agree that the loss of prestige to the UFO project is a disadvantage." This was the beginning of the attempts to end Project Blue Book and the beginning of a chain of events that would lead to the creation of the University of Colorado study that would become known in the UFO community as the Condon Committee. A chain that had a very important link that had been forged in July 1952 over Washington, D.C.

Another volley was fired in 1962, when Lieutenant Colonel Robert Friend, who, at that time was the chief of Project Blue Book, wrote to his headquarters that the project should be handed over to a civilian agency that would word its report in such a way as to allow the Air Force to drop the study. At about the same time, Edward Trapnell, an assistant to the Secretary of the Air Force, when talking to Dr. Robert Calkins of the Brookings Institution, said pretty much the same thing. Find a civilian committee to study the problem, then have them conclude it the way the Air Force wanted it concluded. One of the stipulations, of course, was that this civilian group say some positive things about the way the Air Force had handled the UFO problem for the last fifteen or twenty years. This became, in a very broad sense, the blueprint for the Condon Committee.

Public pressure, which began with the Washington Nationals, was mounting for an independent study of UFOs. The Air Force explanations, often half-explained, and sometimes not completely thought out, resulted in a public perception that the Air Force investigators were hiding the real truth. This was reinforced when people studied the Washington Nationals. The questions that kept coming up were the same and the Air Force answers were seen as inadequate.

Then, for three years in a row, starting in 1964 with a spectacular landing in New Mexico, a series of UFO sightings again grabbed national headlines. The explanations offered by the Air Force, and their scientific consultants, were found by the press and the public, to lack credibility. Gerald Ford, a congressman from Michigan, was demanding congressional hearings about UFOs because his constituents were demanding answers about their sightings in 1966. The wheels were threatening to come off the cart once again.

The outgrowth of this pressure by the public and congress was an allegedly independent and scientific investigation of UFOs by a civilian organization. Heralded in the beginning as just what the UFO phenomenon needed by those inside the civilian flying saucer community, the Condon Committee, organized at the University of Colorado, was funded by more than half a million dollars of Air Force money. Several universities had been approached, but they had all turned down the research grant. The University of Colorado had been way down the list of possible sites, but it was the only university that accepted the

Air Force challenge. That a few arms were twisted to make this work is a common belief that isn't fully rejected.

Scientific director of the project, the man who officially received the Air Force grant, was Dr. Edward U. Condon, a professor of Physics and Astrophysics, and a Fellow of the Joint Institute for Laboratory Astrophysics at the University of Colorado. As a career scientist, Condon had the sort of prestige the Air Force wanted in their scientist.

Dr. Edward Condon

Condon, prior to the Air Force assignment, had a distinguished career as a scientist. He was a former director of the National Bureau of Standards and was a member of the National Academy of Sciences. In 1941, he was named to the committee which established the atomic bomb program. He was a scientific advisor to a special Senate atomic energy committee for Naval Atomic Bomb tests in 1946. Twenty years later, Condon was a professor at the University of Colorado.

As noted by the documentation that appeared after the declassification of the Project Blue Book files, the formation of the Condon Committee was part of an already existing plan. Find a university to study the problem (flying saucers) and then conclude it the way the Air Force wanted it concluded. It is obvious that the first universities approached did not agree to the conditions placed on them by the Air Force contracts and rejected the opportunity to conduct the research.

It was a Set-up from the Beginning

It is important here to understand that the Condon Committee wasn't a legitimate scientific effort. It was a set-up from the very beginning. The evidence for this is more than just idle speculation. It is an established fact. Dr. Michael Swords has spent the last several years studying the history of the Condon Committee and confirms the view that the Air Force used Condon and that Condon was a willing participant in the deception. According to a letter discovered by Swords and written by Lieutenant Colonel Robert Hippler to Condon at the beginning of the investigation, the plan was laid out in no uncertain terms. Hippler told Condon that no one knew of any extraterrestrial visitation and therefore, there "has been no visitation."

Hippler also pointed out that Condon "must consider" the cost of the investigations of UFOs and to "determine if the taxpayer should support this" for the next ten years. This, despite the fact that Samford and others had repeatedly told the press that the cost of investigating UFOs was a minor expense. Hippler warned Condon that it would be another decade before another independent study could be mounted that might end the Air Force UFO project.

Condon understood what Hippler was trying to tell him. Three days after receiving the letter, while in Corning, New York, Condon, in a lecture to scientists including those members of the Corning Section of the American Chemical Society and the Corning Glass Works Chapter of Sigma XI, told them, "It is my inclination right now to recommend that the government get out of this business. My attitude right now is that there is nothing in it. But I am not supposed to reach a conclusion for another year." Such a statement certainly indicates that Condon understood his instructions.

Robert Low responded to Hippler's letter a day or so after Condon's Corning talk, telling him that they, the committee, were very happy, that now they knew what they are supposed to do. Low wrote, "...you indicate what you believe the Air Force wants of us, and I am very glad to have your opinion." Low pointed out that Hippler had answered the questions about the study "quite directly."

Low, who in the UFO literature has become nothing more than Condon's hatchet man, did want to do a proper scientific investigation. In fact, according to Swords, Low had a rather brilliant plan for the investigation that would have entailed the creation of a "case book" containing both new cases and re-investigation of some of the classics such as the Washington Nationals. These were cases that were considered extremely puzzling. Low hinted to those around him that he believed UFOs were a subject worthy of study, although he didn't believe that the study would lead to extraterrestrial visitation. He did seem to believe that something of scientific value could come from a properly conducted investigation. I suspect that he wanted the investigation to land in the hands of civilian scientists.

In 1969, the Condon Committee released their findings. As had all of those who had passed before them, the Condon Committee found that UFOs posed no threat to the security of the United States. Edward U. Condon in Section I, Recommendations and Conclusions, wrote, "The history of the past 21 years has repeatedly led Air Force officers to the conclusion that none of the things seen, or thought to have been seen, which pass by the name UFO reports, constituted any hazard or threat to national security."

After suggesting that such a finding was "out of our province" to study, and if they did find any such evidence, they would, quite naturally, pass it on to the Air Force, Condon wrote, "We know of no reason to question the finding of the Air Force that the whole class of UFO reports so far considered does not pose a defense problem."

Included in the Recommendations, was the idea that "It is our impression that the defense function could be performed within the framework established for intelligence and surveillance operations without the continuance of a special unit such as Project Blue Book, but this is a question for defense specialists rather than research scientists."

Finally, Condon wrote, "It has been contended that the subject has been shrouded in official secrecy. We conclude otherwise. We have no evidence of secrecy concerning UFO reports. What has been miscalled secrecy has been no more than an intelligent policy of delay in releasing data so that the public does not become confused by premature publication of incomplete studies or reports."

The Condon report suggested there was no evidence of extraterrestrial visitation and that all UFO reports could be explained if sufficient data had been gathered in the beginning. This is exactly what Hippler wrote in his January 1967 letter to Condon. Yet, even when they selected the sightings they would investigate, they failed to explain almost thirty percent of them. In one case (over Labrador, 30 June 1954), they wrote, "This unusual sighting should therefore be assigned to the category of some almost certainly natural phenomenon, which is so rare that it apparently has never been reported before or since."

So, there weren't any cases that they found persuasive. They had looked at some of the "classics" including the Washington Nationals. Just what did they find during their investigation of those sightings.

Condon and the Washington Nationals

The Washington National sightings as detailed by the Condon Committee, bore no resemblance to the unbiased reports offered by other investigators. In the Condon report, it was suggested that very few of the pilots sent to look for UFOs on those nights saw anything. Most of the sightings were made on radar and the radar end was explainable as weather related phenomenon. Although they didn't say it, the suggestion was that the timing of the sightings was indicative of a mass hysteria induced in the various observers by discussions of

UFOs and some of the reports that had been published in the newspapers in the days and weeks before the first of the sightings.

The problem with the Condon assessment is the idea there were few visual sightings. The report did quote from a few Air Force personnel who talked of seeing stars but even Ed Ruppelt, head of Project Blue Book during the sightings admitted that those "confessions" seemed coerced. Ruppelt, the man on the inside had published information that Air Force personnel had changed their stories to conform to the Air Force party line, but Condon and the scientists didn't follow up on this suggestion. They weren't supposed to walk down those paths.

Dewey Fournet and Al Chop, who both were present on the second Saturday night set of sightings, knew that visual sightings had been made. Fournet said, "When you combine radar reports with [Lieutenant John] Holcomb's explanations to me about solid returns with reports of the pilots, I think you can conclude they were not reflections from the atmosphere or temperature inversions."

Aware that the Condon Committee had virtually overlooked the visual sightings made by both civilian airline and military interceptor pilots, as well as lock on by on board radars, I asked Fournet about the Condon Committee's suggestion there were few visual corroborations. Fournet said, "The reports we got from at least one of the fighter pilots was pretty gory." He wouldn't elaborate, just saying that "It was pretty interesting."

Fournet made one other point that I found interesting. Although the Condon Committee had spoken to a number of the controllers who had been in the radar room during the Washington Nationals, they didn't search for Fournet. Finding him from scratch was incredibly easy. It took almost five minutes, and I didn't have access to the Air Force personnel records that could have been used by the Condon Committee. The Air Force was sponsoring the investigation and they would have been able to put one of the scientists in touch with Fournet, had anyone asked the question about him.

I asked Fournet if he would have told the Condon Committee investigators what he had told me about his experiences in the radar room that night. Fournet said, "Yes, I would. In fact, I think I would have told them more had I known what they were doing."

During my interview with Al Chop, I asked him if he had been contacted by the Condon Committee during their research. He said that he hadn't been. He would have, of course, provided them with as much information as he had given to me if they had bothered to call him.

Michael Wertheimer, during his investigation in December 1966, spoke to many of the people who had been involved in the sightings including some of the air traffic controllers and the Air Force personnel who reported sightings. He was aware of the visual and radar sightings, that targets were seen, at least once, on radars in three separate locations, and that onboard radars had locked onto the targets as the jet interceptors had chased the UFOs all over Washington.

Wertheimer, in his preliminary report, makes it very clear that the controllers believed they were watching solid targets of craft in the sky and not of reflected radar waves. These men, experienced in the anomalies that could appear on radar were well aware of the Air Force explanation of weather-related phenomenon, but they didn't believe it to be accurate. Paul Petersen, one of

Michael Wertheimer

those controllers, told Wertheimer that he had not seen weather targets like those he saw in July 1952. He also mentioned that he had only seen similar targets on a couple of occasions after those events in July 1952.

Wertheimer did interview Harry Barnes about the sightings. In his preliminary report, Wertheimer wrote, "Mr. Barnes found the experience of discovering unknown radar and visual targets flying over Washington, particularly in the vicinity of the White House, at a small early hour in the morning when there was no known air traffic, quite 'terrifying'. The object made right angle turns on the radar and in other ways executed maneuvers that no self-respecting aircraft could. He indicated that nobody at the time thought it was the Russians or experimental aircraft or Mars-men (sic), but everybody who was involved seemed quite puzzled."

Wertheimer noted that Barnes did not believe that the objects they had seen on the radar that night were "ghosts". The radars were functioning properly. Various radar sets, including those in the jet fighters, detected the UFOs. There were visual sightings to corroborate the radar sightings.

Wertheimer wrote, "Mr. Barnes also indicated that he thought it was very unlikely that the sightings were due to a temperature inversion, because the objects were moving all the time and also didn't have the shape on the radar scope that known temperature inversions produce." In other words, the senior man in the radar room, an experienced radar operator, told the Condon Committee investigator that the objects they had detected did not resemble the weather-related phenomenon they had seen in the past. It was something different.

To be fair here, it is necessary to point out that Barnes told Wertheimer that he didn't believe UFOs represented an extraterrestrial presence, but that he thought they could be explained as natural phenomena. He didn't know how but thought that they might represent some sort of magnetic anomaly.

Wertheimer also interviewed Joseph Reino who had come on duty about the time the UFOs disappeared from the scopes. Reino's duty began in the early morning. Reino told Wertheimer that "A Capital airliner was coming in [to Washington National]; two objects were on the [radar] screen, came up to his starboard side and paced him; the tower asked the pilot if he saw them, and the pilot said he did. As the plane approached Riverdale the pilot turned it right to see if they would follow; they did but went a little faster than the plane. They were clearly not aircraft; he hadn't seen them before - they were saucer or cigar shaped, grayish-green with light coming from the bottom. The pilot couldn't get very close to them, and Mr. Reino wondered whether our type of metal repels them or makes them afraid."

Wertheimer was also told of other incidents, in that time frame, where there was radar contact and visual sightings. Reino told of one incident in which five people were involved in watching a group of objects on the scope and the same objects in the sky overhead. Reino made it clear that some of the standard explanations for the sightings just didn't work because of the experience and training of those involved.

Wertheimer reported, about his trip out to Washington National, "At dusk I was taken to the control tower by Joe Reino, who gave me a brief lesson on how to read the radar. I found out how one goes about identifying whether something is a jet, about where it is, what a flock of birds looks like, what occasional ghosts look like, and became convinced that after extensive experience a radar operator probably can tell what a given object is. Mr. Reino put me through several exercises in which he would point to an object on the radar screen and then ask me to find it in the sky, and I found this wasn't too difficult to do."

Importantly, Wertheimer reported that "Both Mr. Conklin [who had been in the radar rooms during the 1952 sightings] and Mr. Reino confirmed Mr. Barnes's story, and are convinced it couldn't have been temperature inversion, birds, or the like; experienced radar operators can tell these apart easily."

Given Wertheimer's preliminary investigation into the Washington Nationals, it becomes strange that he hadn't bothered to locate and interview Fournet and Chop. Both Fournet and Chop were easy to locate. I did nothing special to find them. Had Wertheimer wanted to speak to them, he could have found them as easily. Since he didn't, the question becomes, why not?

Timing here, is critical. Wertheimer made his preliminary investigation at the beginning of December 1966. Six weeks later, Hippler told Condon exactly what the Air Force wanted. The Washington Nationals investigation apparently ended at that point. And even though they had information that there wasvisual, and radar coordinated sightings, when the final report was written, that information disappeared.

Condon's Contract

To fully understand this, we must examine the contract that was given to Condon. According to Swords, Condon was the "grantee" and was, therefore, the chief scientist. He had the job of writing the conclusions. He was not required to allow the "committee" to review them. In fact, Condon wrote his conclusions based on his personal opinion rather than the scientific facts surrounding UFOs as revealed by the investigation, what little there had been. He had made it clear, before the end of the investigation what his conclusions would be.

Carmon Marano, the last officer at Blue Book.

Discussing this with Dr. Swords, I asked about that, and he said, "The chief scientist will write the summary and he can say whatever he wants in it. The summary for the Condon report is a disaster."

The case book was never written. Low's plan for reviewing a number of cases in-depth is something that never happened, although, as we've seen with Wertheimer's investigation, they did begin the research. According to Swords, fifteen or so cases were written up for the case book, but those treatments had been written by Tad Foster, a graduate law student. These were not technically oriented, and the plan called for the scientists to rewrite them in the proper format. That never happened.

The draft of the Washington Nationals, written by Foster for the ill-fated case book, seems to be quite comprehensive. It lays out the weather data, interviews with the primary participants with the important exceptions of Fournet and

222

Chop, and describes, chronologically, the complex events of July 1952. What is interesting, is the difference in the draft for the case book, and the final description as it appeared in the final draft of the Condon report.

Another thing Condon did was refuse to investigate any of the past, "classic" cases. Whenever it was suggested, Condon said that they had really been investigated and what could they learn that was new? One of those was the comprehensive sightings of a large, egg-shaped craft seen around Levelland, Texas, on November 2, 1957. Although there were multiple witnesses including local law enforcement and Air Force officers, and that close approach to the UFO stalled cars, the committee did not investigate. Levelland is reduced to a couple of lines and the excuse that the cars involved in the sighting would be impossible to find. To Condon and the committee, it was as if this series of sightings had never taken place.

Condon, then, did the job he was hired to do. He attempted to bury the questions about UFOs under a blanket of scientific jargon and supposed objectivity. The Committee report, structured the way Condon wanted it, was then used to halt other scientific investigation into UFOs. It stopped many scientists and journalists from speaking about UFOs in a positive light just as it was designed to do. It also allowed the Air Force to claim that they were closing Project Blue Book. They would not respond to reports of UFO activity.

It is quite clear from the evidence at hand that the Condon investigation of UFOs was not the unbiased, scientific report it was supposed to be. Almost no one accepts, as genuine, the conclusions it draws. Had Low's plan been used, then, according to Swords, "... there were a whole lot of people on the project, including Bob Low who weren't whitewashing. Condon, because he was the grantee and it was a typical Air Force contract, he had the right...[as] the chief scientist [to] unilaterally...write the summary...Condon just takes control." Swords believed that if Low's plan had been used, "You would have had a hell of a lot of different UFO history..."

It is also true that had Low's plan been followed, the history of the Washington Nationals, as told since 1969 would have been different. The sightings were more complex, involving more people and equipment than originally suggested in various press accounts and conferences. The questions still to be answered surrounded radar and its fallibility. Could the problems of weather and radar explain, finally, the Washington Nationals?

CONCLUSIONS

Like so much of the UFO phenomena, the Washington Nationals have become confused and convoluted by those with agendas other than the truth. Air Force officers and Pentagon officials, not wanting to admit that something could invade our airspace without fear of reprisal, attempted to minimize the events. The objects that most thought they had observed over Washington, D.C. were, in fact, false radar returns created by temperature inversion. UFO researchers, wanting to believe in government conspiracy and extraterrestrial visitation, attempted to exploit the events because the objects had been seen on radar and those radar tracks proved the UFOs to be extraordinary. Since no power on Earth could create those sorts of craft, the only possible explanation was with the extraterrestrial.

The truth of the matter lies somewhere in the middle, as it often does. Those on one side overlook the facts that don't fit with their theories, while those on the other see manipulation of the truth. There are a few facts that are undisputed in the case, and from those few facts we can reach a few rational conclusions.

First, everyone agrees that the radars at Washington National Airport did detect something during the sightings. Radars at other locations including Andrews Air Force Base and Bolling Air Force Base also detected strange objects on those nights. Fighters scrambled did achieve, in a limited fashion, onboard radar locks on these objects.

Second, pilots, whether in the cockpits of jet interceptors, or flying commercial airliners, did seen lights in the sky where the radar operators said those lights should be. These seem to provide visual confirmation of the objects detected by the radars at the airfields.

Third, there were temperature inversions all along the Atlantic seaboard that hot and muggy July. Weather records establish the fact. It is the strength of those inversion layers that becomes the important point in the debate over the Washington Nationals.

Finally, in a point that is often overlooked in UFO research, the important national magazines had published stories about flying saucers in the weeks that proceeded the sightings. Although not one of them was heavily "pro-UFO", all of them brought the topic to the forefront of conversation so that, as the sightings began in Washington, those on the "front lines" were ready to interpret the anomalies they were watching as something extraordinary and possibly extraterrestrial.

As we study the case, we do notice that some of the sightings can be explained, often as weather related. For example, one of the pilots, chasing a radar object, noticed that each time the radar controller on the ground said they had maneuvered into a position right on top of the UFO, the aircraft was passing over the river. On the river was a slowly moving boat. The pilots believed that the boat, and the river, accounted for the UFO seen on radar because they could see no corresponding object in the sky. This explanation seems reasonable, given the facts and the observations by the pilots.

But what must be remembered is that a single explanation given to a single sighting does not translate into a blanket explanation that will explain everything. Each sighting must be treated as an individual case. It is only in the aggregate that the Washington Nationals become impressive. If we eliminate some, or even a majority of those cases, there are still others that have not been eliminated. However, if we can sufficiently reduce the numbers, then the case takes on less importance.

One of the most important aspects of the Washington Nationals is the intercepts attempted. We know, from the records, that some of those intercepts resulted in no visual corroboration by the military pilots. We can offer two explanations that seem reasonable. First is that there were no physical objects in the sky where the radars suggested they should be. If that is true, then the weather explanation takes on added weight.

Second, we can suggest that the object, whatever it was, had no lights on it, and therefore would not be readily visible to the interceptor pilots in the dark, night sky. This allows the object to be real and present, but unseen.

For the sake of convenience, let's eliminate those radar reports in which there is no corresponding sighting simply because there is no corresponding sighting. We do this simply because one of the chains of evidence, the visual confirmation, is not present. We have a radar sighting that suggests something in the sky, but nothing that proves it was physically there. Other explanations, such as temperature inversion, are reasonable in these cases.

What we are attempting to do here is reduce sightings to the smallest possible number by eliminating those with reasonable, though not proven explanations, those without visual confirmation, and those that are lacking sufficient data for us to examine. There is a risk that we will reject or overlook a sighting that is

225

valuable simply because our arbitrary criterion eliminates it. However, there are enough good, solid sightings that fit our strict point of view to help us understand all of the Washington Nationals.

One of the best examples of the sightings around Washington, were those spotted on the radar and radioed to Captain Casey Pierman. Here was a group of sightings in which the objects seen on the radar were also seen in the air. Pierman, when told where to look, could see the lights of the UFOs. Radar and visual confirmation.

Another fine example is the attempted intercept on the second night when the pilot found himself virtually surrounded by the UFOs. Those in the radar room, watching the scene as it played out on the scope, could hear the pilot describing the same thing in the air around him. It was obvious that solid objects were surrounding his aircraft.

Fournet and Chop both described, for me, that incident, Fournet suggesting that it had been "real gory." The pilot involved talked about the lights surrounding his aircraft as those on the ground watched the scene played out on the radar scopes. Again, this would seem to suggest a real event rather than a weather-related problem.

A third good example comes from another but failed attempted intercept. The UFOs all disappeared from the radar screens as the jet fighters appeared. This seems to suggest that the UFOs were responding to the presence of the jets. That is something that weather related phenomena would not, or could not, do.

Both Dewey Fournet and Al Chop said that the UFOs reacted to the presence of the fighters. In one case, as the jets arrived on the scene, all the UFOs disappeared. When the interceptors turned to head back to their airfield, the UFOs returned to the scope. That sort of activity, observed by the military representatives as well as the experienced radar operators, argues against the temperature version explanation. Weather related phenomena would not react to the fighters.

Although the Air Force would have us believe that these sightings were also the result of temperature inversions, that simply is not the case. The description provided by Capital Airlines pilot Pierman, along with the radar plots as the object maneuvered around the airliner argues against temperature inversion. If the UFO had remained in one place according to the radar, then the temperature inversion explanation would be reasonable. However, the objects did not remain stationary, seemed to react to the presence of the aircraft, and, according to Harry Barnes in the radar center, seemed to be under intelligent control.

What this means, quite simply, is that once we have adjusted for the sighting reports for those that have plausible explanations, and adjusted for those that have reasonable explanations, and even when we adjust for those that have explanations no matter how far we have to stretch the facts, there is a core of cases that simply cannot be explained. Temperature inversion, pilot and observer hysteria, and misidentification of stars, do not explain the reactions of the UFOs as seen on the radar scopes and by those on the ground and in the air and as reported not only to me during my interviews, but with others over the years.

Radar provides a mechanical means of observing the targets. Operator bias and interpretation certainly can influence those observations, but when the UFOs react to the jet interceptors, or disappear when the interceptors arrive on station, and are observed on the radar screen doing that, then a mechanical instrument has provided confirmation of the outside situation. In other, less complex words, it means that the radar has corroborated what the pilots were reporting and there are now two chains of evidence... mechanical or instrumentation (radar) and eyewitness meaning both the radar operators and the interceptor pilots.

All of this suggests that, while some of the sightings made were clearly misidentifications, there was a body of them that had no explanations. Even the Air Force, which pretended to have explained the sightings as temperature inversions, listed many of the sightings as unidentified in their official files. Even with their readymade solutions, they didn't apply them to all the sightings made during those critical times.

Some fifteen years after the Washington Nationals, the Condon Committee scientist who began an investigation of those sightings, in his preliminary report wrote about "My Current Impressions of the UFO Phenomenon." He analysis said:

> As my sketch of a model indicates, my thinking about UFO reports suggests that they are pretty complex phenomenon. Most of our briefing in the groups has been concerned with the input end, the physical phenomena that can give rise to UFO reports. I learned a great deal during the briefings; I hadn't realized how many different sorts of physical phenomena of which I was unaware, or minimally aware, could, at least occasionally produce UFO

sightings, including balloons and their fragments, ball-lightning, all the rest of the meteorological and astronomical events too.

I've come to the impression that in spite of a tremendous overload of work, and in spite of doing a very good job considering the small number of people involved, that only some proportion of the Blue Book explanations are, if one's going to look at them very carefully, very tenable. In a substantial proportion of cases the explanations are not very plausible. Chances are the detailed study of many of them will suggest that quite a few should be changed, either from explained to unexplained, or from one class of explanation to another being more likely. But, if one takes just the ones that are officially listed as unexplained, but which don't look very well explained, I would guess that if we work real hard, maybe one-third to one-half of these could eventually be put into the "explained" category, in the sense that somebody can come up with a reasonably plausible account of how the sighting might have been induced. I'm also convinced, though, that however much time we or any other group put in on it, eventually there will still remain some that are not very satisfactorily explained. The big question comes in how to interpret that remaining group in the "X" class. Unfortunately, I think it is becoming clear that the fundamental question that the public and the Air Force want answered is just plain unanswerable. The assertion that at least some (one or more) of these are actually caused by objects of intelligent extraterrestrial origin in neither proved nor disproved, neither made more or less likely by the existence of cases in this "X" class. While the data are consistent with that hypothesis than an infinity of other alternative hypothesis, they are no more consistent that hypothesis than an infinity of other alternative hypotheses of the origin of these reports. It would seem far more parsimonious at this point not to entertain the extraterrestrial-origin hypothesis. Just because there is no question, but that sincere and reliable people are reporting complex phenomena that they clearly really did experience and which nobody can explain, there is a vast jump, from my point of view a logically indefensible jump, between the assertion that these reports constitute proof of or evidence for an extraterrestrial intelligent origin of the objects reported.

This report, prepared after the man had reviewed some of the Washington Nationals and after he had seen many of the Project Blue Book files, says,

228

clearly, that the people might have worked hard, been dedicated and honest, their conclusions for the sighting reports were, for the most part, in error. That is a tune that had been played by UFO investigators almost from the moment that it was learned that the Air Force was investigating flying saucers.

It must be noted that he does not agree that the material in the files would lead to the extraterrestrial conclusion, but he does not rule it out. This was a man on the Condon Committee who had talked to a number of men who had been involved in the Washington Nationals. His conclusion was that something happened over Washington, D.C., that the men involved were highly trained and skilled, and that they observations could not be dismissed as easily and cavalierly as the Air Force had done in 1952.

That seems to be where we are today. The evidence is that something extraordinary was seen in the sky over Washington. Radar confirmed the sightings and fighters attempted to intercept these objects. There were visual sightings. And there was pressure by the Air Force to force their personnel to chance their descriptions of the UFOs and their conclusions about the objects.

We can say, with certainty, something was seen by radar and observed visually. There was a physical manifestation over Washington that engaged the interest of the president. If the objects sighted were manufactured craft, then it is clear that they hadn't been built on this planet. The only explanation that fits all the facts is the extraterrestrial. We were so busy arguing the question that we didn't respond to the situation.

The Washington Nationals show that we have been visited. There is no other plausible solution.

Appendix A: The Unidentifieds in the Summer of 1952

May 1, 1952: Moses Lake, Washington. An AEC employee watched a silver object in straight and level flight.

May 1, 1952: George AFB, California. 5:50 p.m. Several Air Force officers, and enlisted men watched five, flat white, disc-shaped objects make a sudden 90 degree turn and disappear.

May 5, 1952: Tenafly, New Jersey. Witnessed by Judson. Carried as an unidentified in the Project Blue Book files.

May 7, 1952: Kessler AFB, Mississippi. 12:15 p.m. Four Air Force personnel saw about ten objects that were cylindrically shaped and looked to be made of aluminum dart in and out of the clouds.

May 9, 1952: George AFB, California. 10:30 a.m. Witness on the ground and pilot of an F-86 saw one silver colored, round object that disappeared to the north. One of a series of sightings at the base on May 9, 11, 13, 14, 20. Some were identified and many were marked as insufficient data.

May 10, 1952: Ellenton, South Carolina. 11:45 p.m. A number of civilians watched four object, yellow in color and disc shape, that few straight and level for a short period. One object was reported to have pulled up to avoid other objects on the ground.

May 14, 1952: Puerto Rico. 7:00 p.m. An attorney, among others, reported two objects, orange in color, spherical, one of which darted around.

May 20, 1952: Houston, Texas. 10:10 p.m. Three Air Force navigators watched an orange-white light coming toward them. Object flew straight except for one turn.

May 25, 1952: Walnut Lake, Michigan. 11:15 p.m. Seven civilians including a witness named Hoffman, reported a white to yellow orange moon-shaped object, which they followed in a car for thirty minutes.

May 28, 1952: Saigon, RVN. 10:30 a.m. A civilian reported a single, white-silver disc-shaped object that was in sight for two minutes.

May 28, 1952: Albuquerque, New Mexico. 1:30 p.m. A city fireman reported two sightings of a light silver and light brown, circular objects that came in from the northeast at high speed, stopped to circle and then climbed out of sight.

May 29, 1952: San Antonio, Texas. 7:00 p.m. An Air Force pilot watched a single object that he described as tubular for about eight minutes.

June 1, 1952: Rapid City, South Dakota. William Beatty, an airman, saw a number of civilians looking into the sky. He turned and saw five or more silver-colored objects that did not resemble airplanes in a box-like formation. He watched them for about 20 seconds, until they disappeared.

June 1, 1952: Walla Walla, Washington. A USAF Reserve Officer watched a single object that was in sight for about seven seconds. The UFO was small, oval shaped and moved rapidly across the sky at about 10,000 to 15,000 feet.

June 1, 1952: Soap Lake, Washington. The unidentified witness (name deleted by the Air Force) saw three glimmering objects that crossed the sky and disappeared in the east. The sighting lasted about ten minutes.

June 2, 1952: Bayview, Washington. Captain Joe W. Donaldson, Major Wesley H. Parks, T/Sgt Oron C. Lott, A/1c William C. Callison, A/1c Bobby J. Lunsford, Bertil Eklin, Richard Christion, Robert Erickson. Witnesses watched an irregular bluish-white or silver sphere that hovered in the sky. The object was observed through a theodolite. An intercept, but a C-47 was attempted, but abandoned with no closure was apparent.

June 2, 1952: Fulda, Germany.

June 5, 1952: Lubbock, Texas. Witnessed by Bacon, among others. Eight unidentified flying objects were sighted during a period of 45 minutes. They were lights like that of a very bright star, were all of a uniform size and color, which was described as a constant yellow.

June 5, 1952: Albuquerque, New Mexico. S/Sgt T.H. Shorey. A large, round object flew quickly over the city. IT was very shiny and made no noise during flight. It crossed above a B-29 that was at 10,000 feet.

June 5, 1952: Offutt AFB, Nebraska. 2nd Lt. William R. Soper. The witness saw a large, bright red object that seem to hover for about five minutes and then disappear at a high rate of speed. No other object was visible.

June 6, 1952: Kimpo AFB, Japan. Carried as an unidentified in the Project Blue Book files. It was also noted in the Master Index that the case file was missing.

June 7, 1952: Albuquerque, New Mexico. Colonel Harold A. Radetsky, Lt. Col. George S. Baylan. A small, metallic, rectangular object crossed in front of their aircraft. They lost sight of it as it passed behind them.

June 8, 1952: Albuquerque, New Mexico. Witnessed by Markland. Four objects in a diamond-shaped formation flew over the city. They were flat and circular and were a very brilliant, whitish-silver color. They made no sound.

June 9, 1952: Minneapolis, Minnesota. Carried as an unidentified in the Project Blue Book files. It is also noted in the Master Index that the case file was missing.

June 12, 1952: Fort Smith, Arkansas. Witnessed by two military officers (names deleted by Air Force). Both officers saw an object best described as cigar-shaped, with an orange glow at the front, and a long, glowing tail at the rear. The object was in sight for about 10 or 15 minutes and was watched through a pair of binoculars.

June 12, 1952: Marrakech, Morocco. T/Sgt Adams. An unidentified object was observed on radar. The UFO was above 60,000 feet and moving at 625 knots.

June 13, 1952: Middletown, Pennsylvania. Witnessed by Thomas. Air Force investigation suggested that this might have been a balloon on its way down. The object was described as round in shape and orange in color. It was noted that the witness had held a penny at arm's length so that it was determined that the object was two times the size of a full moon. Unfortunately, the witness said that he had some knowledge of astrology and thought the object might be an exploding star.

June 15, 1952: Louisville, Kentucky. Witnessed by Edward Duke. A cigar-shaped object, blunt on the front and lighted at both ends, with a red glow at the rear, maneuvered in the area for about 15 minutes. The speed was estimated at between 400 and 500 mph.

June 16, 1952: Walker AFB, Roswell, New Mexico. A group of UFOs were sighted about one mile south of the airfield. There were gray in color and were flying about 5,000 feet above the ground, moving at between 500 and 600 mph.

June 17, 1952: McChord AFB, Washington. Series of sightings around the base on the 17th, 19th, and 23rd of June. Object was silver to yellowish-white, always described as a light and very bright.

June 17, 1952: Cape Cod, Massachusetts. Carried as an unidentified in the Project Blue Book files.

June 18, 1952: Columbus, Wisconsin. Carried as an unidentified in the Project Blue Book files.

June 18, 1952: Pontiac, Michigan. Witnessed by Hoffman. Carried as an unidentified in the Project Blue Book files.

June 19, 1952: Goose AFB, Labrador. 2nd Lt. A'Gostino. The object was described as being a red light moving in a wobbly manner. It turned white and disappeared. GCA radar confirmed the sighting.

June 19, 1952: Yuma, Arizona. Object was spotted as it was overhead, disappeared into the sun, and then reappeared. It was white, about the size of a silver dollar and round in shape.

June 20, 1952: Korea. Sgt. James Kinner and Sgt. A. P. Moore. A small object, only four feet in diameter, flew over an airfield in Korea. It was described as little more than a bright light.

June 21, 1952: Kelly AFB, Texas. T/Sgt. Howard Davis. An arrow-shaped object with a pointed nose and an oval trailing edge was sighted over the air base. There was a trail of reddish sparks and streaks that began behind the object.

June 22, 1952. Korea. Carried as an unidentified in the Project Blue Book files.

June 23, 1952. Spokane, Washington. Many people in the area saw a fiery ball of light that could have been a meteorite.

June 23, 1952: McChord AFB, Washington. See report from McChord AFB dated June 17, 1952.

June 23, 1952: Kirksville, Missouri. Carried as an unidentified in the Project Blue Book files. It is also noted in the Master Index that the case file is missing.

June 23, 1952: Oakridge, Tennessee. Carried as an unidentified in the Project Blue Book files.

June 23, 1952: Near Owensboro, Tennessee. A contractor named Depp heard a sound like aircraft and looked up to see two round objects, described as looking like soap bubbles, flying one behind the other. They disappeared in about five seconds.

June 25, 1952: Tokyo, Japan. Carried as an unidentified in the Project Blue Book files.

June 25, 1952: Chicago, Illinois. One bright yellowish to white egg-shaped light slightly larger than Venus with occasionally visible red taillight traveling in a large continuous circle at slow speed.

June 25, 1952. Japan, Korea area. US Naval vessel recorded a number of strong radar plots that were about the size of a B-29 but were considerably faster. No allied aircraft were in the area, and the location suggests that enemy fighters would not have the range.

June 26, 1952. Terre Haute, Indiana. Carried as an unidentified in the Project Blue Book files.

June 26, 1952: Pottstown, Pennsylvania. Five UFOs were sighting over a period of 30 minutes. First two objects were flying in tandem. The first had steady lights and the second had flashing lights. About 15 minutes later two more objects appeared flying in the same configuration. And 15 minutes after that, a single object appeared. There was no sound and the objects moved steadily across the sky.

June 27, 1952: Topeka, Kansas. 2nd Lt. Kerwin F. Kelly. Pilot saw one object that hovered and pulsated a brilliant red. Shape varied from circular to oval in the vertical dimension as the object pulsated.

June 28, 1952: Lake Kishkonoug, Wisconsin. One silver white sphere was observed over the lake. The object made a 180 degree turn and became elliptical turning the turn and then a sphere.

June 28, 1952: Nagoya, Honshu, Japan. Military witnesses saw a single, purplish-blue object that was elliptical. It maintained constant flight until it disappeared.

June 29, 1952: O'Hare Airport, Chicago, Illinois. Witnesses saw one oval object which was very bright and smooth like highly polished silver. After a time, object moved at a high rate of speed and disappeared like a light bulb being shut off.

July 3, 1952: Selfridge AFB, Michigan. The witness watched two circular-shaped lights, about twenty feet in diameter, traveling horizontally at a tremendous rate of speed.

July 3, 1952: Chicago, Illinois. Two disk-shaped objects flew one behind the other, each described as about the size of one-third of the full moon. The objects were a "bright pastel green with non-persisting luminescent trails and were traveling much faster than a jet but slower than a meteorite."

July 5, 1952: Norman, Oklahoma. An Oklahoma State Trooper, flying near Norman, saw three disk-shaped, dark objects in a formation, hovering. As he watched through binoculars, the objects diminished in size and then disappeared.

July 6-12, 1952: Governors Island, New York. Amateur photographer Neff was making time exposures didn't see the object until the film was developed.

July 9, 1952: Colorado Springs, Colorado. Witnessed by two military pilots. The object was described as resembling one-half of a conventional airfoil with a chopped off trailing edge. The object was a bright, glowing white. It traveled in a slow and erratic way before disappearing.

July 9, 1952: Kutztown, Pennsylvania. Photographs taken by Mittl. He took three photographs of the object, which made no noise. After he took the pictures, the object disappeared.

July 12, 1952: Annapolis, Maryland. Witnessed by Washburn. Four elliptical-shaped objects, about a third the size of a transport aircraft, in a four abreast formation, appeared at a high rate of speed, stopped momentarily, executed a right-angle turn, picked up their high speed and then disappeared in mid-air.

July 13, 1952: Kirksville, Missouri. Object seen on military radar and case file accompanied by scope photographs. The object was recorded as traveling at 1500 knots. There was no visual sighting, and the file suggested a possible weather solution, but the sighting is carried as unidentified.

July 14, 1952: Norfolk, Virginia. This is the Nash-Fortenberry sighting. Carried as an unidentified in the Project Blue Book files.

July 15, 1952: West Palm Beach, Florida. One object, gray in color but sometimes appearing slightly yellow and looked like a "flattened out donut without the hole" approached very fast. It slowed to a hover and after about a minute and a half, picked up speed and disappeared.

July 16, 1952: Beverly, Massachusetts. This is the photographic case that is normally labeled as Salem, Massachusetts. Pictures were taken by Shell R. Alpert.

July 17, 1952: Lockbourne AFB, Ohio. Witnessed by Stevenson and one other man. "A circular object that giving the appearance of a star appeared somewhat smaller than an average airplane." The object's rim gave off an orange and green glow. The object appeared and disappeared over a period of four hours.

July 17, 1952: White Plains, NY. A civilian woman saw two large flying saucers which made a whirring sound and that were flying on edge. They were in sight for only five or six seconds.

July 17, 1952: Rapid City, South Dakota. A master sergeant reported 12 to 14 objects that he described as glowing orange. They flew straight and level and seemed to fly faster than jet aircraft.

July 18, 1852: Lockbourne AFB, Ohio. Elliptical object with pinpoint of flame in the rear which would periodically "flare" was seen by two military men. The object had a resonant beat as it moved through the sky at high speed.

July 18, 1952: Miami, Florida. Witnessed by Raymer. The sound of an aircraft drew his attention to the sky where he saw a spherical bubble about five feet in diameter moving across the sky. It finally disappeared into the clouds.

July 18, 1952: Patrick AFB, Florida. Fred England, A.R. Lasenby and E.W. Taylor. One to five lights were seen over about an hour by both military and civilians on the base. The objects resembled weather balloons but maneuvered erratically and appeared in groups of twos, threes and fours.

July 19, 1952: Williston, North Dakota. A civilian pilot watched a round object that was very high and very distant, and it maneuvered for about five minutes. Finally, it climbed out of sight.

July 19, 1952: Elkins Park, Pennsylvania. An Air Force pilot saw two objects that looked like stars move through the sky. They stopped to hover and then disappeared after about five to seven minutes.

July 20, 1952: Lavalette, New Jersey. Witnessed by Spoomer. Spoomer, a chemistry professor saw lights that he described as resembling those seen over Washington, D.C.

July 21, 1952: Wiesbaden, Germany. Captain Edward E. Dougher and Lt. Joesphine J. Strong. The two officers, in separate locations watched two or four long, slender objects for between ten to fifteen minutes. The objects were described as bright yellow lights.

July 21, 1952: San Marcos, Texas. 1st Lt. Wayne D. Scott, S/Sgt Samuel R. Locke, S/Sgt Thedford R. Townsend, A/1c David McKenzie, A/2c Frank R. Norred and A/1c Paul M. Nelson, Jr. A singular, perfectly circular object, giving off a brilliant blue-white light was sighted by the Air Force personnel listed. The object moved at various speeds and hovered briefly. It disappeared as if a light had been extinguished.

July 21, 1952: Randolph AFB, Texas. Two witnesses, one military and one civilian, saw a silver-colored cigar-shaped object at a low altitude but traveling at a high rate of speed. It made an abrupt turn and then climbed vertically out of sight.

July 21, 1952: Holyoke, Massachusetts. Witnessed by Burgess and two others. Three people saw a round, orange-yellow object flash downward.

July 22, 1952: Rockville, Indiana. A triangular-shaped object the size of a C-47 flew across the sky, stopping to hover for about half a minute. It resumed flight and disappeared in the distance.

July 22, 1952: Uvalde, Texas. The witness, a weather observer, saw a large, round object of silver, about 30 feet in diameter, moving at a speed estimated at over a thousand miles an hour. It seemed to climb and finally disappeared into a cloud.

July 22, 1952: Los Alamos, New Mexico. Don R. Wiens and two others. Wiens the tower operator saw eight round, aluminum-colored objects fly a straight and level course and then begin erratic maneuvers. The man watched them through binoculars.

July 23, 1952: Pottstown, Pennsylvania. 8:40 a.m. The two-man crews of three USAF F-94 jet interceptors saw a large silver object, shaped like a long pear with two or three squares beneath it, flew at 150-180 KTS, while a smaller object, delta-shaped or swept back, flew around it at 1,000 - 1,500 KTS.

July 22, 1952: between Boston and Provincetown, Massachusetts. 10:47 p.m. Pilot and radar operator of USAF F-94 jet interceptor. One round blue light passed F-94, spinning.

July 23, 1952: Altoona, Pennsylvania. 12:50 p.m. Two-man crews of two USAF F-94 jet interceptors at 35-46,000' altitude. Three cylindrical objects in a vertical stack formation flew at an altitude of 50-80,000 feet.

July 23, 1952: Trenton, New Jersey. Jet interceptors made fourteen different visual sightings of bluish- white lights. One sighting was made by radar.

July 23, 1952: South Bend, Indiana. 11:35 p.m. USAF pilot Capt. H. W. Kloth. Two bright blue-white objects flew together, then the rear one veered off after about 9 minutes.

July 24, 1952: Carson Sink, Nevada. 3:40 p.m. Two USAF LTCs McGinn and Barton in a B-25 bomber watched three silver, delta-shaped objects, each with a ridge along the top, crossed in front of and above the B-25 at high speed, in 3-4 seconds.

July 24, 1952: Travis AFB, California. T/Sgt. T.B. Mezo, M/Sgt L. E. Hanson, S/Sgt D.C. Steen. Mezo was the first to see the bright, orange light that looked as if it was landing at the base. It seemed to hover and then made a slow turn to the west and moved off at a high rate of speed.

July 26, 1952: Washington, D.C. 8 p.m. until after midnight. Radar operators at several airports, airline pilots and military pilots saw strange lights. Many unidentified blips tracked by radar all over Washington area, at varying speeds. Pilots spotted unidentified lights.

July 26, 1952: Kansas City, Missouri. 12:15 a.m. USAF Capt. H. A. Stone, men in control towers at Fairfax Field and Municipal Airport watched the UFO. One greenish light with red-orange flashes was seen for 1 hour as it descended in the northwest from 40* elevation to 10* elevation.

July 26, 1952: Andrews AFB, Maryland. This was a continuation of the extensive sightings and radar tracking reports reported throughout the Washington, D.C. area, all night long.

July 26, 1952: Kirtland AFB, New Mexico. 12:05 a.m. Airman 1st Class J.M. Donaldson. Eight to ten orange balls in a triangular or V-formation flew very fast for 3-4 seconds.

July 26, 1952: Williams, California. Case missing from official files.

July 27, 1952: Selfridge AFB, Michigan. 10:05 a.m. Three B-29 bomber crewmen on ground. Many round, white objects flew straight and level, very fast. Two at 10:05, one at 10:10, one at 10:15, one at 10:20. Each was seen for about 30 seconds.

July 27, 1952: Wichita Falls, Texas. 8:30 p.m. Mr. and Mrs. Adrian Ellis. Two disc-shaped objects, illuminated by a phosphorus light, flew at an estimated 1,000 mph for 15 seconds.

July 28, 1952: Heidelberg, West Germany. 10:20 p.m. Sgt. B.C. Grassmoen, WAC PFC. A.P. Turner. One saucer-shaped object having an appearance of light metal and giving off shafts of white light, flew slow, made a 90^ turn and climbed away fast after 4-5 minutes.

July 28, 1952: McGuire AFB, New Jersey. 6 a.m. Ground Control Approach radar operator MSGT W.F. Dees, and persons in the base control tower tracked on radar a large cluster of very distinct blips. The visual observation was of oblong objects having neither wings nor tail, which made a very fast turn and at one time were in echelon formation.

July 28, 1952: McChord AFB, Washington. 2:15 a.m. TSGT Walstead, SSGT Calkins of the 635th AC&W Squadron saw a dull, glowing, blue-green ball...the size of a dime at arms' length, flew very fast, straight and level.

July 29, 1952: Osceola, Wisconsin. 1:30 a.m. Radar operators on ground, pilot of F-51 Mustang in flight saw several clusters of up to 10 small radar targets and one large target. Small targets moved from southwest to east at 50-60 KTS. following each other. The large one moved at 600 KTS. Pilot confirmed one target.

July 29, 1952: Langley AFB, Virginia. 2:30 p.m. USAF Capt. D.G. Moore, of military air traffic control system. One undescribed object flew at an estimated 2,600 m.p.h., below 5,000' altitude, toward the air base for about 2 minutes.

July 29, 1952: Langley AFB, Virginia. 2:50 p.m. Mr. Moore, Gilfillan electronics representative W. Yhope. One radar target tracked moving away, stopped for 2 minutes, again moved very, very fast.

July 29, 1952; Merced, California. 3:44 or 4:35 p.m. Herbert Mitchell and one employee. One dark, discus-shaped object, trailed by a silvery light 2 lengths

242

behind, tipped on its side, dove, hesitated and then circled very fast during the 2-minute sighting.

July 29, 1952: Wichita, Kansas. 12:35 p.m. USAF shop employees Douglas and Hess at Municipal Airport. One bright white circular object with a flat bottom flew very fast, and then hovered 10-15 seconds over the Cessna Aircraft Co. plant, during the5-minute sighting.

July 29, 1952: Ennis, Montana. 12:30 p.m. USAF persons, alerted that UFOs were coming from the direction of Seattle, Wash did see two to five flat disc-shaped objects one of which hovered for 3-4 minutes, while the others circled it.

July 30, 1952: Albuquerque, New Mexico. 11:02 p.m. USAF 1st Lt. George Funk saw an orange light remained stationary for about 10 minutes.

July 30, 1952: San Antonio, Texas. 10 a.m. E.E. Nye and one other person watched as one round, white object flew slow and then sped away after 20-30 minutes.

Aug.1, 1952: Lancaster, California. 1:14 a.m. Sheriff's deputies and other persons, one named Mallette saw two brilliant red lights hovered and maneuvered for 5 minutes.

Aug. 2, 1952: Lake Charles, Louisiana. 3 a.m. USAF 1st LT W.A. Theil, one enlisted man. One red ball with a blue flame tail flew straight and level for 3-4 seconds.

Aug. 4, 1952: Phoenix, Arizona. 2:20 a.m. USAF A3C W.F. Vain. One yellow ball which lengthened and narrowed to plate shape, flew straight and level for 5 minutes.

Aug. 4, 1952: Mt. Vernon, New York. 11:37 a.m. One woman, two children. One object, shaped like a lifesaver or donut, emitted black smoke from its top and made a 15' arc in 1.5 minutes.

Aug 5. 1952: Haneda AFB, Japan. 11:30 p.m. USAF F-94 jet interceptor pilots lLT W.R. Holder and lLT A.M. Jones, and Haneda control tower operators. Airborne radar tracked a target for 90 seconds. Control tower operators watched 50-60 minutes while a dark shape with a light flew as fast as 330 kTS. (380 mph), hovered, flew curves and performed a variety of maneuvers.

Aug. 6, 1952: Tokyo, Japan. This is a continuation of the Haneda AFB sightings. The case is missing from the official files.

Aug. 6, 1952: Belleville, Michigan. Case and card seem to be missing from the official files.

Aug. 6, 1952: Port Austin, Michigan. Although the case missing from official files, the project card is available. According to it, "Radar unit at Port Austin, Michigan observed several objects which were very large and flew at speeds in excess of 1200 knots - Objects were in vicinity of Gore Bay, Canada."

Aug. 7. 1952: San Antonio, Texas. 9:08 a.m. Mrs. Susan Pfuhl. Four glowing white discs: one made a 180* turn, one flew straight and level, one veered off, and one circled during the 70-minute sighting.

Aug. 9, 1952: Lake Charles, Louisiana. 10:50 a.m. USAF A3C J.P. Raley. One disc-shaped object flew very fast and then hovered for 2 seconds during a 5–6-minute sighting.

Aug. 13, 1952: Tokyo, Japan. 9:45 p.m. USAF Marine Corps pilot Maj. D. McGough. One orange light flew a left orbit at 8,000' and 230 m.p.h., spiraled down to no more than 1,500', remained stationary for 2-3 minutes and went out. An attempted interception was unsuccessful.

Aug. 18, 1952: Fairfield, California. 12:50 a.m. Three policemen watched one object changed color like a diamond and changed directions during the 30-minute sighting.

Aug. 19, 1952: Red Bluff, California. 2:38 p.m. Ground Observer Corps observer Albert Lathrop saw two objects, shaped like fat bullets, flew straight and level, very fast for 25 seconds.

Aug. 20, 1952: Neffesville, Pennsylvania. 3:10 a.m. Bill Ford and two others saw an undescribed object flew at 500' altitude for several minutes.

Aug. 21, 1952: Dallas, Texas. 11:54 p.m. Jack Rossen, ex-artillery observer saw three blue-white lights hovered then descended and then, 1 and a half minutes later, one of them descended more.

Aug. 23, 1952: Akron, Ohio. 4:10 a.m. USAF 2nd Lt. H.K. Funseth, a ground radar observer, and two U.S. Navy men saw a single pulsing amber light was seen to fly straight and level for 7 minutes.

Aug. 24, 1952: Hermanas, Mexico. 10:15 a.m. Georgia Air National Guard F-84G jet fighter pilot Col. G.W. Johnson saw two 6' silver balls in abreast formation, one turned grey rapidly, the other slowly. One changed to long grey shape during a turn. Sighting lasted about 10 minutes.

Aug. 24, 1952: Tucson, Arizona. 5:40 p.m. Mr. and Mrs. George White watched one large round, metallic, white light with a vague lower surface, flew slowly, then fast with a dancing, wavering motion, for about 1 minute.

Aug. 24, 1952: Levelland, Texas. 9:30 p.m., 10:30 p.m. Mr. and Mrs. Elmer Sharp saw a single object, shaped like a spinning top, changing color from red to yellow to blue, and with a fiery tail, hovered for 20 minutes, whistling, then flew away. It, or another like it, returned an hour later.

Aug. 25, 1952: Pittsburg, Kansas. 5:35 a.m. Radio station musician William Squyres saw a single dull aluminum object, shaped like two meat platters, face to face, estimated at 75 feet long, 45 feet wide, and 15 feet thick. Through a window in the front section shone a blue light; the head and shoulders of a man could be seen. The mid-section had numerous windows through which could be seen some kind of regular movement. A series of small propellers were spaced close together along the outer edge of the object, revolving at high speed. The object was hovering about 10' above the ground, 100 yards off the road, with a slight rocking motion. It then ascended vertically with a sound like a large covey of quail starting to fly at the same time. Vegetation showed signs of having been disturbed under the object.

Aug. 25, 1952: Delaware, Ohio. An astronomer sighted an object that remained in place for one hour and fifteen minutes. A bright light that was yellow was as bright as Jupiter and the red light flashed.

Aug. 25, 1952: Holloman AFB, New Mexico. 3:40 p.m. Civilian supervisor Fred Lee, foreman L.A. Aquilar watched a single round silver object flew south, turned and flew north, made a 360 turn and flew away vertically after 3-5 minutes.

Aug. 26, 1952: Lathrop Wells, Nevada. 12:10 a.m. USAF Capt. D.A. Woods. One large, round, very bright object with a V-shaped contrail having a dark cone in the center, flew very fast, hovered, made an instantaneous 90 turn, followed by a gentle climb and finally sudden acceleration.

Aug. 26, 1952: Biloxi, Mississippi. The object was in the sky east southeast of town, was round and flat and reddish-orange. The observer suggested it was nine feet by fifteen feet and he gave no estimate of altitude or speed. There were two trails behind the object, similar to jet vapor trails. The object was in sight for seventy-five minutes and twenty-three pictures were taken. Unfortunately, the film was badly underexposed.

Aug. 28, 1952: Chickasaw and Brookley AFB, Alabama. 9:30 p.m. USAF control tower operators, officer from USAF Office of Special Investigations, and others. Six objects, varying from fiery red to sparkling diamond appearance, hovered, flew erratically up and down for 1 hour and 15minutes.

Aug. 29, 1952: Colorado Springs, Colorado. 8:35 p.m. Pilot C.A. Magruder. Three objects, 50' in diameter, 10' high, aluminum with red-yellow exhaust, flew in trail at estimated 1,500 mph for 4-5 seconds.

Aug. 29, 1952: west of Thule, Greenland. 10:50 a.m. Two U.S. Navy pilots flying a P4Y-2 patrol plane. Three white disc-shaped or spherical objects hovered, then flew very fast in a triangular formation, in 2-3 minutes.

Bibliography

Air Defense Command Briefing, Jan 1953, Project Blue Book Files.

Air Intelligence Report No. 100-201-79, "Analysis of Flying Object Incidents in the U.S., 10 December 1948.

Alberts, Don E. and Putnam, Allan E. *A History of Kirtland Air Force Base 1928-1982.* Albuquerque: 1606th Air Base Wing, 1985.

Alexander, John B. *UFOs: Myths, Conspiracies, and Realities.* New York: St. Martin's Press, 2011.

Asimov, Issac. *Is Anyone There?* New York: Ace Books, 1967

ATIC UFO Briefing, April 1952, Project Blue Book Files.

Baker, Raymond D. *Historical Highlights of Andrews AFB 1942 - 1989.* Andrews AFB, Maryland: 1776th Air Base Wing, 1990.

Barnes, Harry G. "Washington Radar Observer Relates Watching Stunts by Flying Saucers." *New York World-Telegram* (July 29, 1952).

Baxter, John. and Atkins Thomas. *The Fire Came By.* Garden City, N.Y.: Doubleday, 1976.

Binder, Otto. *What We Really Know About Flying Saucers.* Greenwich, Conn.: Fawcett Gold Medal, 1967.
------. *Flying Saucers are Watching Us.* New York: Tower, 1968.
------. "The Secret Warehouse of UFO Proof." *UFO Report,* 2,2 (Winter 1974),16 – 19, 50, 52.

"Blips on the Scopes." *Time* (August 4, 1952).

Bloecher, Ted. *Report on the UFO Wave of 1947.* Washington, D.C.: Author, 1967.

Blum, Howard. *Out There: The Government's Secret Quest for Extraterrestials.* New York: Simon and Schuster, 1991.

Blum, Ralph, with Blum, Judy. *Beyond Earth: Man's Contact with UFOs*. New York: Bantam Books, 1974.

Bowen, Charles (ed). *The Humanoids*. Chicago: Henry Regency, 1969.

Braenne, Ole Jonny. "Legend of the Spitzbergen Saucer." *International UFO Reporter* 17, 6 (November/December 1992), 14 – 20.

Briefing Document: Operation Majestic 12, November 18, 1952.

Britton, Jack, and Washington, George, Jr. *Military Shoulder Patches of the United States Armed Forces*. Tulsa, Okla.: MCN Press, 1985.

Brown, Eunice H. *White Sands History*. White Sands, N.M.: Public Affairs Office, 1959.

Brown, Harold. "C.A.A. Chief Debunks 'Objects', Radar Probably Spotted Trucks." *New York Herald Tribune* (July 30, 1952).

Bullard, Thomas E. *The Myth and Mystery of UFOs*. Lawrence, KS: University of Kansas Press, 2010.

Burleson, Donald R. "Levelland, Texas, 1957: Case Reopened," *International UFO Reporter*, 28, 1 (Spring 2003) 3 – 6, 25.

-----. "Deciphering the Ramey Memo," *International UFO Reporter* 25,2 (Summer 2000): 3 –6, 32.

Candeo, Anne. *UFO's The Fact or Fiction Files*. New York: Walker 1990.

Cannon, Martin. "The Amazing Story of John Lear." *UFO Universe* (March 1990): 8.

Carey, Thomas J. "The Search for the Archaeologists." *International UFO Reporter* (November/December 1991): 4-9, 21.

Carpenter, Joel. "The Senator, The Saucer, and Special Report 14." *International UFO Reporter* 25,1 (Spring 2000): 3 – 11, 30.

Carpenter, John S. "Gerald Anderson: Truth vs. Fiction." *The MUFON UFO Journal* no 281 (September 1991): 3-7, 12.

Catoe, Lynn E. *UFOs and Related Subjects: An Annotated Bibliography*. Washington, D.C.: Government Printing Office, 1969.

Chaikin, Andrew. "Target: Tunguska." *Sky & Telescope* (January 1984):18-21.

Chester, Keith. *Strange Company: Military Encounters with UFOs in WW II.* San Antonio, TX: Anomalist Books, 2007.

Clark, Jerome. *UFO's in the 1980s.* Detroit: Apogee, 1990.
------. *The UFO Encyclopedia, Third Edition.* Detroit: Omnigraphics, 2018.
------. *Hidden Realms, Lost Civilizations and Beings from Other Worlds,* Detroit: Visible Ink Press 2010.

Committee on Science and Astronautics, report, 1961.

Cohen, Daniel. *Encyclopedia of the Strange.* New York: Avon, 1987.
------. *UFOs - The Third Wave.* New York: Evans, 1988.

"Could the Scully Story Be True?" *The Saucerian Bulletin* 1,2 (May 1956), 1.

Creighton, Gordon. "Close Encounters of an Unthinkable and Inadmissible Kind." *Flying Saucer Review.* (July/August 1979).

Davison, Leon, ed. *Flying Saucers: An Analysis of Air Force Project Blue Book Special Report No. 14.* Clarksburg, Va.: Saucerian Press, 1971.

Davies, John K. *Cosmic Impact.* New York: St. Martin's, 1986.

Davis, Richard. "Results of a Search for Records Concerning the 1947 Crash Near Roswell, New Mexico." Washington, D.C.: GAO, 1995

Dennett, Preston. "Project Redlight: Are We Flying the Saucers Too?" *UFO Universe,* May 1990: 39.

"DoD News Releases And Fact Sheets," 1952 – 1968.

Dolan, Richard M. *UFOs and the National Security State.* Charlottesville, VA.: Hampton Roads Publishing Company, 2000.

------. *UFOs and the National Security State: The Cover-Up Exposed, 1973 – 1991.* Rochester, NY: Keyhole Publishing, 2009.

Editors. "Flying Saucers." *Look* (1966).

Edwards, Frank. *Flying Saucers - Here and Now!* New York: Bantam,1968.
------. *Flying Saucers - Serious Business.* New York: Bantam, 1966.

------. *Strange World*. New York: Bantam, 1964.

Eighth Air Force Staff Directory, Texas: June 1947.

Endres, Terry and Pat Packard. "The Pflock Report in Perspective." *UFO Update Newsletter*, 1,5 (Fall 1994) 1-6.

Estes, Russ (producer) "Quality of the Messenger." *Crystal Sky Productions*, 1993.

"Experts Say a Meteor Caused Flash of Fire," *Deseret News* (April 19, 1962): 1.

Fact Sheet, "Office of Naval Research 1952 Greenland Cosmic Ray Scientific Expedition," October 16, 1952.

Fawcett, Lawrence and Barry J. Greenwood. *Clear Intent: The Government Cover-up of the UFO Experience*. Englewood Cliffs, N.J.: Prentice-Hall, 1984.

Final Report, "Project Twinkle," Project Blue Book Files, Nov. 1951.

Finney, Ben R. and Eric M. Jones. *Interstellar Migration and the Human Experience*. CA: University of California Press, 1985.

First Status Report, Project STORK (Preliminary to Special Report No. 14), April 1952.

"Flying Saucers Again." *Newsweek*, April 17, 1950, 29.

"Flying Saucers Are Real." *Flying Saucer Review* (January/February 1956) 2-5

Foster, Tad. Unpublished articles for Condon Committee Casebook. 1969

Fowler, Raymond E. *Casebook of a UFO Investigator*. Englewood Cliffs, N.J.: Prentice-Hall, 1981

"Flying Saucers Are Real," *Flying Saucer Review*, (January/February 1956).

Genesce County (Michigan) telephone directories 1945-1950.

Gevaerd, A. J. "Flying Saucer or Distillation Machine?" *Brazilian UFO Magazine*, November 2006.

Gillmor, Daniel S., ed. *Scientific Study of Unidentified Flying Objects*. New York:

Bantam Books, 1969.

Goldsmith, Donald. *Nemesis*. New York: Berkley Books, 1985.
------. *The Quest for Extraterrestrial Life*. Mill Valley, Calif.: University Science Books, 1980.

Good, Timothy. *Above Top Secret*. New York: Morrow, 1988.
------. *The UFO Report*. New York: Avon Books, 1989.
------. *Alien Contact*. New York: Morrow, 1993.

Graeber, Matt. "The Reality, the Hoaxes and the Legend." The Author, 2009.

Gribben, John. "Cosmic Disaster Shock." *New Scientist* (Mar 6, 1980):750-52.

Gross, Loren E. UFOs: *A History – 1952: June – July 20th*. Fremont, CA: The Author, 1986.
------. *A History – 1952: July 21st– July 31st*. Fremont, CA: The Author, 1986.

"Guidance for Dealing with Space Objects Which Have Returned to Earth, Department of State Airgram, July 26, 1973.

Hall, Michael. "Was There a Second Estimate of the Situation," *International UFO Reporter*, 27,1 (Spring 2002), 10 – 14, 32.

Hall, Michael and Wendy Connors. Captain Edward J. Ruppelt: Summer of The Saucers – 1952. Albuquerque, NM: Rose Press, 2000.

Hall, Richard. *Uninvited Guests*. Santa Fe, NM: Aurora Press, 1988.
------. ed. *The UFO Evidence*. Washington, D.C.: NICAP, 1964.

Hanrahan, James Stephen. *History of Research in Space Biology and Biodynamics at the Air Force Missile Development Center 1946 - 1958*. Alamogordo, NM: Office of Information Services, 1959.

------. *Contributions of Balloon Operations to Research and Development at the Air Force Missile Development Center 1947 - 1958*. Alamogordo, NM: Office of Information Services, 1959.

Hastings, Robert. *UFOs and Nukes*. Bloomington, Ind.: Author House, 2008.

Hegt, William H. Noordhoek. "News of Spitzbergen UFO Revealed." *APRG Reporter* (February 1957): 6.

Hippler, Robert H. "Letter to Edward U. Condon," January 16, 1967.

"History of the Eighth Air Force, Fort Worth, Texas," (Microfilm) Air
    Force Archives, Maxwell Air Force Base, AL.

Hogg, Ivan U. and J. B. King. *German and Allied Secret Weapons of World War
    II.* London: Chartwell, 1974.

Hughes, Jim. "Light, Boom a Mystery. *Denver Post*, 12 January 1998.

Huyghe, Patrick A. "The 1952 UFO 'Raid' That Panicked Washington, D.C.
    UFO Report 4 no. 4 (August 1977)

Hynek, J. Allen. *The UFO Experience: A Scientific Inquiry.* Chicago: Henry
    Regency, 1975.

Hynek, J. Allen and Jacques Vallee. *The Edge of Reality.* Chicago: Henry
    Regency, 1972.

Jacobs, David M. *The UFO Controversy in America.* New York: Signet, 1975.

Jung, Carl G. *Flying Saucers: A Modern Myth of Things Seen in the
    Sky.* New York: Harcourt, Brace, 1959.

Strange Creatures from Space and Time. New York: Fawcett, 1970.

Keyhoe, Donald E. *Flying Saucers from Outer Space.* New York: Henry Holt and
    Company, 1953.
------. *Aliens From Space.* New York: Signet, 1974.

Klass, Philip J. *UFOs Explained.* New York: Random House, 1974.
------. *The Public Deceived.* Buffalo, NY: Prometheus Books, 1983.

Knaack, Marcelle. *Encyclopedia of U.S. Air Force Aircraft and Missile
    Systems.* Washington, D.C.: Office of Air Force History, 1988.

LaPaz, Lincoln and Albert Rosenfeld. "Japan's Balloon Invasion of America,"
    Collier's, January 17, 1953, 9.
Library of Congress Legislative Reference Service, "Facts about UFOs," May
    1966.
Lore, Gordon, and Harold H. Deneault. *Mysteries of the Skies: UFOs
    in Perspective.* Englewood Cliff, N.J.: Prentice-Hall, 1968.

Lorenzen, Coral and Jim Lorenzen. *Flying Saucers: The Startling Evidence of the*

Invasion from Outer Space. New York: Signet, 1966.

------. *Flying Saucer Occupants*. New York: Signet, 1967

------. *Encounters with UFO Occupants*. New York: Berkley Medallion Books, 1976

Low, Robert J. "Letter to Lt. Col. Robert Hippler," January 27, 1967.

Maccabee, Bruce. "Hiding the Hardware." *International UFO Reporter.* (September/October 1991): 4.

------. "What the Admiral Knew." *International UFO Reporter.* (November/ December 1986).

"McClellan Sub-Committee Hearings," March 1958.

"McCormack Sub-Committee Briefing," August 1958.

McDonald, James E. UFOs – An International Scientific Problem. Tucson, AZ: The Author, 1968.

McDonough, Thomas R. *The Search for Extraterrestrial Intelligence*. New York: Wiley & Sons, 1987.

Menzel, Donald H. and Lyle G. Boyd. *The World of Flying Saucers*. Garden City, NY: Doubleday, 1963.

Menzel, Donald H. Ernest Taves. *The UFO Enigma*. Garden City, New York: Doubleday, 1977.

Moseley, James W. and Karl T. Pflock. *Shockingly Close to the Truth*. Amherst, N.Y.: Prometheus Books, 2002.

Mueller, Robert. *Air Force Bases: Volume 1, Active Air Force Bases within the United States of American on 17 September 1982*. Washington, D.C.: Office of Air Force History, 1989.

National Security Agency. Presidential Documents. Washington, D.C.: Executive Order 12356, 1982.

Neilson, James. "'Secret U.S./UFO Structure." *UFO*, 4,1, (1989): 4-6.

NICAP, *The UFO Evidence*. Washington, D.C.: NICAP, 1964.

"No Sign of 'UFO' – *NSRI*. News24, 5 May

Oberg, James. "UFO Update: UFO Buffs May Be Unwitting Pawns in an Elaborate Government Charade," *Omni* 15, no. 11 September 1993: 75.

Olive, Dick. "Most UFO's Explainable, Says Scientist." *Elmira (NY) Star-Gazette* 26 January 1967, 19

Papagiannis, Michael D., ed. *The Search for Extraterrestrial Life: Recent Developments.* Boston: 1985.

Peebles, Curtis. *The Moby Dick Project.* Washington, D.C.: Smithsonian Institution Press, 1991.
------. *Watch the Skies!* NewYork, N.Y.: Berkley Books, 1995.

Legacies." In Walter H. Andrus, Jr., ed. *MUFON 1995 International UFO Symposium Proceedings* Seguin, TX: MUFON, 1990: 154-68.

Press Conference - General Samford, Project Blue Book Files, 1952.

"Project Blue Book" (microfilm). National Archives, Washington, D.C.

"Radar and the Saucers." *Washington Post.* (July 25, 1952).

Randle, Kevin D. "Mysterious Clues Left Behind by UFOs," *Saga's UFO Annual*(Summer 1972).
------. "The Pentagon's Secret Air War Against UFOs," *Saga* (March 1976).
------. *The UFO Casebook.* New York: Warner, 1989.
------. *Conspiracy of Silence.* New York: Avon, 1997.
------. *Project Moon Dust.* England: Lume Books, 2022.
------. *Scientific Ufology.* New York: Avon, 1999.
------. *Reflections of a UFO Investigator,* San Antonio, TX: Anomalist Books, 2012.

Randle, Kevin D. and Cornett, Robert Charles. "Project Blue Book Cover-up: Pentagon Suppressed UFO Data," *UFO Report* 2 no. 5 (Fall 1975).

Randles, Jenny. *The UFO Conspiracy.* New York: Javelin, 1987.

"Rocket and Missile Firings," White Sands Proving Grounds, Jan - Jul 1947.

Rosignoli, Guido. *The Illustrated Encyclopedia of Military Insignia of the 20th Century.* Secaucus, N.J.: Chartwell, 1986.

Ruppelt, Edward J. *The Report on Unidentified Flying Objects.* New York:

Ace, 1956.

Russell, Eric. "Phantom Balloons Over North America," *Modern Aviation*
    (February 1953).

Sagan, Carl and Page, Thornton, eds. *UFO's: Scientific Debate*. New York:
    Norton, 1974.

Sanderson, Ivan T. "Meteorite-like Object Made a Turn in Cleveland,
    O. Area," *Omaha World-Herald* (December 15, 1965).
------. "Something Landed in Pennsylvania." *Fate* 19,3 (March 1966).
------. *Uninvited Visitors*. New York: Cowles, 1967.
------. *Invisible Residents*. New York: World Publishing, 1970.

Saunders, David and R. Roger Harkins. *UFOs? Yes!* New York: New American
    Library, 1968

Sheaffer, Robert. *The UFO Verdict*. Buffalo, NY: Prometheus, 1981.

Simmons, H.M. "Once Upon A Time in the West." *Magonia* (August 1985).

Slate, B. Ann "The Case of the Crippled Flying Saucer." *Saga* (April
    1972): 22-25, 64, 66-68, 71, 72.

Smith, Scott. "Q & A: Len Stringfield." *UFO* 6,1, (1991): 20-24.

"The Space Men at Wright-Patterson." UFO Update.

Special Report No. 14, (Project Blue Book) 1955.

Spencer, John. *The UFO Encyclopedia*. New York: Avon, 1993.

Spencer, John and Evans, Hilary. *Phenomenon*. New York: Avon, 1988.

Status Reports, "Grudge - Blue Book, Nos. 1 - 12."

Steiger, Brad. *Strangers from the Skies*. New York: Award, 1966.
------. *Project Blue Book*. New York: Ballantine, 1976.
------. *UFO Missionaries Extraordinary*. New York: Pocket Books, 1976.
------. *The Fellowship*. New York: Dolphin Books, 1988.

Steiger, Brad and Steiger, Sherry Hanson. *The Rainbow Conspiracy*. New
    York: Pinnacle, 1994.
------. *Conspiracies and Secret Societies*. Canton, MI: Visible Ink Press, 2006.

------. *Real Aliens, Space Beings, and Creatures from Other Worlds.* Canton, MI: Visible Ink Press, 2011.

Stone, Clifford E. *UFO's: Let the Evidence Speak for Itself.* Calif: The Author, 1991.

------. "The U.S. Air Force's Real, Official Investigation of UFO's." private report: The Author, 1993.

Stonehill, Paul. "Former Pilot Tells of Captured UFO." UFO 8,2 (March/April 1993): 10 —11.

Story, Ronald D. *The Encyclopedia of UFOs.* Garden City, New York: Doubleday, 1980.
------. *The Encyclopedia of Extraterrestrial Encounters.* New York: New American Library, 2001.

Sturrock, P.A. "UFOs - A Scientific Debate," *Science* 180 (1973): 593.

Sullivan, Walter. *We Are Not Alone.* New York: Signet, 1966.

Summer, Donald A. "Skyhook Churchill 1966," *Naval Reserve Reviews* (January 1967): 29.

Swords, Michael D., ed. *Journal of UFO Studies*, New Series, Vol. 4. Chicago: CUFOS, 1993.
-----. "Too Close for Condon: Close Encounters of the 4th Kind," *International UFO Reporter*, 28,3 (Fall 2003) 3 – 6.

Swords, Michael and Robert Powell. UFOs and Government. San Antonio: Anomalist Books, 2012

Tech Bulletin, "Army Ordnance Department Guided Missile Program," Jan 1948.

Technical Report, "Unidentified Aerial Objects, Project SIGN," Feb. 1949.

Technical Report, "Unidentified Flying Objects, Project GRUDGE," August 1949.

Templeton, David., "The Uninvited," *Pittsburgh Press* (May 19, 1991):

U.S. Congress, House Committee on Armed Forces. Unidentified Flying

Objects. Hearings, 89th Congress, 2nd Session, April 5, 1966. Washington D.C.: U.S. Government Printing Office, 1968.

U.S. Congress Committee on Science and Astronautics. Symposium on Unidentified Flying Objects. July 29, 1968, Hearings, Washington, D.C.: U.S. Government Printing Office, 1968.

Vallee, Jacques. *Anatomy of a Phenomenon*. New York: Ace, 1966.
------. *Challenge to Science*. New York: Ace, 1966.
------. *Dimensions*. New York: Ballantine, 1989.
------. *Revelations*. New York: Ballantine, 1991.

War Department. Meteorological Balloons (Army Technical Manual) Washington, D.C.: Government Printing Office, 1944.

"Washington Blips" Life (August 4, 1952).

Wilkins, Harold T. *Flying Saucers on the Attack*. New York: Citadel, 1954.
------. *Flying Saucers Uncensored*. New York: Pyramid, 1967.

Wise, David and Ross, Thomas B. *The Invisible Government*. New York: 1964.

Zeidman, Jennie. "I Remember Blue Book." *International UFO Reporter* (March/April 1991): 7.

Index:

THE BEST OF

PROJECT
BLUE
BOOK

KEVIN D. RANDLE, LT. COL. USAR (RET)

LEVELLAND

BY
KEVIN D. RANDLE, LT. COL. USAR (RET)

UNDERSTANDING ROSWELL

THE TRUE STORY OF WHAT HAPPENED IN ROSWELL IN JULY 1947

KEVIN D. RANDLE, LT. COL. USAR (RETIRED)